Employee-Assistance Programs

Employee-Assistance Programs

Philosophy, Theory, and Practice

Martin Shain
Judith Groeneveld
Alcoholism and Drug Addiction
Research Foundation of Ontario

LexingtonBooks
D.C. Heath and Company
Lexington, Massachusetts
Toronto

Library of Congress Cataloging in Publication Data

Shain, Martin.
Employee-assistance programs.

Bibliography: p.
Includes index.
1. Employee assistance programs–United States. 2. Employee assistance programs–Canada. I. Groeneveld, Judith, joint author. II. Addiction Research Foundation of Ontario. III. Title.
HF5549.5.E42S5 658.3'82 78-20375
ISBN 0-669-02737-5

Published simultaneously in Canada.

Printed in the United States of America.

International Standard Book Number: 0-669-02737-5

Library of Congress Catalog Card Number: 78-20375

Contents

List of Figure and Tables

Preface and Acknowledgments

Several excellent books and numerous articles have appeared in the last few years on the subject of alcoholism and its treatment in the workplace. Prominent among these is Trice and Roman's reissued *Spirits and Demons at Work* (1978). Its reappearance is a tribute to the original comprehensive treatment of the subject by the authors who continue to lead the field in exploring this area. Schramm, too, in edited works (1977*a*) and original material with Mandell and Archer (1978), has made major contributions to the study of alcoholism and the development of its treatment in industry. Follman (1976) has given an overview of the field from a broad, practical base.

This book is not an attempt to replicate the work of these and other writers. Rather, our purpose is to build upon the foundations established by their efforts. Without such seminal material, this book could not have been written.

We are indebted to the following staff members of the Alcoholism and Drug Addiction Research Foundation of Ontario for their invaluable assistance in gathering data for this book: N. D'Amour, J. Danic, B. Finlay, E. Freedberg, J. Hassan, H. Jupiter, A. Moss, R.D. ONeill, J. Simon, and H. Suurvali. The research reported in chapter 7 concerning alcoholism-prevalence estimates in a provincial ministry and a psychiatric hospital would not have been possible without the painstaking community-development work of R.H. Gray and L.M. Poudrier.

Ken Bennett was of great assistance to us in obtaining obscure but important materials; he was in touch with more people in the EAP field than either of us thought existed.

We are especially grateful to Peggie Walden, with whom we shared the task of writing appendix A, "Employee-Assistance Programs as Conflict-Avoiding Devices." Ms. Walden was graduated from the Osgoode Hall Law School of York University in Canada in 1977 and is currently a member of the Ontario bar. She is in practice in Toronto.

We are most grateful to our secretary, Mary Duarte, who coped with the manuscript in an exemplary fashion.

Although they cannot be named, we owe a great deal to the many employers and union officers in both the private and public sectors who gave time and energy to help us arrive at our present understanding of EAPs. We hope that we have done justice to their efforts and that the result in the form of this book, will be useful to them.

Introduction

This book is concerned with the philosophy, theory, and practice of employee-assistance programs (EAPs). By necessity, a variety of cousins to these programs will be considered, since the term EAP means many things to many people. Indeed, a characteristic of these programs is that they adapt themselves to local needs and conditions. Generally, however, EAP is a generic term used to describe the various methods found in the workplace for the control of alcoholism, drug abuse, and certain mental-health problems that adversely affect job performance. These methods typically involve both rehabilitative and disciplinary components. Their goals include the restoration of job performance to expected levels as well as the restoration of health to a better condition.

The search for a definition of EAP that captures the variety of methods found in practice has culminated in the term *ideal model*. This definition describes the necessary and sufficient conditions for effective and efficient launching and maintenance of an EAP. The majority of the larger health-oriented organizations concerned with control of alcoholism and drug abuse in the workplace (as part of broader mandates) have tried to define the key elements of successful EAPs. This is the case in both the United States and Canada. Indeed, the issues discussed in this book draw on materials from both countries, since the similarities and occasional differences prove instructive for an understanding of EAP as a transcultural method of job-performance and substance-abuse control.

A major goal of this book is to engender debate about the utility of the ideal-model approach, which has become an established part of the ideology of many who wish that industry, business, and other employment sectors would opt for EAP and of an influence group in the workplace which would like to disseminate the model on a widespread basis. This neither implies that everyone concerned with such industrial problems subscribes to the ideal-model approach nor is it a slur on the good faith of those who do subscribe. We contend that in the long run such an approach may rigidify and therefore render less useful a method of great value but of which too much may be expected.

Consequently, another goal is to focus attention on ways in which the purposes of EAPs may be served by auxiliary or alternative methods. These suggestions flow from a reconceptualization of what organizations need in terms of job-performance-control policies and of what employees, unions, and public-health agencies can and do expect from such policies. To do this, we will review the very nature of organizations and how change comes about in them.

The overall purpose of raising doubts about the present EAP approach and of suggesting auxiliary and alternative methods is to assist groups concerned with both controlling and bringing assistance to impaired workers to set reasonable expectations for the performance of EAPs or related techniques and to maintain reasonable standards for their evaluation. The discussion will be of value to policymakers in government, implementers in management, catalysts and coimplementers in unions, and interventionists in public-health capacities. Each group has its own emphasis and set of priorities with respect to the development and implementation of EAPs. We hope this book will help to clarify the interests of the different groups and enable them to recognize both the strengths and limitations of present employee-assistance programming as they seek new methods and new solutions. However, an intervention or solution that pleases one party may not please another. For example, it is often claimed that EAPs can achieve primary prevention of alcohol, drug, and other mental-health problems. This means that the employer should be able, ideally, to create a situation in which employees "at risk" for problem development seek help voluntarily. This is not an agenda that causes excitement among many employers, but some public-health interventionists are committed to the development of such possibilities and experience failure when they do not eventuate. Much of the literature dealing with the success or apparent failure of these programs avoids the issue of different interest groups with different types or levels of investment in program outcomes. This matter is a central theme of our book.

The plan of the book is, first, to provide a theoretical overview of the employee-assistance concept, identifying issues of central importance, and, second, to present a body of information based on our research, various aspects of which are keyed to the identified issues.

Employee-Assistance Programs

1 Theory and Philosophy

Although employee-assistance programs (EAPs) mean many things to many people, in general EAPs refer to policies and procedures adopted by employers in order to identify problem employees, including those with alcoholic involvement, as manifested by deteriorating job performance. Once identified, such employees are steered to a variety of agencies (both inside and outside the workplace) for the express purpose of receiving treatment or rehabilitation. The means of identification varies, but usually line supervisors or union officials are involved at least in documentation and identification, and often in confrontation and referral. However, the latter function may be performed by a specially designated group or individual. Implicit in the definition of EAP is the potential threat of dismissal if the employee does not cooperate. This blend of assistance and duress is often referred to as "constructive coercion." The ideal outcome of EAPs, however, is that employees will come forward voluntarily with their problems and be dealt with accordingly. Job security is supposedly guaranteed if the employee cooperates. There are other quite variable features of EAP, such as whether or to what extent the union is involved in policy development and implementation and whether there is allowance for followup and aftercare. Occasionally, supervisors are minimally involved, and identification is done by computer-reading of attendance and medical records. This description of EAP is by necessity quite broad in order to accommodate the wide variation in its actual application.

In recent years the literature dealing with EAPs and the broader concept of occupational programming has burgeoned. Since several excellent reviews of this literature exist, we will not replicate that work. Nonetheless, we will examine the themes and issues which the reviewers have identified as a context for the discussion in this book. There is considerable thematic commonality in these reviews of which no less than three have appeared since 1975. They are by Archer (1977), Hitchcock and Sanders (1976), and Hayward, Schlenger, and Hallan (1975). There were, of course, earlier reviews. One of the most important and notable is that of Trice and Roman (1972). This work, entitled *Spirits and Demons at Work*, has been reissued (1978) but the authors maintained its original structure and it is convenient to subsume under the same headings the issues raised in that excellent volume. The field of occupational programming is currently blossoming with research, much of it still unpublished. Whether the themes chosen by the reviewers will remain adequate to deal with the emerging results is as yet unclear, but there is some evidence that the framework is straining at the seams. This is, however, a desirable process in a field which has tended to have been underconceptualized. The new introduction to Trice and Roman (1978) provides a further elaboration of this point.

The reviews selected for discussion here concern themselves with many themes in common. To simplify the process of analysis, the review by Hayward, Schlenger, and Hallan will be taken as the basic framework for organizing the literature. Additions to this base or theoretical departures from it will be noted where they occur. The following major components appear in all three reviews, though sometimes they are introduced in different ways.

Context and Rationale for Occupational Programs

Reviews of the literature in occupational programming frequently begin with estimates of the prevalence of alcoholism at the national level. Costs to industry and to society in general are touted. It is argued that we have progressed a long way from a view of the alcoholic as a skid-row bum and we know that most alcoholics are employed. Since this impaired group represents a major drain on the economy in costs to the health system, in lost productivity, and in many social agency and transfer costs, and since many of this group are employed, it makes eminent sense for industry to take the bull by the horns and deal with the problem on its own ground on its own terms. After all, the threat of "economic capital punishment" through dismissal is likely to be the most effective means of breaking through what is perceived to be the ironclad denial system of the alcoholic. Get alcoholics into treatment while they still have something to lose, something at stake, becomes the motto.

It is argued also that the earlier a person can be contacted during the development of a problem, the better the chance for recovery. This is the basic logic of early intervention and it is typically presented in an uncritical manner. One exception to the bland acceptance of this rationale is to be found in Archer's review. She argues that much of this reasoning depends on seeing alcoholism as a progressive disease. That is, the early intervention argument supposes that every episode of problem drinking will eventually become a case of chronic alcoholism. The term *early* presupposes the idea *late*. Archer points out that this view has been challenged repeatedly and convincingly. However, she notes the development of a vested interest group which is sometimes referred to as the "alcoholism industry," a term first made current by Trice and Roman (1972). This group has a remarkable capacity for resisting the notion that alcoholism is anything other than a disease. The National Institute on Alcohol Abuse and Alcoholism (NIAAA) and the National Council on Alcoholism have vigorously opposed arguments that alcoholics can learn to drink socially. Needless to say, Alcoholics Anonymous (AA), a strong voice in occupational programming, have similarly resisted this concept. Nonetheless, some have argued cogently that the practice if not the principle of early identification is open to abuse and that people can be prematurely labeled as alcoholics who are nothing of the kind. Worse, labeling may reinforce behavior which left alone or treated might have diminished by itself. Archer notes that pressure on the disease concept of alcoholism appears to have been associated with the growth of so-called broad-brush programs and a movement away from alcohol-specific policies in industry. She cites Roman and Trice (1976) particularly in this regard. Roman and Trice hypothesize that NIAAA's advocacy of broad-brush policies is an attempt to legitimize the "alcohol worker" as professional change agent or consultant, thus eschewing the former image of social worker or do-gooder.

In spite of the fact that certain aspects of the rationale for EAP have been accepted with surprising readiness and are often regarded simply as "givens," there is a convergence of opinion among the varied interest groups concerned with this mode of intervention with respect to its value relative to existing alternatives. Basically, most interest groups would agree that the fundamental principle of EAPs is that they are more effective and efficient in altering the problem behavior of employees than purely disciplinary methods. The current variation in opinions about the worthwhileness of EAPs tends to emerge not on the basis of this principle but rather on the basis of how effective and how efficient such ultradisciplinary methods really are. It is nevertheless important to establish at least the *principle* of EAP as being grounded in practical reality. This principle can be given no better demonstration than by an examination of its antithesis, that is, the "discipline only" approach to the management of problem employees. The logical conclusion of the disciplinary process, where it has failed to correct the problem behavior of employees, is firing. However, if unionized, employees may elect to challenge the termination (or other severe discipline) and constrain the union to grieve on their behalf.

In the case of discharges involving claims of alcoholism two studies were conducted in order to look at the outcome of such grievances where they result in arbitration. One study was reported by Trice and Belasco in 1966 in the United States; the other by Adams in 1978 in Ontario. The results are remarkably similar: cases involving discharge for alcoholism (in Adams' study, these were 9 percent of all cases reviewed) were found to have the *highest rates of reinstatement* (55 percent in the Ontario study) but the *worst prognosis* for future work adjustment. Within two years, in the Ontario study, 50 percent of those reinstated had been fired—this time for good, presumably; 21 percent had quit; and 20 percent had received further discipline. The offenses covered by the heading "alcoholism" meant, in this study, intoxication at work; possession of alcohol on company premises; improper conduct at work due to intoxication; and absenteeism related to alcoholism.

It is extremely important to note that arbitrators are as unhappy with this outcome as employers, employees, or unions. Time and again arbitrators, in written decisions, rail against the uselessness of the grievance process as a *primary* means of solving work problems due to alcoholism. This should not, of course, be taken to mean that they would remove the grievance mechanism or that they oppose the use of discipline—far from it. Their argument is simply that the disciplinary process is not suited to the task of problem solving and that in the case of alcoholism particularly, problem solving is often what is needed. If that is what arbitrators think, one may well question why they reinstate discharged employees when they feel so pessimistic about the outcome. The answer is simple: they have no choice. When arbitrators review a discharge for "just cause" they want to know several things, at least where the offenses were not clearly a breach of safety regulations or were not criminal in nature. They want to know, for instance, whether the employee had been given warnings of the likely outcome of such continued behavior; whether other employees demonstrating similar behavior had been treated in like fashion; and whether the evidence of witnesses was corroborative. In fact, these conditions are often not met by employers since in order to do so they would have to have a *clear, explicit, and consistently enforced policy* on management of problem employees.

In addition, arbitrators may take the view that the employees' prior work record should be taken into account. In the case of those who have worked fifteen years for a company with an unblemished record and taken a plunge only in the last two years, this type of consideration again counts against the employer who has failed to pursue a policy of corrective discipline. Adams feels that entry into a treatment program should be made a condition of reinstatement if arbitrators are going to take this position but that the better alternative would be for employers to use ultradisciplinary methods before things get to the grievance stage. It is hard to miss the similarity between the conditions set up by arbitrators to support a just-cause discharge and the typical content of an EAP. Both emphasize the need for clear, consistent policy on management of the problem employee. Also many arbitrators feel that the treatment alternative should be introduced before the threat of termination. The relationship between arbitral decisions in alcoholism cases and the development of EAPs is more fully examined in appendix A.

Disciplinary action, especially where it results in grievances, is time-consuming, disruptive, and expensive. If it is also ineffective, the argument for the use of ultradisciplinary methods gains strength. It would seem that the interests of the employer, the employee, or the union are not accommodated by the disciplinary process. Even in nonunionized settings, the use of the discipline-only approach with *valued* employees who demonstrate problem behavior is likely to fail if the postreinstatement behavior of discharged alcoholics is anything to go by. However, unionized and nonunionized settings cannot be directly compared when it comes to the rationale for EAP.

History and Proliferation of Occupational Programs

The history of occupational programs for alcoholism is usually traced to the 1940s during which era certain pioneering companies undertook to manage their alcoholics by means other than dismissal. In spite of promising beginnings and prompting by the National Council on Alcoholism these programs were slow to grow: only as alcoholism became more "destigmatized" and as the huge cost of the condition became known did the momentum pick up. There was a quantitative jump in activity with the passage of the Hughes Act in 1970 in the United States and the creation of the NIAAA. Also in the United States legislation setting up programs in the federal government and the military provided a quickened spur to programming activity. The growth of private consulting became marked in this area while the Association of Labor Management Administrators and Consultants on Alcoholism (ALMACA) created a national organization of alcoholism service entrepreneurs. Again the only critical note in the recent reviews is struck by Archer as she amplifies Roman and Trice's point about the growth of the alcoholism industry. Later, it will be argued that we need to expand such critical commentary to the point at which we have a functional, socioanthropological perspective on occupational programming. This analysis would push further into the past for roots of what has in essence become a social movement, whose purpose and nature are rarely studied but may have practical implications for the future.

Description of Occupational Programs

In one way or another the reviews take us through some kind of framework for organizing the published material describing occupational programs. Hayward, Schlenger, and Hallan invite us to follow a "conceptual road map" which delineates the major descriptive dimensions as follows.

Program Approaches

The major variations are alcoholism-only policies and the broad brush or employee (troubled employee) assistance program concepts. In fact, these types represent end points on a practical continuum.

Program Components

All the reviewers agree that the following with varying degrees of emphasis are touted as the major components of occupational programs where they were successfully operated: written policy; labor-management involvement; company-wide information and education program; supervisory training; uniform identification and referral procedures; availability of treatment resources; and follow-up procedures.

Program Characteristics

Variations in programs can be usefully described according to the degree of emphasis on early detection; use of constructive confrontation; location of program in organizational structure; and nature of relationship with treatment facilities.

The overwhelming consensus in the reviews on the components is such that the resultant composite EAP takes on the dimensions of an "ideal model." Indeed, the practitioner's approach to EAP appears at times to be driven by an ideological fervor which may not be functional for this form of intervention in the long run. During the course of this book, it will be necessary to raise certain doubts concerning the practicality of the ideal model. Consequently the central importance of the concept of an ideal model of EAP warrants a more thorough analysis at this stage than can be found in any of the existing reviews. The next section is therefore devoted to an elaboration of what is meant by the ideal model.

Components of the Ideal Model

Dating back to the early 1950s and the "Yale plan" (Henderson and Bacon 1953), attempts have been made to define the ideal EAP. During the 1970s this seems to have become an obsession, with most of the major agencies in the United States and Canada concerned with occupational alcoholism turning their attention to the development of models for EAP. It is difficult to summarize these efforts. A simple summative listing of all the ideal components of EAPs tends to be misleading because the whole amounts to more than the addition of the parts. However, something of the kind has to be done in order to give a flavor of the extensiveness and comprehensiveness of what is meant by an EAP in the late 1970s. One of the most noticeable characteristics of the ideal EAP is that it places considerable demands on host organizations. Table 1-1 lists the key elements as synthesized from the models of EAP developed by the National Council on Alcoholism and the NIAAA and endorsed recently by the Addiction Research Foundation (ARF) of Ontario. These elements are presented both in terms of events that are supposed to take place (writing a policy) and in terms of attitudes thought to be necessary (willingness to see alcoholism as a treatable condition).

Table 1-1
Hypothesized Key Elements and Their Implementation: The Ideal Model

	EAP Goals/Imperatives	*Related EAP Activities Methods*	*Required Organizational Orientation, Conditions*	*Necessary EAP Consulting Skills*
Written Policy Re Joint Development and Promulgation (where union exists)	A written policy governing the management of problem employees, including rights and duties of employer and employee should be jointly developed by management and union.	1. Management/union committee must be struck. 2. Joint statement must be issued. 3. Joint procedures must be established.	History of good management/union relations must exist.	Ability to recognize when union/management relations are within reach of the EAP goal.
Prerequisite Attitudes	The employee who demonstrates problems with job performance or work-related behavior must be recognized as potentially suffering from a variety of mental, physical, behavioral, or social problems.	Where relevant, insurance coverage should be obtained for the treatment of alcoholism, drug abuse, mental illness, disturbance, and so on.	Key executives and union officials must recognize that a wide range of mental, physical, behavioral, and social problems can be remedied or alleviated. Human-relations style detectable in some coherent if not consistent form.	Knowledge of programs aimed at remediation or alleviation of the noted range of problems. Belief that they can be effective. Access to persuasive techniques. Credibility with industry.
Early Identification	Such problem employees should be identified as soon as possible.	Case finding and referral by organizational identifiers, usually supervisors, or other formally designated persons.	1. Economic foresight or vision. 2. Supervisors are held accountable for observation and documentation of deteriorating work performance	1. Awareness of the economic realities of the workplace and understanding of cost-effective accounting. 2. Ability to recognize when an organization is within reach of this level of functioning.
Skills of Identifiers	The identifiers should know what to do and when to do it.	Supervisors and union officials must be trained in skills of documentation, confrontation, referral, and followup.	Organization must have a training function, service, or department.	Knowledge of techniques of communication and of content area sufficient to conduct training if requested.

Table 1-1 continued

	EAP Goals/Imperatives	*Related EAP Activities Methods*	*Required Organizational Orientation, Conditions*	*Necessary EAP Consulting Skills*
Support for Identifiers	Management and union must support the identifiers.	Written guidelines must be developed which make identification of problem employees part of the identifier's job description.	1. Written job descriptions and performance reviews must be normative. 2. Discretionary power of line supervisors must be recognized and valued. 3. Communication channels must be fairly free both up and down.	Ability to recognize organizational signs which indicate that control and communication functions are compatible or within reach of compatibility with EAP goals. Skills of organizational diagnosis and consultation are involved.
Identification Keyed to Job Performance	Legitimate signs of problem behavior are only those related to work performance.	Supervisors must be trained to keep good records of job performance.	1. Personnel recordkeeping must be geared toward identification of deteriorating job performance. 2. Span of supervisory control must permit attainment of this objective.	1. Ability to comprehend record-keeping systems and make recommendations for change. 2. Organizational diagnosis, as outlined relative to *support*.
Choice of Treatment or Risk of Discipline	Treatment alternative to discipline must be clearly spelled out and made credible and visible.	Routes into treatment (medical or psychosocial) must be established. Key role for coordination of referral and treatment must be created.	History of functional management must exist, or the precedent must be established (far more difficult). Human-relations ideology must be detectable at senior levels.	1. Ability to recognize dead ends: it is probably too ambitious to expect conversion to functional management where no precedent exists. 2. Knowledge of various models for cutting in the treatment alternative into disciplinary model. 3. Understanding of discipline and grievance procedures of client organization.

Self-Recognition and Referral	Self-recognition of impending job crisis is better than management-induced crisis.	Pathways to care must be publicized, credible, and visible.	Reputation of treatment program must be established with regard to effectiveness and trustworthiness.	1. Public relations work with respect to treatment agencies in the community. 2. Persuasion of client organization to launch publicity campaign.
Crisis Induction Through Mandatory Referral	Failing self-recognition, a crisis must be induced in the problem employee's life through threat of job or status loss.	Skills of constructive confrontation and coercion must be introduced.	Job performance evaluation of supervisors must include skills of constructive coercion and confrontation. Supervisors must feel supported in their confrontive, coercive roles. (*support*)	Ability to demonstrate alternative methods of performance evaluation in promising situations (in organizations within reach of compatibility with EAP).
Availability of Treatment	Treatment facilities must exist and be available.	Treatment facilities must be located and agreement to admit referred employees secured.	History of involvement in community affairs might extend to active development of treatment facilities in some cases.	Knowledge of available resources and ability to establish liaison between key coordinator and such resources.
Nondiscrimination	All employees should be eligible for and subject to company policy coverage.	Policy terms must explicitly relate to blue- and white-collar workers, men and women	A history of nondiscrimination must be demonstrable.	Recognition of limitations of this philosophy in specific situations.
Employee Education	All employees should know the terms and benefits of the policy.	The policy's terms must be disseminated to all employees.	Mechanism for credible, direct contact between management, union, and employee must exist.	Facilitation of employee education campaign. Ability to recognize organizational limitations with regard to dissemination of information.
Benefits Coverage	Clearly stated benefits must exist for problem employees.	Package must be examined for coverage of alcoholism and other problems related to mental health and revised if necessary.	Broad sense of social responsibility or long-range economic vision must be detectable at senior levels.	Ability to demonstrate the favorable relationship of program costs to program benefits in terms of absenteeism, accidents, and productivity.

Table 1-1 continued

	EAP Goals/Imperatives	*Related EAP Activities Methods*	*Required Organizational Orientation, Conditions*	*Necessary EAP Consulting Skills*
Protection of Reputation	Employees' reputation must be protected if treatment route is chosen.	Records of treatment and background to the problem must be confidential.	Key coordinator or designated official should be responsible for the safekeeping and release of information.	Should be able to advise on systems of confidentiality used elsewhere.
Guarantee of Clean Slate	Employee participation in the assistance program must not jeopardize future career opportunities after successful completion of the program.	Provision must be made to protect career opportunities in the policy itself.	Joint management/union committee should act as an appeal board in cases of complaints about career blocking.	Familiarity with recorded cases in arbitration where this has been an issue.
Program Monitoring and Accountability	Operation of the program must be recorded for progress reports and accountability of responsible personnel.	Monitoring function must be introduced.	1. Recognition of the need for monitoring must exist. 2. Mechanism for monitoring must exist.	Knowledge of monitoring systems or resources which can advise.
Followup	Followup component to treatment/management program must exist.	Supervisors/union need to be persuaded of the importance of continuity and reinforcement.	Stability of supervisory work force, permitting continuity of treatment.	Persuasiveness. Knowledge of management systems in which such continuity can be maintained.

In emphasizing the existence of the ideal-model approach to EAP, the voices of dissent which have always been detectable—sometimes louder, sometimes softer—may be drowned out. This would be a most unfortunate by-product of a concentration on the prevalent mode of approaching EAP. Indeed, an examination of existing alternative approaches to assisting employees focuses attention more sharply on philosphical assumptions which do not emerge even in the detailed portrayal of the ideal model just completed. In a recent survey of consultants employed by the ARF of Ontario it was found that although the majority believed that the success of EAP depended largely on the implementation of the key elements listed in table 1-1, there was a minority group (about 30 percent in a group of fifty-five people) who believed that an alternative conceptualization of substance abuse and its management in industry was warranted. It is interesting, however, that both the majority who subscribed to the "individual model" (the philosophical basis of the ideal model) and the minority who subscribed to the "environmental model" felt they were practitioners of EAPs. The basic distinctions between the two approaches, sketched as extremes, are as follows:

Individual Model

1. The excessive use of alcohol is considered wholly dysfunctional to the individual.

2. The causes of alcoholism may be largely sought within the individual's own psychological makeup.

3. The prescribed treatment for the condition of alcoholism is some form of rehabilitation focusing on the individual's psychological makeup. Many variations on this theme are possible, including psychoanalysis, behavior therapy, casework, crisis intervention, reality therapy, and transactional analysis. The concern of some interventions is improved psychosocial functioning; that of others, simply improving job performance.

Environmental Model

1. The excessive use of alcohol is considered *under certain conditions* to be functional for the individual: relief from monotony, stress, or feelings of powerlessness. Also the "drunk" role may be part of a broader social role which is important in the industrial peer group situation (Dentler and Erickson 1959).

2. The causes of alcoholism may be sought not only or even mainly in the individual, but also in the social context (economic or political disadvantage) and in the specific organizational context (the nature of some kinds of work, or the structure of some types of organization).

3. The prescribed treatment may not be for the individual but for society and for the specific organization within which alcoholism is found. A reorientation of the worker to the means of production (control over) may be more relevant than psychotherapy.

It follows in theory and it can be shown in practice that such fundamentally divergent philosophies result in radically different approaches to the problem of alcoholism and drug abuse in industry. Clearly, there is disagreement about who *owns* the problem: is it the individual, industry, or society? Certainly, such differences can and do make a great deal of difference to the way in which EAP is marketed, as in the following example.

In the individual model, the EAP consultant's goal is to locate an EAP in any industry which is prepared to develop basic procedures, namely, documentation, coercion, referral, and sometimes followup.

In the environmental model, the EAP consultant's goal is to change the organization of an industry so that it does not *promote* mental health disorders.

Again these descriptions are extremes, though both may be found in reality. However, in the more common situation the EAP consultant operates at some indefinite midpoint between the extremes: a midpoint which is beset with theoretical and practical contradictions. We must return to this theme presently. For the moment, let us simply be aware that EAP is not the single philosophical, theoretical, and practical package that it appears to be. It is in fact a title for a variety of different approaches. We can begin a closer look at this by examining variations in expectations of EAP.

Variations in Program Expectations

There appears to be general confusion about how much can be expected of EAP. The concepts around which much of this confusion centers are primary, secondary, and tertiary prevention. Claims are made for each of these levels of prevention under the heading of EAP, as evidenced in a study of consultants at the ARF (Shain and Groeneveld 1976, 1977). It is important, therefore, that we examine the definitions of these terms to provide a context within which we may reconsider realistic and ethical goals for EAP. The three levels of prevention were defined by Swisher in testimony to the U.S. Senate Committee on Labor and Public Welfare: Subcommittee on Alcoholism and Drug Abuse (1977), as: the tertiary level (after the fact) involves treatment or rehabilitation; secondary level (during the fact), involves crisis intervention, early diagnosis, and crisis monitoring; and primary level (before the fact), involves education and development.

The main question which arises from this definition of terms is whether EAP, as defined in the ideal model, can be expected realistically to achieve primary prevention. That is, can it be expected that EAP should contain procedures for educating the entire work force of host organizations in such a way that employees who may one day be at risk in relation to substance abuse modify their lifestyles to the extent that this risk is avoided? Indeed, substantially more is implied by the concept of primary prevention than the requirement in the ideal model that the EAP policy and its procedures be disseminated to all employees. More is meant, in fact, than the notion of substance abuse education in industry (Payne, Monti, and Winer 1976). Primary prevention is held increasingly to refer to methods of encouraging healthy personal development and growth such that problems do not have a chance to flourish. Vicary (1978) reports that this definition of primary prevention now appears in policy statements of federal government agencies concerned with drug and alcohol abuse. One thing is clear: primary prevention of this sort is not a logical extension or continuation of procedures used in EAP with respect to secondary and tertiary prevention. In the latter forms of intervention, emphasis is placed on *identification of problems* by either supervisors or the troubled individuals themselves. In either case, the benefits provided under the terms of the policy are activated on the employee's acceptance of the need for help. In primary prevention, identification of problems plays no part and it clearly involves a set of activities not considered in the ideal model.

There is, however, a question about the role of identification even at the secondary prevention level. Since the concept of early identification rests upon the notion that it is possible and desirable to detect alcoholism and other problems at early stages of development—the province of secondary prevention—it becomes relevant to consider whether the idea is as wholesome and benign as it first appears. The problem emerges as we look more closely at the meaning of early signs or early warnings. The trouble is that in order to be on safe ethical ground we must assume that all *early* signs and warnings eventually mature into *later* signs and fulfilled prophesies. That is, we must assume that alcoholism is a deteriorative condition without spontaneous remission which is guaranteed to progress to a chronic stage. We must also assume that we know what all the early signs and symptoms are. This is a deterministic view of alcoholism. The fact of the matter is, however, that not every person who exhibits early-warning signs will become alcoholic whether some intervention occurs or not. Therefore, the earlier the alleged "sign," the more we are dealing in probability rather than certainty.

The business of secondary prevention is sometimes described in terms of predicting who will become an alcoholic or drug abuser. Yet we know for certain that even the best predictive devices misclassify people when they are used to identify individuals who are suspected of being higher risks for developing certain undesirable conditions. Secondary prevention subjects have from time to time come to the attention of the courts. In the same testimony to the U.S. Senate Committee, Swisher cited a decision by a court in Montgomery County, Pennsylvania, in which an injunction was issued against a program which sought "early identification of high-risk drug abusers." (*Merriken et al.* v.

Cressman et al. Civil action #72-2057, U.S. District Court, Eastern District, Pennsylvania, September 1973.) The objections to these programs usually concern the danger attendant upon giving a person a label (potential drug abuser or alcoholic) solely on the basis of some clinical or statistical probability. It has been demonstrated in many areas (delinquency and mental health disorders) that the premature ascription of a label such as "thief" or "schizophrenic" can be influential in consolidating the labeled person's identity around these negative definitions; that is, by calling a person a name before he deserves it, one can create a situation in which that person comes to *act as though* he really possessed the attributes ascribed to him by the labeler. It is basically a case of the self-fulfilling prophesy. The process is a circular one. As the labeled individual takes on more of the characteristics of the ascribed label, so other people in their environment begin to react to the resultant behavior. An example of how labels can affect judgment was given by Swisher in his testimony. He cites Rosenthal and Jacobsen (1968), who performed an experiment in which teachers were told that students who were "bright" were "below average." Teacher evaluations of these students tended strongly to reflect the label—below average rather than the reality—bright.

The relevance of all this to EAP is that early intervention relative to problem employees in industry may be subject to labeling problems. There are, however, some interesting differences in EAP which in theory go some way toward a resolution of these problems. First of all, identification in EAP is officially tagged to deteriorating job performance. This means, in theory, that if an employee has every problem under the sun but his work performance is not affected, he cannot be confronted and exposed to constructive coercion. Since many people doubt whether alcoholism affects job performance until its later stages, there appears to be a logical, theoretical limitation to the penetration of EAP; that is, deteriorating job performance may not be an early sign but rather a late sign of alcoholism. In that case, the whole idea of secondary prevention under EAP is meaningless. However, there are just as many people in the EAP field who believe that if job performance is monitored carefully enough, the early signs of emerging problems are there. Nevertheless, even the advocates of this point of view usually admit that the quantity and quality of employee supervision have to be high in order to pick up early signs. Even then, a slight deterioration in an excellent performance record may not be sufficient grounds for confrontation in the eyes of the employee, the supervisor, or the union. However, all these objections proceed on the notion that the employee is going to be confronted and then constructively coerced into rehabilitation.

The second major difference in EAP which distinguishes it from other early identification systems is that an ideal of such interventions is the emergence of *self-referrals* rather than mandatory referrals. This is the theoretical key to the ethical problems of labeling just noted. If the individual employee, knowing he is in trouble but knowing equally well that it is showing up only insignificantly in job performance, chooses to come forward and make use of the company EAP, this resolves the ethical dilemma of making a mandatory referral on the basis of very early work-related signs.

The problem remains, however, that there is a very fuzzy area between the point at which job performance is clearly affected and constructive coercion is warranted, and the point at which job performance is so barely affected that only a self-referral would fit the ethical requirements noted earlier. This, in fact, may be an area which gives supervisors the greatest difficulty in practice. They often simply do not know what to do in marginal cases. Very possibly, the implication of this state of affairs could be that more effort should be put into the generation of self-referrals from industry. However, this would require an approach which differs from the customary present approach in that we would need to begin from the employee level rather than the managerial level. One can conceive of a form of public health education for employees in industry which might achieve this objective, but it would involve the deployment of expensive resources since the activities would be identical to those discussed in relation to primary prevention: life skills and health development, decision making, values clarification, and information giving. Such a line of thought imposes quite a strain on our assumptions about the motivation of employers to be interested and involved in EAP.

Compatibility of Public Health and Industrial Goals

Just how interested is industry in EAP? In terms of levels of prevention, what level of penetration is industry likely to be satisfied with? The trouble here is that we cannot be sure at what point individual industries will make an economic cutoff. How cost-efficient is it, for example, to launch a primary prevention program in industry? The payoff may seem too remote. At the other end of the spectrum, it may make economic sense to refer chronic problem employees into treatment. Savings of quite remarkable sums have been reported at this level of intervention. Again it is the fuzzy area in between these extremes which presents problems. Is early identification worth the trouble to industry? Is it cost-efficient? The point here is simply that the worthwhileness of EAPs is likely to be considered from different perspectives by public health agencies on the one hand and industry and other employers on the other. In many cases, by trying to "sell" EAP, its practitioners are trying to accommodate a health-oriented system of intervention into a profit-oriented system of production. This deceptively simple observation is the key to understanding the extent to which we can expect public health goals, in the form of EAP, to be implemented in the context of production goals. It is probably not too far from the truth to say that industry is interested in public health only insofar as it serves some economic goal. Such economic goals may be shortsighted or longsighted but it does not alter their nature. It has been suggested by Bartell (1976) that the origins of the human-relations movement in industry must be seen in the light of how it serves the interests of the power elite. He cites Davis (1967) who defines "human relations" in the context of industry as, "the integration of people into a work situation that motivates them to work together productively, cooperatively and with economic, psychological and social satisfactions." Bartell sees the industrial human-relations movement—of which we must consider EAP to be a part—as a response by industry to various kinds of environmental pressure. Most important among these pressures are:

1. A broad social movement emphasizing the social responsibility of industry, and desire by industry to prevent government from legislating such responsibility
2. Growth of psychological theory stressing higher human needs and the importance of their being fulfilled (job satisfaction or a sense of purpose)
3. Growth of labor unions
4. Increased size of organizations and resultant bureaucratization with greater spans of control (with resulting problems of maintaining control)
5. Increased education of workers and higher worker expectations
6. Increased specialization of workers and greater costs of training
7. Growth of a specialized group in industry whose role was to negotiate between labor and management; Bartell refers to this group as "a prime consumer of human relations ideology"
8. Recognition by industry that a happier worker is a more productive worker, with the corresponding investment of money in studies to that effect
9. Growth of industrial relations schools in major universities, often subsidized by industry

In other words, human relations made sense to industry in terms both of meeting social demands and of greater productivity within this changing social context.

In addition to the influences above, Trice and Belasco (1966) noted that EAPs seem to be tailor-made to fit increasing legal demands exerted upon industry. In particular, they say that in many states the courts have increasingly tended to make employers *absolutely* liable for employee disabilities to the point where many mental health disorders are compensable under the workmen's compensation acts. Specifically, there are numerous cases in which courts have allowed compensation for injuries from the intoxicated state of an employee. Trice and Belasco feel that it is only a matter of time before alcoholism itself is treated as a compensable disease. If employers are going to be liable for alcoholism in the United States, it makes sense for industry to prevent the development of alcoholism in the workplace. EAPs are a good way of doing this.

Trice and Belasco also observed that arbitration law in the United States is becoming such that it is very unlikely that a dismissal will be upheld unless the company has been able to meet certain strict criteria. Some of these are (1) evidence against the employee must be consistent among witnesses; (2) disciplinary procedures of the kind in question must have been consistently applied against other employees; and (3) mitigating circumstances must have been taken into consideration, such as prior good work record or joining AA after discharge.

Trice and Belasco interpret the trend in arbitration as one where dismissal will be upheld only where inability to change has been shown by the employee. Again the spirit of EAP is that of documentation of deteriorating work performance, uniformity of practice, or giving employees a chance. The essence of EAP, then, is very similar to the essence of the criteria which Trice and Belasco report are used in arbitration law in the United States. So an employer who followed EAP practices to the letter would meet such arbitration criteria when firing eventually became inevitable. It is therefore a useful policy to have if employers wish to avoid fruitless and costly reinstatements of problem employees. The costs of such reinstatements take many forms, among which are backpay, sometimes awarded for several months; partial productivity, which can go on for years until an incident catalyzes the discharge procedure again; time and money spent in grievance proceedings; absenteeism after reinstatement; and diverted management energies.

All these costs represent pressures on industry—and indeed on unions—to deal constructively with such problems.

These social and legal pressures lead to the conclusion that EAPs are a useful and appropriate response to them. However, it must also be expected that this response will be generated only insofar as it is compatible with economic pressures on industry. One could not predict, for example, to what level of EAP activity these social and legal constraints would drive a specific work organization. It would depend on numerous factors, such as the size and location of the organization, the type of work it is engaged in, its union status, the type of workers employed, and many others.

Further, in considering the likelihood of their being adopted by an organization and the extent to which EAPs will be implemented, it is necessary to weigh the larger issue of the compatibility of EAP, which assumes in philosophy and practice the existence of a human-relations orientation, with the particular industrial organization at hand. Frequently, practitioners are disillusioned by a predictable failure to sell EAP to non-human-relations-oriented organizations. This does not mean that such industries cannot profit from EAP. It means rather that it is a waste of time dealing with specific policies, such as EAPs, if the general organizational basis for them does not exist. A strong current of opinion urges EAP consultants to think of themselves as organizational diagnosticians and, if invited, organizational change agents (Trice and Roman 1978, Roman 1978). This shift requires, however, that we unlearn some old ways of doing things and absorb some new ways. One does not learn to diagnose and consult with total organizational systems overnight. Yet if we are to identify those industries and agencies whose way of doing business is compatible or, more importantly, within reach of compatibility with EAP, these skills must be acquired.

A quite common example of the disappointments encountered by EAP consultants because of failure to recognize the relationship between public health and economic goals is as follows. An industry is identified (often through its own request) as being interested in the idea of EAP, perhaps because of a current crisis with a problem drinker. The economic arguments seem quite attractive to the managers, insofar as they are aware of them. The consultant is pleased because there appears to be genuine interest in EAP, and perhaps there is; but often EAP is the first real example of a human-relations style of management that the client has seen. His organization is simply not geared to the goals and systems of people-oriented management. If the EAP consultant is only dimly aware of this problem, he cannot bring it to the attention of the employer, let alone negotiate for a position which will enable him to make legitimate and credible observations about the client's organization *as a functional whole*. All too often, the EAP consultant, out of habit or despair, will agree to one of the most common ways of introducing EAP to an industry: training line supervisors.

In our study of EAP at the ARF (Shain and Groeneveld 1977), we discovered that, with very few exceptions, the number of supervisors trained had *no effect* on reported rates of referral. Various explanations have been offered for this phenomenon. The most promising explanation argues that all too often we miss the boat in supervisory training by concentrating on attitude change rather than on behavior and, most importantly, on the organizational constraints on supervisory behavior. In short, though supervisors are often well-intentioned with regard to identification and referral of problem employees and may even learn the necessary skills in role-play situations, they are thwarted by the often unsupportive organizational climate in which they are expected to carry out the policy: unidirectional lines of communication, huge spans of control in which supervisors barely know their subordinates, or highly specific divisions of labor in which responsibility for more than a short series of small tasks is virtually unknown. Often, problems between management and union can thwart the attempts of either to exercise newly learned skills. The introduction of EAPs into such climates can be a frustrating business because the ingrained organizational problems of client industries are often beyond the reach of current skill levels and terms of reference among occupational alcoholism consultants. Yet it is important to realize that although the EAP consultant may be frustrated, the client industry may be getting as much as it wanted out of the policy. That is, the consultant may want a policy that gets down to early identification; the industry may simply want to clean up a backlog of multiproblem employees. The client organization may simply not have the economic foresight and the managerial style to relate to anything more than tertiary prevention.

Summary

The issues in the philosophy and theory of EAPs can be summarized in terms of certain classes of factors which influence the genesis and development of these programs and sometimes act as determinants of their potential impact. The balance of this book is devoted to an exploration of these issues at a more practical level.

Philosophical Influences

The world views of EAP consultants vary considerably. This radically affects the ways in which they conceive of problem drinking in industry. Some feel that alcoholism is a problem for which the *individual* is primarily responsible, others that *environment* (society at large or industry in particular) is primarily responsible.

The resultant styles of EAP consultants in approaching industry and their styles of intervention vary dramatically. This variation can be expected to influence the impact of EAP considerably, because in effect a number of quite different approaches to industry are being considered as though they could all be referred to as EAPs. Some may be effective, some may not be. Most of this chapter, however, has been concerned with the potential and problems of the individual model of EAP.

Logical Determinants

Certain problems concerning the logic of EAP were identified. A policy which is tagged to job performance has implicit limitations relative to early identification. Early identification itself, even if achievable, has some *ethical* problems associated with the ill effects of labeling unless it is based on self-referrals. It was argued that in practice this is a very fuzzy area of which supervisors and union officials are often aware, making them unwilling to act. It is an ethical limbo.

Economic Determinants

It was argued that industry and unions are aware in differing degrees of the extent to which EAPs save money at the three levels of prevention. It was suggested that the goals of public health practitioners, including EAP consultants, may be more far-reaching and ambitious than is often realistic in the context of production goals. Nevertheless, it is possible that changes in workmen's compensation and arbitration law will make it worthwhile to industry to accommodate these more ambitious public health goals because it will be in their best economic interests. It was argued that even if this happens, a new approach will have to be found to deal with secondary prevention which will emphasize generation of self-referrals. Such a new approach, based on education rather than identification, might also be functional at the primary prevention level. A more precise accounting system would enable consultants to introduce EAP not only from the viewpoint of saved production costs but also of saved workmen's compensation and arbitration costs. This is, however, an area in which there is generally an insufficiency of precise information.

Organizational Determinants

It was argued that EAP, in order to be disseminated successfully, must be considered as a *system* of intervention with its own philosophy, goals, and methods. These goals and methods are based on human-relations-management principles and are related to public health objectives which we expect somehow to accommodate in the womb of production goals and systems. Since EAP is sometimes an industry's first practical introduction to human-relations management, it is argued that the EAP consultant must be able to judge whether the client organization is compatible or within reach of compatibility with the proposed system of intervention. This involves skills of organizational diagnosis and possibly consultation. The EAP consultant is an organizational change agent in many cases.

Failure to reconceptualize EAP in these terms probably leads to bogging down policy implementation at a fairly early stage unless the client organization is already operating on human-relations principles, in which case the challenge for the EAP consultant is not all that great anyway. Preaching to the converted has limited satisfactions.

Implications

1. EAP cannot be properly evaluated unless the underlying philosophy of its advocates is made clear. Evaluation proceeds on the basis of clearly stated objectives in relation to which outcomes are compared. When it is not clear who wants what and to what extent, it is impossible to speak clearly of outcome, successful or otherwise. The objectives of different interest groups (employers, unions, and public health agencies) need to be clarified in relation to specific programs. In the process of clarification it is likely that the expectations of the interested parties will become more balanced and realistic.

2. Assuming that a common goal of all interested parties turns out to be (in one degree or another) the assistance of impaired employees in their attempts to recover their health and economic status, it may become necessary to reconceptualize the current approach to the dissemination of EAP by shifting emphasis from managerial identification of problem employees to self-identification through education. This will overcome the logical and ethical limitations on EAP as it seeks to work down to the secondary prevention level. Unions would have to be involved very intensively in such an approach.

3. In disseminating EAP we need in general to become more aware of the variety of economic arguments other than those related to production which could influence both management and union in developing EAPs, such as workmen's compensation and arbitration costs. It should be borne in mind that the accommodation of public health to industrial goals will be keyed to the economic interests of the employer. If economic reasons can be found for developing primary and secondary prevention strategies based on education rather than identification, emphasis should be placed upon this goal in the future.

4. It will be necessary to conceptualize the role of the EAP consultant as that of the organizational change agent. This involves the definition and acquisition of a new range of skills for many people involved in EAP, but it seems to be the inevitable implication if this form of intervention is not to lose headway as we move into the 1980s.

2 Occupational Programs in Practice

Studies of employee-assistance programs (EAPs) to date have been characterized chiefly by the smallness of their number and the narrowness of their theoretical bases. The reviewers cited in chapter 1 (Archer 1977; Hitchcock and Sanders 1976; Hayward, Schlenger, and Hallan 1975) inform us that the evaluative literature in the field of occupational programming is usually concerned with issues of effectiveness and efficiency but in a manner which leaves much to be desired. This observation is examined and developed in the present chapter.

Effectiveness of Occupational Programs

Two major questions are typically addressed in the study of effectiveness in occupational programs: first, to what extent is the population at risk penetrated (penetration rates) by the program; and second, to what extent are changes (success rates) wrought among the people who are identified as having problems and with whom some intervention is attempted?

Penetration Rates

There appears to be a growing acceptance among students of occupational programs that the formula proposed by Schlenger and Hayward (1976) is more useful than the older, cruder methods. The older method chose to do one of two things: it related the size of the *identified* problem group in a given industry to the size of the work force as a whole in that industry or it related the identified group to an estimated population at risk within that work force. Schlenger and Hayward point out that most of these prevalence estimates are guesses and identify this as one of the chief difficulties in the literature. They urge that if such estimates are to be used we can at least make them somewhat less crude when entering them into a penetration-rate formula. They suggest that the formula should control for annual turnover and for the people who have already passed through the program successfully and remain in the employ of the organization. This idea is rarely if ever acted upon in studies of occupational programming. In Hitchcock and Sanders' review (1976) not one study utilizes an approach similar to that advocated by Schlenger and Hayward. Hitchcock and Sanders provide a full account of studies in which penetration rates have been estimated. They array their analysis of the literature in such a way that the studies are tabulated according to method and findings. They demonstrate that the overall penetration of occupational programs ranges from 0.01 to 0.006 percent of the various work forces if the known referrals are averaged over the life of the programs. How many of these reported programs really correspond to the description of the ideal model EAP cannot be concluded from the available data. This picture of penetration rates overall seems rather dismal at first glance, especially when compared to the popular estimates of alcoholism in society at large which often range from 5 to 10 percent of the population as a whole. However, 5 to 10 percent is itself an enormously wide range. Clearly, it makes a world of difference in assessing the effectiveness of an EAP, or other control measure, whether the population at risk accounts for 5 percent or 10 percent or some other proportion of the work force. For example, a study by the Comptroller General (1970) of heavy and light industry claimed that the prevalence of alcoholism could vary as much as 10 percent to 1.5 percent depending on the type of work being done.

Success Rates

Either or both indicators are typically used to denote success in dealing with the employed alcoholic: improvement in job-related behavior, or modification of drinking behavior. Hitchcock and Sanders echo Hayward, Schlenger, and Hallan in deploring the variation in how these indicators are defined. One of the worst problems in judging success is in the incomparability of findings between studies. Comparisons are virtually impossible because:

1. Definitions of problem behavior are not sufficiently specific; the term *alcoholic* means different things to different people. Rarely is anything other than job-related evidence given for degree of alcoholic involvement.
2. Criteria for successful rehabilitation are rarely given and certainly not in terms which would allow one program to be compared with another; the term *absenteeism* can and does mean many things. Even the term *accident* is not without ambiguity.
3. Client characteristics and variations are rarely described or used to discriminate successful from unsuccessful cases, or those who dropped out of or refused treatment from those who remain.
4. Followup intervals vary enormously even when they are given. The percentage of the eligible total who were successfully contacted is rarely given.

This is very unfortunate because there does appear to be considerable agreement in the literature on the *dimensions* of job performance which should be used in program assessment. What is missing is a consistent set of indexes and criteria that can be applied to these dimensions.

Hitchcock and Sanders point out that an evaluation of effectiveness would properly include a comparison of the tested program against the "spontaneous recovery or remission" effect. Pursuing a similar theme, Hayward, Schlenger, and Hallan urge that certain questions need to be addressed if the field is to become more sophisticated: Do treated groups do better than comparable groups of untreated people; how much intervention is enough to achieve the stated goals of the program; and if effects are seen, to what components of the intervention are they attributable? They note that there are no studies of the third type of question, hardly any of the second, and but a handful of the first.

In the light of these observations it seems rather premature to conclude, as Hitchcock and Sanders do, that overall the success rates of occupational programs are quite encouraging. However, they extrapolate studies in which job-performance improvement is used as the principal criterion and in those cases the success rates vary from 65 to 80 percent depending on the rigor of the criterion used and the length of time over which improvement was monitored. This is good news, perhaps, but we must be realistic and put these results together with those concerning penetration rates. Together, the results appear to be that occupational programs (including EAPs) enjoy considerable success once identification and referral have taken place but that the referred population represents only a small fraction of those who, according to public health estimates, need help. In addition, the only evidence of success appears to be in an area which is of most interest to the employer, namely, job performance. Nonetheless, the fact should not be dismissed lightly that in spite of numerous, theoretically devastating methodological criticisms there are many studies of varying degrees of sophistication which support the value of occupational programs (EAPs among them) once a case is referred for treatment.

There is a major discrepancy between the requirements for a meaningful evaluation as touted by the reviewers and the level of information that actually finds its way into the literature. To a great extent, the reasons for this discrepancy are probably to be found in the different interests which the various parties to a program evaluation might be expected to have. It might be anticipated, however, that the employer would at least share the public health researcher's interest in whether all the cases eligible for the EAP were getting into it and whether they were improving more rapidly than they would if dealt with exclusively by disciplinary means. There are, no doubt, employers who genuinely want the answers to those questions, but the average employer is likely to be satisfied with much less information if the overall effect of the EAP's operation for him and his managers is to reduce the "noise" typically generated by highly visible, alcoholic employees. This may seem shortsighted to those who have a mandate to utilize the workplace as a public health hunting ground for the walking wounded and perhaps in some ways it is. After all, some who are drinking immoderately now will be problem drinkers tomorrow, causing disruptions in production, scheduling, and morale. However, the employer seldom has the luxury of sitting back and planning how to head off possible problems of tomorrow when today is full enough with difficulties. The employer may be aware that among a given group of at-risk employees only a critical few will become actual problems. It may be less trouble to cope with the emergent few than to try to reach the potential many. There is, in fact, some evidence to support the effectiveness of a policy which deals only with major casualties and leaves the rest from a purely economic viewpoint. Edwards (1975) draws attention to the findings of Cahalan and Room (1972) which show that 10 percent of all males in a national survey had a problem of minimal severity on the job as a result of drinking while 6 percent had a problem of higher severity if the recall period is held for the last three years. When respondents were asked if they had *ever* had a problem on the job as a result of drinking, 21 percent said they had had a problem of minimal severity and 13 percent a more severe problem. Edwards notes the significance of this finding as being that "a large proportion of people move into and out of the problem drinking population in a three year period" (p. 46). This appears to be evidence against a deterministic theory of drinking in which increased consumption will lead automatically to alcoholism. The Cahalan and Room data suggest at least the existence of a remission rate and probably of a spontaneous recovery rate if the additional studies of Bergin (1971) and Smart (1975-1976) are brought to bear on the issue. The employer, then, is behaving reasonably when he argues that it is more efficient to wait for problems to become florid before taking remedial action. Reasonable behavior is not necessarily the most efficient or most effective.

In addition, the employer may gain some support from several studies which, if read together, lend credence to the view that at any one time it is a special subgroup of the alcoholic population who will cause trouble. We will refer frequently to the concept of the "critical few" (Bird and Loftus 1976) in the course of our examination of EAPs. Edwards (1975) draws attention to three studies which warrant this interpretation, though he does not conclude that they might be used to support a very limited concept of EAP. Pell and D'Alonzo (1970) compared the frequency and severity of disabilities for known, suspected, and recovered alcoholics and for a control group of randomly selected "normals" whose basic characteristics were matched with those of the problem groups (n = 764). The average frequencies of absence (days of disability) per annum were for known alcoholics (19.4), suspected alcoholics (10.8), recovered alcoholics (11.7), and controls (5.8).

Evidently the problem groups as a whole had higher rates of absence from work, but it is crucial to note that 55 percent had a reasonably good attendance record during the year of study. Cole and Shupe (1970) in their study of the job performance of schizophrenics, neurotics, and matched controls found that four years after the initial diagnosis, there were a substantial group among the patients who were doing as well or better than the normals but there were a few very deviant cases who did much worse. The simple comparison of mean scores on the work performance inventory which was used to discriminate between the groups was found to be misleading because of the effect wrought by this highly deviant group. Trice (1962) made certain observations about the job behavior of problem drinkers which can be seen in a similar light. In surveying 750 male members of AA by questionnaire Trice attempted to reconstruct their work experience prior to the occurrence of crises which led to their formal identification as problem employees. The purpose of this effort was to provide some bearings on the actual relationship between the development of alcoholism and deterioration of work performance. Among Trice's findings were two of significance to the present line of inquiry. Respondents reported that their work efficiency had declined, but blue-collar workers tended toward absenteeism more often than before while white-collar workers tended toward less. Similarly, accidents occurred at less than the expected frequency for the employee group as a whole. This report may be criticized on the grounds that it is based on self-report data, but it is nonetheless important in an area where few such studies are even attempted.

Ten years after Trice's observations, a study by Borthwick (1977), employing official records as the data source, confirmed the tendencies noted in the earlier study. This is an important study which has implications of many kinds for EAP. For the present, suffice it to say that Borthwick noted among navy personnel a strong tendency for the sickness and accident rates of a majority of those who eventually found their way into treatment to be lower than average during the year before referral while the comparable rates during the same period among a critical few (about 20 percent) exceeded the norm dramatically. However, the effect of early warnings on the majority group may have accounted for their better records during this period before referral to treatment. In addition, the data say nothing about the quality of work performed. Being at work is obviously only a prerequisite for satisfactory job performance. It is of great interest, however, to observe that the responses of problem employees to confrontation and documentation of job performance vary dramatically: some react protectively and try at least to keep up appearances by not being absent and not getting into accidents while others (a minority in the navy study) react by falling to pieces. At all events, the approach which avoids looking at the problem group as an entity, exemplified in the above studies, seems preferable to those which announce that "alcoholics cost X times the amount represented by normal employees in sickness, accidents, and time out." Although this may be true, it is true only in a limited sense. The study by Winslow et al. (1966) is of the latter type. Valuable and important as they were in making people aware that alcoholics do cost industry money, such studies should now give way to more sophisticated approaches, such as that adopted by Borthwick.

Efficiency of Occupational Programs

Noting that efficiency (cost-effectiveness) is an issue "seldom adequately documented in the literature," Hayward, Schlenger, and Hallan classify the questions as the costs of problem drinking to the employer and the costs of operating a program to correct the problem.

Usually, an attempt is made to ascribe some monetary value to changes in job-performance indicators, such as reduced absenteeism, accidents, sickness benefits, visits to the medical department, disciplinary action, grievances, and supervisory ratings. The exact method of cost estimation is rarely given in the published studies. These "savings" may then be juxtaposed with the estimated costs of running the programs which are attributed with having brought about these changes. Unfortunately, the costs of such programs are rarely reported and, indeed, they are difficult to estimate especially where they involve reallocation of existing organizational resources. For example, how much is it worth to transfer executive A from a key position to that of alcoholism program coordinator, even on a part-time basis? The study which stands head and shoulders above any other to date is Borthwick's cost-benefit analysis of the navy alcoholism rehabilitation programs (1977). The unique aspect of this work is that Borthwick developed a cost-benefit formula which weighs the known probability of future military service for personnel in various age groups against the known likelihood of rehabilitating problem personnel in the same age groups. The formula enables us to evaluate the cost-efficiency of trying to rehabilitate personnel with different service records. Generally, younger men are not expected to remain in the service for as long as men who have already served a certain number of years; it is therefore necessary to achieve a *higher* rehabilitation rate with the younger people in order to recover costs due to a larger proportion of them leaving the service. Also, of course, the cost of replacement goes up as a person becomes more senior and competent. This is the kind of accounting which would be needed in order to make clear statements about the cost-efficiency of EAPs in the civilian employment world. It has not been done in spite of the fact that the ability to do it is clearly present.

One may well question with Roman (1978) whether absolute efficiency is quite as important to employers as the EAP philosophy seems to imply. An alternative explanation is that the kind of accounting utilized by employers when it comes to dealing with alcoholism is not properly understood by those who are trying to implement EAPs. It is evident that much more needs to be understood about employer motivation in adopting EAPs and the way in which they approach the costing of these programs. Later, we present our studies which attempt to define a more realistic view of the employers' perspective on such matters. In general, the situation becomes clearer once the principle of differential interests outlined earlier in this chapter is applied to the question of cost-efficiency. We suggest that much of the confusion about costs derives from the tendency of those outside industry to second-guess the motivations of those in industry concerning the adoption of EAPs or other control policies. It appears that those outside industry are often convinced that producers of goods and deliverers of services are motivated solely by the pursuit of profit. They appear to reason that this pursuit of profit is done in obvious, direct ways so that the value of implementing an EAP would be assessed by employers only on the basis of whether the costs of running the program would be more than offset by the savings generated through rehabilitated employees in reduced absenteeism, benefits paid, or accidents recorded.

To a limited extent, this kind of reasoning may go on among employers; certainly employers who are proud of their programs tend to present their results in cost-benefit terms. However, the fact that the results are presented in this manner is not necessarily evidence of the use of these considerations in policy implementation. Essentially, when employers opt for an EAP they are often opting for a *method of job-performance control* which is expected to deal with certain kinds of problems for which alternative solutions (discipline, dismissal, retiring, or retraining) are becoming increasingly impractical. The drying up of alternatives may be a result of increased union pressure to deal constructively with employee problems; adverse decisions of arbitrators who reinstate employees who once would have stayed dismissed; the increased costs of finding and retraining skilled employees, with an inevitable delay; the added pressure from government not to create a pool of unemployables; and the simple desire to look good in the community and attract business.

It is interesting and no doubt revealing that reviewers do not deal with costs to any group other than the employers. It does not, however, reflect the whole of reality by any means. Berry and Boland (1977) tried to rectify this situation by estimating the extent of lost productivity through a calculation of reduced earnings of employees with alcohol problems. Their admittedly crude methods led them to conclude that lost productivity in terms of lost earnings is substantial—approximately $9.8 U.S. billion per annum. This estimate is derived from Cahalan and Room's national survey data (1974) for noninstitutionalized males between the ages of 21 and 59. This study showed that households which contained male drinkers with high consequences (effects of excessive drinking) had typically lower incomes than households without a male alcohol abuser; for example, median 1 (households without male alcohol abuser) earned $9,861, whereas median 2 (households with a male abuser), $7,931.

Berry and Boland point out that in both cases nonlabor income is represented: transfer payments, interest income, and so on. These factors cannot be controlled for in their data. An attempt was made to control for the effects of socioeconomic influences on the differences noted above by applying a corrective factor estimated by Luft (1975) who, in a study of health status, claimed that nearly 24 percent of income differences between well and sick workers were accounted for by such factors.

Even if Berry and Boland's estimates are crude, they draw attention to an area of costs which are rarely mentioned in connection with the possible impact of EAPs. It is evident from their data that the impact of the $9.8 billion loss goes beyond the direct effect on the worker. For example, other services must be withdrawn (child care, house care, and meal preparation and other family-produced services and goods) in order to compensate for the losses incurred by the removal of the male alcohol abuser from the work force even if this is a temporary situation. Clearly, the costs to employees and their families and to society at large must be considered in an appraisal of the impact of EAPs and must be added to the already strong social rationale for the encouragement of such policies. It is important to distinguish between the social benefits of EAPs and the benefits to the employer, as indicated in our discussion of the differential interest principle.

On the whole, reviewers have been much more critical of evaluations of effectiveness in occupational programs than of the rationale and social functioning of these programs. To some extent this is understandable: it is perhaps unfair to talk about the latter until some evidence has been accrued concerning the effectiveness of these programs. However, a counterargument is that evaluation attempts may be directed toward illusory or unrealistic program objectives and that negative results may obscure the social role of these programs. For example, if it is discovered that occupational programs do not achieve more than tertiary prevention, shall we call them a failure? A perspective guided by the view that occupational programs *should* penetrate to the *primary* prevention level would lead to the conclusion that if only tertiary prevention is achieved, the program failed. A perspective guided by the view that tertiary prevention was all that the employer wanted in the first place would tend to modify this picture of failure. Further inquiry might reveal that the occupational program was adopted by the employer largely to avoid the trouble and expense of grievances, hearings, and arbitrations spawned by alcoholics. There is some evidence (Trice and Belasco 1966) that employers may see occupational programs in that light. Adams (1978) showed that dismissals for alcohol-related offenses at work are the most likely to be overturned by arbitrators and yet reinstatements for these cases have the worst prognosis. This should act as a stimulus to employers to protect themselves with an alcoholism policy. This does not mean, however, that the employer wants early identification or primary prevention. It means that he wants a more effective and cost-reducing way of dealing with clearly definable problem drinkers.

One of the missing perspectives in the literature is a consideration of the variation in the *objectives* of the different parties who have an interest in occupational program development and implementation. What may be a rationale for program development to an occupational programming consultant (increased productivity) may be no more than a rationalization to the employer who is more interested in cleaning up a backlog of multiproblem employees who cause a lot of difficulty to everyone. The social control value of occupational programs to industry has not received much emphasis in the literature and yet it is a perspective which could substantially modify the scope of objectives in occupational programming. Similarly, it would tend to modify the interpretation of evaluations of effectiveness in this area.

It is likely that a broader historical approach to occupational programs would serve also to modify our expectations. Bartell (1976) showed that the human-relations ideology in industry was essentially incorporated as an adaptation to swift social change. The ideology was used defensively and was self-serving. It is argued that occupational programming should be seen in the context of the growth of human-relations ideology in industry. This would take us back to the nineteenth century rather than to the 1940s where most "histories" begin. In addition, there is a wealth of literature pertaining to the manifestations of corporate social responsibility (Neubeck 1974, Silk and Vogel 1976, Capitman 1973, Heald 1970, Cohn 1971). Such a perspective suggests that we consider occupational programming to some extent in the same light as corporate involvement in urban renewal, equal opportunity hiring, and community programs for the disadvantaged. This is by no means a cynical exercise. Its purpose is to adjust our sights when looking to industry as the medium through which the solution to alcoholism treatment may be found.

3 A Reconceptualization of Programs and Their Evaluation

The treatment of the philosophy, theory, and practice of employee-assistance programs (EAPs) in the preceding chapters has largely respected the kinds of issues and concerns that have recommended themselves to the attention of recent reviewers of the state of the art in occupational programming (Archer 1977; Schlenger, Hallan, and Hayward 1976; Hitchcock and Sanders 1976). This approach was considered sound enough as a reflection of the kinds of issues and concerns actually found in the literature. It is time now, however, to step back from the framework employed in the foregoing sections in order to consider whether it is in itself a broad enough context for a proper understanding of EAPs and their results. Several intimations have been made that it is not.

A major source of difficulty in opening up the discussion of EAPs is the tendency to dwell on the relatively narrow idea of "program" rather than on the broader concept of "employee assistance." Much of our knowledge about EAP in practice is mediated by researchers and students of the field who accept the area of employee-assistance *programs* as an appropriate subject of inquiry. Consequently, much of the discussion revolves around the effectiveness and efficiency of programming as though these matters could be studied in a vacuum of theory about the intended and actual functions of employee assistance. It is true that within this limited context many useful observations have been made about the apparent impact of EAPs, and many sound proposals for improving our understanding of them. Nonetheless, little definitive information has been gathered to explain the notable *variation* in the results of occupational programming. Most efforts to explain variation in results have cited the following factors as contributors.

1. Failure to ensure that similar programs are actually being compared. There is a tendency to assume that the alikeness of programs has prevailed so that partly implemented policy results are compared with fully implemented ones, or alcohol-specific programs are compared with broad-brush ones and those that fall between these extremes. Further, little attempt has been made to document the presence or absence of theoretically important policy and procedural elements in the programs reviewed. The works of Trice et al. (1978) and Roman (1978) are exceptions to this tendency.

2. Failure to define the nature of the inquiry in terms that allow results of one program to be compared with those of another. Basic terms such as alcoholic, drug abuser, problem employee, absenteeism, accident, improvement, and success are often not defined at all.

3. Failure to employ methods of inquiry (beyond definitional problems) which are adequate for drawing conclusions about effectiveness and efficiency and which vary from study to study, contributing to sometimes spurious variations in results. Williams and Tramontana (1977) recommend that a standard procedure for program evaluation should include comparison of the identified problem group with a control group selected at random from the same work force or on the basis of matched characteristics. Or a comparison of the problem group should be made with the population norms for the whole organization on such dimensions as sickness rates, absenteeism, turnover rates, or accidents. It is the exceptional study that tries to implement these recommendations.

4. Variation in the prevalence of the problem to which the measured program effects are supposed to relate. The prevalence of alcoholism may vary considerably from one industrial environment to another (Comptroller General 1970). Consequently, the bland comparison of penetration rates (usually expressed as the percentage of the total work force in a given organization represented by the identified problem group) is quite misleading if on the one hand a 1 percent problem group is being related to a 3 percent prevalence rate or to a 10 percent prevalence rate of the same problem. Schlenger and Hayward (1975) made specific recommendations for improving the calculation of penetration rates but the usefulness of their formula depends on exact knowledge of the prevalence of the problem (alcoholism, for example) in specific industrial situations. As already observed, most estimates of prevalence are merely guesses.

These explanations of the variation found in the results of EAPs both in terms of penetration and success rates are, however, largely concerned with shortcomings in the *methods* of inquiry and comparison which have been brought to bear on program efforts to date. It is, therefore, difficult to know how much variation would remain to be explained if these methodological problems could be dealt with satisfactorily. It can be said with confidence, however, that some variation would remain simply because EAPs are wanted by different interest groups for different reasons leading to differences in effort and expectations of results. It was pointed out that a level of program activity that is satisfactory to one employer might be entirely inadequate for another, too much for still another, and unsuitable altogether for yet another. Unions and employees on the other hand might take up a position quite different from any adopted by employers since their definition of success may be couched in terms that go considerably beyond job-performance indicators to embrace a more holistic concept of recovery and improvement. Unfortunately, the literature on program results has concentrated on employer-related criteria for success, assuming for the most part that all employers want the same things from an EAP. Similarly, the implied or explicit criticisms of low referral, identification, and success rates of problem employees have assumed the existence of some absolute criterion for effective program functioning which appears to be no less than 100 percent identification, 100 percent recovery. This laudable goal is rarely explicit. It may be found to originate more in the public health sector than in industry, business, or commerce whose expectations are more limited and geared to a multitude of other economic considerations.

In a significant way, the tendency for students of EAPs to ignore the role of different interest groups in the variations in expected and observed outcomes of these programs is an indicator of a more basic oversight concerning the *function* of employee assistance within an organizational context. That is, the avoidance of the subject of variable expectations is a product of conceptualizing the industrial or commercial organization in too simplistic a fashion. Similarly, it is a product of seeing EAP as a mode of intervention which will fit any organization with equal facility given the employer's good-will and motivation. In short, it may well be that we have been asking the wrong questions of EAPs. Rather than asking, how successful are EAPs? we should be asking, what are the functions of EAPs according to the various parties who have an interest in them? Once a satisfactory answer can be given to that question, we can consider what evidence exists concerning the manner in which these various functions are discharged. Consequently, the balance of this chapter will be directed toward the following objectives: (1) a reconsideration of EAPs as *systems of intervention*; (2) a reconsideration of work organizations in the light of modern theory about their functions; and (3) the presentation of a framework for the evaluation of EAPs which is compatible with the reformulations attempted in the first two sections.

The EAP as a System of Intervention

The typical approach to measuring the impact of an EAP has been to assume that EAP is a form of job-performance control and employee rehabilitation which can be tacked on to almost any organization's mode of operation. This assumption is distilled in the constant use of the term *program* to describe carrying out an employee-assistance policy. This is most unfortunate since the proponents of EAP are often disillusioned by the failure of their programming efforts to take hold in certain organizations or by the tendency for the program to peter out after one or two years of functioning. The fact is, however, that many such failures could be predicted from a proper formulation of the problem at hand. An EAP is not just a loose piece of program material that can be wedged into the chinks of the armor that is the public face of most organizations: it is a whole system of organizational intervention with its own philosophy, theory, and practice. When introducing this system to a company, the consultant is proposing not just a way of "rounding up the drunks" but rather a way of running the organization so that current, acute difficulties with problem employees are dealt with and future problems are recognized in their infancy and corrective action applied. For many organizations this is not a minor adjustment; it is a change in management methods. Some companies already employ a form of management which, with little effort, can be extended to cope with problem employees at some level. For employers who do not operate in such a manner, however, the question is whether or to what extent they should change their management methods to cope with the problem employee in a rehabilitative rather than a purely disciplinary manner. The response of the majority of consultants to business and industry who are charged with the responsibility of disseminating EAP has been unequivocal, judging from the wealth of exhortative material in the literature: industry needs EAP and that means change. Perhaps this advocative posture could go unchallenged and could indeed be heralded if the results were more encouraging. The fact is, however, that employers in both the private and the public sector do not appear to respond wholeheartedly to this approach, which leads us to consider what it may be that we are doing wrong.

Certain insights into this problem are provided by the eminent theorist and organizational consultant Argyris (1970). He urges us first of all to realize that change itself is not a primary intervention task and that it should not be assumed that change is necessary or desirable. The need for and the direction of change should be determined by carrying out three primary intervention tasks as follows.

1. Ensure that *valid information* is collected about the client and his system, with its strengths and weaknesses. In the process of collecting this information, "the interventionist needs to be careful that he does not, unrealizingly, see all the clients' problems in terms of his own repertoire of solutions" (p. 31).

2. The interventionist (a term Argyris uses in preference to "change agent" for obvious reasons) should ensure that the client does not look to the consultant for solutions and in that way come to depend on him. At all times, the client system's autonomy must be maintained and action on the client's part must be taken as the result of *free, informed choice*.

3. Before further collaborative action is taken, the interventionist must ensure that any course of action reflects an *internal commitment* on the part of the client system. Even if it is management who approaches the interventionist with the initial request for help, it is ultimately the *system* that becomes the client. Naturally, this embraces the interests of unions and employees. Argyris recognizes that this is a value position but argues that little lasting improvement in a system will result from supporting one interest group in the face of opposition from others. This view is consistent with what appears to be Argyris' more general view of intervention as a public health activity whose basic element is educating clients about "organizational health and illness" (p. 16). Consequently, the underlying goal of intervention is to restore the ability of the client organization to regulate its own functioning. This view

of self-regulation implies a great deal about the health of organizations. In particular, it suggests that the health of an organization can be defined usefully in relation to the manner in which it lives in harmony with its environment. This seemingly abstract idea will receive more attention as we proceed and it will be shown to lie at the roots of an alternative and more realistic approach to helping employers cope with problem employees while maximizing the public health impact of their interventions.

Argyris returns frequently to the point that the success of an intervention is a highly relative business–relative, usually, to the different dimensions and criteria for success employed by the various client groups and the interventionist. "For example, low turnover and absenteeism could be signs of system illness as well as health. In some cases the organization may have minimal turnover and absenteeism because the people are not required to be responsible for being productive. In other cases, high absenteeism may be necessary because it provides the involved and committed people a periodic respite from extreme pressure. Without absenteeism they might quit or become less involved" (p. vii).

Clearly, Argyris is taking a position quite different from advocates of EAP who argue that there is an ideal model of employee assistance which simply has to be sold to employers. Even if it could be shown that the ideal model was an excellent representation of how a fully functioning, healthy organization went about dealing with problem employees, it would not imply that client organizations could appreciate this fact or be motivated to achieve this condition. Argyris, in fact, argues that client organizations can be expected to do no more than *move toward* the goal of better functioning and this concept must be defined relative to the particular needs of the organization at the time. Even then, this relative success is only achievable if the prerequisites to effective action, defined by Argyris' three primary intervention tasks, are met.

According to Argyris' concept of useful intervention, the prevalent strategic error implicit in the dissemination of EAPs has been the strong tendency to "market" EAP as though it were a "thing" or a package for sale rather than to develop a *process of consultation* with clients which would enable all concerned parties to consider what the presenting problem really was and what might be done about it. In those terms, the problem with EAP has been its emphasis on selling a program rather than implementing a helping process within client organizations. It has been as though EAP could, by dint of its powerful rationale in the eyes of public-health-minded people, defy the principles of sound organizational consultation.

The Nature of Work Organizations

Theory concerning the nature of work organizations has undergone considerable change during the course of the twentieth century. In many ways such theory has appeared to be very much a product of the times during which it was generated. For example, the "machine theory" of organizations, first clearly conceptualized as principle by Taylor (1911), saw the worker as no more than a resource to be exploited. The job should be designed and then the worker should be fitted to it. This line of reasoning became known as scientific management and lodged itself in the popular imagination in the form of time-and-motion studies where the predominant concern was to get the most out of a worker in the shortest possible time. It is important to note, with Glen (1975), that not all theorists saw the world in those terms even in Taylor's time: for example, Munsterberg (1913) was one of the earliest advocates of job-person matching—an approach which has now become part of a new discipline, ergonomics.

The human-relations movement in organizational theory developed largely as a reaction to machine theory, emphasizing the importance of psychological and social factors in work. Mayo's Hawthorne studies, reviewed by Roethlisberger and Dickson (1939), were instrumental in bringing such factors to the attention of a wide audience, particularly an awareness of how the informal structure within an organization operated to affect the behavior and motivation of workers. The informal structure refers to the patterns of association among workers independent of the relationships required to complete their tasks. Patterns of association, with shared meanings and understandings, can operate to facilitate or obstruct accomplishment of the organization's tasks. No analysis of an organization's level of functioning can be complete without an understanding of how this informal structure works. The human-relations school was responsible for several key observations which are reviewed by Glen (1975) following Simon (1955) as follows: (1) the act of studying a phenomenon such as worker behavior can change the phenomenon itself (the Hawthorne effect); (2) the opportunity for interaction among employees increases both morale and productivity (the interaction hypothesis); (3) the likelihood of change in group behavior covaries with the degree to which those affected by the proposed change are involved in its planning and execution (the participation hypothesis); and (4) personal conflict results from exposure to two or more groups with conflicting values and attitudes (the cross-pressures phenomenon).

Valuable as these contributions to organizational theory were (and familiar as they may seem now), there was a tendency to overgeneralize from specific studies, and too much emphasis was placed on the individual-group level of analysis (Kelly 1969). Although theories of organization still reflect the human-relations school's impact, there has been an increasing emphasis in the literature on the importance of organizational structure—in particular the varying effects of different arrangements for ensuring control over the quantity and quality of production. This line of inquiry takes into account the different methods for division of labor, management of communication, and control over job performance and technological processes. In addition, certain theorists have extended this structural line of inquiry to incorporate the socioeconomic milieu in which organizations operate, with a view to determining the interaction between the two (Trist and Bamforth 1951, Emery and Trist 1960, 1965). This concern with what amounts to environmental interaction with organizations is part of a larger trend toward "system" thinking as exemplified by Emery (1969). It, too, is a reflection of our times much as machine theory was a reflection of Taylor's time.

Perhaps it is a unique expression of our own era, however, when we find warnings not to regard any theory as valid for all times and places. As Woodward (1965) says, "The danger lies in the tendency to teach the principles of administration as if they were scientific laws, when they are little more than administrative expedients found to work well in certain circumstances but never tested in any systematic way." Notwithstanding these observations, organization theory has matured so that today it embraces a wider range of social and economic factors in its attempt to piece together a useful picture of how organizations function. Of particular importance is open-system theory first popularized by Von Bertalannfy (1950), but with roots in the 1930s. Its point of departure from closed-system theory is its insistence upon the importance of interaction with the external environment as a requisite to understanding organizational behavior. Central to the notion of organizations as open systems are the now familiar (if widely misused) concepts of steady state, input, throughput, and output, and the fundamental idea of mutual permeation of environment and organization.

Steady state has to be differentiated as a characteristic of open systems from the related concept of equilibrium, a characteristic of closed systems. The difference is more than semantic: an open system implies that the internal sociotechnical structure and process of an organization are inextricably linked with the external environment; mutual permeation in turn implying that the fate of the organization is tied up with *changes* in the environment. Equilibrium describes a balance between interdependent parts of a closed system; that is, its components are wholly independent of the external environment.

A steady state defines the capacity of an organization to respond to variations in both the available input (in terms of labor or raw materials) and output requirements, such as market demands. The health of an organization may be defined as its ability to spontaneously reorganize at another, different level, itself characterized as a steady state, *without* the need to modify its basic structure (Emery and Trist 1960). It may be recalled that this concept of organizational health appears prominently in Argyris' discussion of the goals of effective intervention. An organizational consultant must understand and respect these concepts in order to be useful to a client, and so must the EAP consultant. Consequently, recommendations for dealing with a specific problem such as alcoholism must be based on an understanding of the organization's overall functioning. It must not be assumed that an organization can or should change or that EAP is the only system available to prospective employers.

Within the context of open-system theory, a body of data exists that exemplifies the various ways in which an organization and environment interact. One major theme of research in this area has been a study of the way in which technology represents the response of the organization to the demands of the environment (Emery 1969, Woodward 1970, Perrow 1967). Technology, according to this school of thought, exercises a major, influential role in the type of sociotechnical structure that can appear in a work organization. The relationship is not, however, deterministic in that there are often choices available to managers with respect to the nature of the arrangements that can be made for getting the job done. While the range of choices may be limited, they may vary considerably in terms of their effects on productivity, employee behavior, and performance. Early studies by Trist and Murray (1948) demonstrate this point. These investigations were concerned with the various methods of coal-getting in mines. When different social systems relating to the same technology in the same place were compared, it was found that one set of arrangements was superior in terms of both productivity and stress indicators (absenteeism of various kinds). In this case, the despecification of roles and the creation of more interdependent work groups proved more effective than the highly specific division of labor which had been traditional. Open-system theory explains that the flexible social system is simply more responsive to the changes occurring constantly in the underground environment. However, Trist and Murray do not claim an absolute value for a flexible division of labor. The term *flexible* simply describes the work relationships found to be most effective in the situation studied. In other situations (for example, where the task at hand requires specialized, nonsubstitute skills) a more rigid division of labor may be the most appropriate. Furthermore, it is not argued that flexible work roles—in this case, part of the composite social system—are effective in the mining situation because they facilitate friendship patterns and informal social interaction. Rather, it is claimed, the fact that the composite system leads to the provision of adequate resources to do the job properly *in turn* leads to conditions under which task-related relationships based on mutual respect can emerge. It is interesting that Trist and Murray go to such lengths to disabuse their readers of the notion that they are taking a political, value-laden position rather than reporting scientifically ascertained facts.

It is indeed unfortunate that the terms used to describe work relationships are usually value-laden. It is very important, however, to keep an open mind on such matters, particularly so when the implications of the present discussion are brought out in relation to EAP. Chapter 1 noted that the prevalent but not exclusive approach to EAP has been to assume that alcoholism and drug abuse are mainly problems of the individual rather than induced or exacerbated by the work environment. Based on this assumption, EAP seeks to identify individuals who can be removed if necessary from the workplace in order to control the problem. While this approach can be justified on many grounds, it must be appreciated that it is based on expedience rather than an absolute notion of effectiveness. This can be demonstrated by reference to the various ways of controlling absenteeism. It is often urged by proponents of EAP that an employer who tolerates a high proportion of alcoholics must, by definition, be tolerating a high absenteeism rate. Control alcoholism and you will control absenteeism, appears to be the message. To some extent, the validity of this claim has been substantiated by research which demonstrates that absenteeism, overall, is higher among alcoholics and that EAP and related techniques appear to be effective in reducing this consequence. As a strategy for dealing with absenteeism, however, EAP has competition. One cogent example is provided by the Trist and Murray study cited previously. Under the conventional system absenteeism without reason had run at 4.3 percent and had been reduced to 0.4 percent under the new composite system. Sickness and accident absences had been 8.9 percent and 6.8 percent under the old division of labor and had been reduced to 4.6 percent and 3.2 percent, respectively, after the introduction of the new methods. These figures represent percentages of possible (scheduled) shift time lost through the various causes listed. It should be noted that in this example absenteeism was high to begin with.

It is apparent that structural changes can have a major impact on organizational problems of this order. Beyond a certain stage, however, it may be that such an approach reaches a point of diminishing returns. For example, it may be twice as hard to halve an absenteeism rate of 8.2 percent as it is to reduce the rate from 20 to 8.2 percent. Indeed, structural means may not be the answer in this case. The question which faces the conventional EAP consultant in this context is whether the ideal package discussed in chapter 1 is likely to meet the needs of a client organization faced with an absenteeism rate (combined causes) of 20 percent as opposed to one of 8.2 percent. It is likely that the same number of alcoholics were on the payroll in the case of both the conventional and the composite work systems investigated by Trist and Murray. Had the client organization been persuaded to attack the 20 percent absenteeism problem through alcoholism control, it is improbable that it would have been reduced to 8.2 percent. On the other hand, once the major structural problems had been attended to, it may have made sense to approach a fine-tuning of the system through an EAP-type intervention.

The general point to emerge from this discussion is that EAP may not be an appropriate solution to all the organizational problems of which alcoholism and drug abuse may be apparent symptoms. Consequently, it can be argued that it is essential for the EAP consultant to recognize the differences between these presenting problems. Similarly, the employer needs the best advice on whether the problems he is faced with are amenable to programmatic solutions of the EAP type or to structural solutions involving an overhaul of basic control systems as demonstrated by Trist and Murray. Further, following Argyris, it is important to recognize when the limits of intervention have been reached and when no intervention is warranted or likely to succeed.

A Reformulation of the Evaluative Task

The discussion in the preceding two sections has implications of a basic nature for the evaluation of EAPs or for the evaluation of any kind or organizational intervention. We will now explore these implications.

Just as it is essential for the EAP consultant to weigh several considerations before deciding on a course of action (including doing nothing), so it is for the evaluator of any intervention which has been launched in response to a client organization's expressed needs. The evaluator cannot afford to accept the relevance of the attempted solution to the apparent problem as given any more than he can afford to assume that the problem itself is as stated by the principal parties. This is not an exercise in cynicism but rather a precaution against applying results against criteria or expectations that are nonexistent, not shared by all the parties involved, or not really meant to be taken seriously. These are admonitions of a type long since found in the general literature on program evaluations. Williams and Tramontana (1977) bring this approach into the arena of EAP evaluation when they cite Deniston et al. (1968) as a model for the evaluative exercise. The points which they make seem very basic—so much so that they are frequently ignored, to the detriment of the quality of the resulting studies. In approaching the evaluation of any program, however, it is crucial to ascertain, by reference to the principal parties involved, basic facts, as follows.

1. To what problem is the program intended to be a solution? This is far from clear in many cases, especially when several interest groups were involved in program development and may not have seen it in the same way. It is an appropriate point at which to consider the manner in which the interventionist (for example, an EAP consultant) conceived of the presenting problems of the client organization. Did the employer see the problem as absenteeism; the consultant as alcoholism? Did the union have yet another opinion?

2. What is the target group for the program under review? Is it alcoholics or all who manifest absenteeism rates above a certain level, or the one through the other? Do all the concerned parties agree on the target group?

3. What expectations are held by the various interest groups in relation to the target group? Does the employer expect to identify only manifest alcoholics, reduce absenteeism to X percent, while the interventionist wants to identify not only alcoholics but those in danger of becoming so, hoping thereby to reduce absenteeism to Y percent?

4. What activities are seen as being expressly directed toward the achievement of these objectives?

5. What resources (personnel, funds, and materials) are seen as being available for the pursuit of these objectives? Opinions may vary on this, depending on the interests of the respondent. The personnel department may be charged with responsibility for an EAP but see itself as being already overburdened and consequently not emphasize its assigned extra role. The medical department may not be responsible for program administration but may in practice make most of the referrals because of the professional orientation of the staff. The union may feel that certain resources are available according to their agreement or understanding with management but consider that in practice these resources are not available.

6. Is the target problem an area of high priority relative to other problem areas? If management is concerned primarily with meeting government antipollution standards, how much energy will they expend on alcoholism control?

If the union is preoccupied with noise, heat, and vibration abatement, will it support an alcoholism control policy wholeheartedly?

7. Is the program broad enough in scope to address the problem for which it was designed? If the problem is accidents (personal and property), is an EAP broad enough to attack this problem or will it only scratch the surface?

Within the context of adequate answers to these questions, it is then relevant to consider the questions of effectiveness (whose objectives were achieved and to what extent?) and efficiency (at what cost?). A consideration of the latter questions without attention to the prerequisites to evaluation is likely to be a fruitless affair. Indeed, where the results produced by a study that has not paid attention to these matters are not entirely useless, they may be actually harmful: it can be quite misleading and potentially damaging to announce that a certain result was not achieved if none of the parties to the program had expected that result to be achieved.

In a sense, the evaluator has to go through the same logical steps as the interventionist should have gone through in planning his strategy with the client organization. Similarly, the evaluator must have an awareness of the context within which the client organization operates according to the principles discussed in the previous two sections, otherwise no sensitivity will be developed concerning the way in which the program objectives were formulated. The evaluator must know a great deal about the total functioning of the organization in the context of open-system theory to understand the degree to which the intervention is compatible with the needs of the client's system as it seeks a dynamic balance with its environment. A company producing heavy steel in a highly industrialized area but under severely competitive conditions and in a situation where most eligible males are employed may opt to control only those drinkers whose behavior is obviously affecting their work, leaving any attempt at earlier intervention to a time when production demands are not so pressing and selection of personnel can be made from a larger pool of eligibles. Conversely, a company specializing in the production of custom-built precision instruments for a space contract may, under similarly competitive conditions, decide to search long and hard for even incipient problem drinkers. Mistakes in such a highly skilled environment can be annihilating for the firm and sudden absenteeism or unreliability of a uniquely skilled employee can create major problems for replacement and retraining.

These are examples of situations in which the technology of the organization interacts with the demands of the environment in terms of both input (labor) and output (customer requirements) to create fairly specific needs in controlling a specific problem. The response to such a situation may be either structural or programmatic, depending on the results of detailed assessment. Thus an evaluation—much like an intervention—must take into account the overall functions of an organization in the context of its environment in order to appreciate the factors which influence a specific attempt at a structural or programmatic solution to the client's problem. Ultimately, the value of such solutions should be related to the extent to which they are successful in restoring the client system's ability to regulate its own functioning in a manner that is satisfactory to the concerned parties.

The considerations outlined so far serve as a framework within which the study of more specific questions for research becomes meaningful. Given that the appropriate overall, guiding question for this pursuit is, what are the various functions of EAP and how effectively are they performed? it is possible to list a series of questions which (if asked and answered in the context proposed in the foregoing) should serve to develop a picture of EAP not just as a programmatic device but as a means of social control and as a unique creation of the social and cultural fabric from which it is cut.

1. What is the prevalence of alcoholism and other problems in specific industrial settings?
2. To what extent have alcoholism recovery and EAPs been successful in penetrating the populations at risk identified by such prevalence studies?
3. What are the selective factors which operate to yield some people at risk for treatment and not others; is the profile of the identified group similar to that of the unidentified group?
4. What are the characteristics of the most successful systems for the identification, referral, and treatment of alcoholic and drug-dependent employees?
5. What are the various stages of EAP development and implementation; what factors are crucial to the survival of such programs?
6. What is the relationship between job-performance deterioration and alcoholic (or other) impairment?
7. Once identified and referred (by voluntary or mandatory process), what are the short-term and long-term outcomes of such referrals?
8. Does it make any difference in outcome what kind of treatment the employee is exposed to?
9. Are some occupational groups more prone to certain problems than others?
10. Do some industrial situations spawn more problems than others; do certain kinds of people select themselves into certain industrial situations?
11. What is the most effective method of improving an organization's ability to detect and deal with its problem employees? This inquiry should embrace both programmatic and structural approaches.
12. Is the readiness of an organization to adopt EAP a function of its own managerial style, its size, the nature of its business, the characteristics of the consultant, or some combination of these?
13. Can EAPs be expected to achieve primary as well as secondary and tertiary prevention objectives?
14. What motivates private industry to adopt EAPs?
15. What motivates the public sector to adopt EAPs?
16. Are voluntary referrals more desirable than mandatory, and if so, how can they be increased?

17. Is there any difference in outcome between voluntary and mandatory referrals?
18. What are the cost-benefit ratios for alcoholism recovery and EAPs?

Obviously, efforts have been made to address some of these questions. Valuable though these efforts have been and continue to be, they have lacked an overall theoretical perspective within which specific results can become more meaningful by being related to a conceptual whole. This state of affairs is likely to prevail unless an organized effort is made to standardize the ways and means by which studies of EAP and its cousins are made.

In attempting to improve the level of conceptualization and comparability of such studies, much of our information will continue to be based on studies of individual programs and their effects. If this is the case, the methods and procedures used must be capable of yielding comparable information under the following headings.

1. The kinds of people identified.
2. The kinds of people acted upon (or who accept treatment).
3. The kinds of people who refuse treatment and drop out of the program.
4. The relationship of the groups mentioned above to the population at risk in whatever problem category is being investigated (alcoholics). Juxtaposition of the characteristics of the four groups above yields some idea about the selective factors operating in a program in a specific workplace and it gives a proper basis for the computation of penetration rates.
5. The kind of program actually in effect as opposed to what is in writing or what is said by the principal parties. What are the identifiable components of the program?
6. The kind of organization in which the program is located. This involves an analysis of the goals and systems of the employing organization, including some typification of division of labor, power structure, and communication methods. The type of work undertaken by the organization and the environment in which it functions must be characterized in some meaningful way.

Information in areas 5 and 6 is necessary for a study of how organizations accept or reject occupational programs as well as for a study of how programs are actually used.

Although the emphasis of the approach suggested is on *programmatic* solutions to specific problems, opportunities should also be sought for the study of *structural* solutions to the same problems, as exemplified earlier in this chapter. Naturally, comparisons of various approaches should be undertaken where possible. Ideally, these comparisons should be made according to an experimental design following the recommendations of Edwards (1975) among others.

Evaluative Dimensions, Indicators, and Criteria

The information headings just listed are more useful if they are utilized in a general framework for the evaluation of program endeavors. We will now present such a framework. This model arranges information about program performance according to the level of the client organization at which relevant activities take place. Consequently, in order of progression the following activities should be reviewed: (1) the rate and type of case finding; (2) the rate and type of case disposition; and (3) the nature, quality, and rates of desirable and undesirable outcomes. To discuss the evaluation of these activities, it will first be necessary to clarify certain terms which are used repeatedly.

The term *criterion* means a standard which can be used to make decisions (Webster). Standards or criteria are in turn related to the *expectations* or, more concretely, *objectives* of various groups of people who have an interest in the outcome of EAP. There are at least five such *interest groups*: employers, employees, unions, public health agencies, and entrepreneurial agencies such as the Association of Labor-Management Administrators and Consultants on Alcoholism, the NIAAA, and the National Council on Alcoholism.

The criteria or standards are applied to three dimensions of EAP outcome or performance just outlined. The five different interest groups may relate to the same dimensions of outcome or performance but they tend to apply different criteria or standards to them in order to judge success. Success is defined as the degree of relationship between the expected or targeted outcome (judged by the use of a criterion) and the observed outcome. The criteria or standards are applied to the dimensions of performance or outcome through the medium of indexes which are used to measure them. Consequently, we end up with four terms which serve to define the evaluative exercise.

Dimensions ←	*Indexes* ←	*Criteria/Standards*
of performance or outcome (the rate and type of case finding).	of performance or outcome (the relationship of an identified group to the population at risk).	of performance or outcome (two self-referrals for every one mandatory; 70 percent of the population at risk identified).

Based on the knowledge of whether criteria have been met;

Judged Success is a function of the relationship between *observed* performance/outcomes and *expected or targeted* performance/outcomes.

An evaluative model can therefore be built by using the dimensions of case finding, case disposition, and case outcome, relating appropriate indexes to each and then applying the criteria of the different interest groups to them.

Appendix 3A presents this model in its basic terms. It must be remembered throughout, however, that the *interpretation* of results from this undertaking has to be made in reference to the total functioning of the organization in question and according to explicit knowledge of the interest groups' objectives relative to each dimension of program performance.

Appendix 3A Dimensions of Performance

#1: Rate and Type of Case-Finding

Index

1. *Ratio* of identified cases to population(s) at risk. Requires knowledge of *prevalence* of problems (for example, alcoholism) in a given work force.
2. *Correspondence* between characteristics of population at risk and identified cases in terms of:
   Age
   Sex
   Occupation
   Length of service
   Level of job performance (including absenteeism, accidents, and sickness)
   Level of alcohol involvement
   Degrees of mental, physical, and social impairment
   Number of grievances lodged

Purpose

Investigation of selective factors in the recruitment of people into the EAP in terms of the framework in figure 3A-1. See relationship between areas 1 and 2.

Criteria

A. Employer: Criteria are likely to be expressed in terms of *felt satisfaction* with control over employee job performance. The point at which this satisfaction is experienced will vary from one employer to another depending on conditions outlined earlier. Some employers will be content with identification of employees with many, chronic problems while others will push for some form of earlier intervention.
B. Employee: Probably does not care enough to apply a criterion, but if it were found relevant it might be stated in negative terms, for example, don't go so far that you interfere in people's private affairs; avoid "witchhunts."
C. Union: May be interested in identifying people at *early stages* of problem development, but will probably say that identification of a formal kind should be linked only to *job performance* (protection of employee). Wants to avoid bias in identification.

1	Population(s) at Risk (Alcoholics)				
2	Identified Cases (self or other)				Unidentified Cases
3	Acted-on Cases		Not Acted-on Cases		Unknown
4	Good[a] Outcome	Bad Outcome	Bad[a] Outcome	Good Outcome	Unknown

[a]These terms are used here solely for convenience. They are not intended to have any absolute meaning.

Figure 3A-1. The Situation in Many EAPs

D. Public Health Agency: Ideally wants to identify 100 percent of the population at risk.

E. Entrepreneurial Groups: May represent all manner of considerations without always identifying their origins, since all the above interests are represented here.

Note: The dimension of program performance referred to here usually forms the basis for what has become known as the "penetration" rate of case-finding activity. Schlenger and Hayward (1976) have developed a formula for assessing this rate which accounts for work-force turnover and for the successful rehabilitation of a proportion of the identified problem employee group. Thus, the penetration rate equals

$$\frac{PD_1}{A(E+H)-C}$$

PD_1 = number of problem drinkers identified and referred to treatment in a given time period.
A = estimated proportion of problem drinkers in the work force.
E = number of employees at the beginning of the time period.
H = number of employees hired during the same period.
C = number of people who are successfully treated and retain their jobs.

It should be noted that the precision of this formula is only as good as the accuracy of the prevalence estimate (A in the formula). There are no examples in the literature of attempts to *measure* the prevalence of alcoholism in a specific work force so as to provide a basis for the penetration rate. There are many examples of guessing about such prevalence. Sometimes these guesses are based on deductions from national prevalence statistics. In a specific work force, however, it will make a great deal of difference if the prevalence of alcoholism is 6 percent rather than 4.5 percent if this figure is to be used as the basis for estimating the penetration rate of the program.

#2: Rate and Type of Case-Disposition

Index

1. *Ratio* of "acted-on" cases to identified cases.
2. *Correspondence* between acted-on to not acted-on cases in terms of:
   Age
   Sex
   Occupation
   Length of service
   Level of job performance (including absenteeism, accidents, and sickness)
   Level of alcohol involvement
   Degrees of mental, physical, and social impairment
   Number of grievances lodged
3. *Ratio* of voluntary to mandatory referrals, number of refusers.
4. *Differential* use of control options—for example, treatment or discipline.

Purpose

Investigation of selectivity and differential management in the operation of the EAP in terms of the framework described in figure 3A-1. See relationship between areas 2 and 3.

Criteria

A. Employer: Restoration of control over employee job-related behavior is the goal. Therefore, if identification is in itself sufficient to this end, the employer will not care if no further action is taken. Selectivity and differential management are pragmatic, not moral issues.
B. Employee: Is likely to be acutely aware of selectivity and differential management, wanting to minimize it. Prefers options which lead to job retention.
C. Union: Is likely to be alert for signs of discrimination and would urge across-the-board application of procedures.
D. Public Health Agency: Is likely to take the view that all identified cases should be acted on because program objectives include restoration of health

and social functioning as well as job performance. Selectivity is likely to be abhorred. Differential management may be endorsed if the objective is overall rehabilitation in the most effective way.

E. Entrepreneurial Groups: Represent a variety of interests, not always clearly. All the positions in A-D are to be found here.

#3: Nature, Quality, and Rates of Desirable and Undesirable Outcomes

Index

1. *Outcomes* relative to those who accepted help and those who refused it in terms of:

Before, during, and after intervention (if any):

- Age
- Sex
- Occupation
- Marital status
- Length of service
- Employment status
- Level of alcohol involvement
- Job-performance level
- Criminal involvement
- Disciplinary action
- Accidents on the job (workmen's compensation claims)
- Accidents off the job
- Sick leave; sick benefits
- Grievances
- Unauthorized absences
- Marital stability[a]
- Relationship with children[a]
- Levels of psychological and social functioning[a]

2. *Comparisons* of characteristics of those who succeeded or failed or dropped out in the terms listed in (1).

Purposes

Determination of what kinds of people respond favorably or unfavorably to a given program.

[a]These are off-the-job indexes which are typically not included in research studies but which will require investigation in future work if the public health aspects of EAP are to be properly understood.

Determination of the duration of effects.
Provision of the basis for a cost-effectiveness analysis.

Criteria

A. Employer: Will probably emphasize the need for a more effective, efficient employee in the following terms:

1. Improved work performance (including everything from quality and quantity of production to relationships with supervisors and coworkers).
2. Reduced costs due to:
   Absenteeism
   Discipline (including arbitration and grievance activity)
   Sick leave
   Accidents (workmen's compensation premiums and disbursements)
   Training new employees (replacements).
3. Greater employee predictability (planning of shifts).
4. Improved managerial control of personnel by means of:
   Accurate identification of all problem employees whose work performance is affected;
   Effective and appropriate disposition of identified cases (maximum return for costs, without repercussions from employee or union);
   Maximum rate of generation of self-referrals;
   Minimum use of mandatory referrals (less supervisor time).

B. Employee: Will probably emphasize greater stability, welfare, adjustment, "happiness" in the following terms:

1. Maintenance of employment.
2. Maintenance of employment benefits (pay levels, seniority, advancements).
3. Improved physical, emotional health (probably only possible through reduced drinking, abuse of drugs).
4. Reduced financial difficulties (less debts, credit, more income).
5. Reduced legal involvement.
6. Improved family life (wife, children, relatives).
7. Improved relationships with friends, fellow workers, neighbors, community.

C. Union: Will probably emphasize a satisfied membership in the following terms:

1. Protection of membership with respect to:
   Victimization
   Protection of employment
   Employment benefits
   Confidentiality
2. Attraction of new members and affiliates with respect to the advantages listed in (1).
3. Minimization of costs to membership by keeping grievance activity to a minimum.

4. Maintenance of effective bargaining posture with management.

D. Public Health Agency: Will probably emphasize the public's welfare in these terms:

1. Reduced prevalence and incidence of alcoholism and problems due to alcoholism (physical, mental, social).
2. Reduced costs to the state and to the taxpayer resulting from these problems (health, welfare costs, lost production).
3. Protection of jobs, less unemployment.
4. Earliest possible identification and treatment of developing problems due to alcoholism.

E. Entrepreneurial Groups: Will emphasize different things to different people at different times.

4 Studies of EAPs in Industrial Communities

Current Knowledge in the United States

Whatever value may be ascribed to the principle of rehabilitation in the management of problem employees, it becomes a largely academic matter if employers do not endorse it. While it is clear that certain well-known, large industrial, commercial, and business organizations have adopted the principle of employee-assistance programs (EAPs) at least to some degree (Roman 1977), it is far from clear to what extent employers in general have done so. It is quite misleading to assume that the majority of employers would follow in the giants' footsteps. A confounding element in any inquiry launched to discover the prevalence of EAP is the definition to be used in identifying employer practices which go beyond the simple expedient of discharging problem employees. When used in its full sense of an ideal model, EAP is a comprehensive term. The ideal model requires that client organizations manage their affairs in very specific ways that are consistent with the humane philosophy of EAP. If we were to apply the ideal-model criteria against employer practices at large, we would probably find that they were met in very few cases. However, such an inquiry has not been made except in very large employing organizations where over half of the approximately 500 surveyed had some form of EAP in that various key elements associated with the ideal-model approach were found (Roman 1977).

If the criteria for what constitutes an EAP are relaxed to include all employers who incorporate ultradisciplinary practices in their management of problem employees, two further studies are worthy of note. Habbe (1969) inquired into the practices of 160 private organizations through questions directed at their executives. About 62.5 percent reported little or no use of a rehabilitation approach; 25 percent were in the initial stages of developing an ultradisciplinary control policy; and 16 percent had a program in operation that was working well. Unfortunately, the characteristics of these organizations are not described. Schramm (1977b) conducted an inquiry into the content of 500 collective agreements and found that only 46 had some language which related to alcoholism. Specific clauses were found in only twenty-nine cases. Of the twenty-nine, twelve contracts provided only for immediate discharge for a number of specific offenses related to drinking. Fourteen had some kind of disciplinary action short of discharge.

Schramm's study was based on an almost random sample of agreements. As such, it may well have missed certain classic contracts between employers of large work forces and unions, but the picture so presented is probably a good reflection of the general situation as demonstrated in joint union-management agreements. However, many ultradisciplinary policies, procedures, and practices are in effect that do not involve unions in a direct way or are not reflected in collective agreements. The desire to keep ultradisciplinary measures out of the agreement is a matter of principle among certain union spokesmen (Perlis 1977). Similarly, management may wish to keep such practices out of the agreement in order not to become locked-in to a position over which arbitration could arise. Consequently, though Schramm's study is a useful account of the extent to which the ideal-model principle of joint union-management policy construction is represented in collective agreements, it is almost certainly an underestimate of actual collaboration between the relevant parties.

An estimate by the National Institute on Alcohol Abuse and Alcoholism (NIAAA; 1977) suggested that in 1977 there were approximately 1,000 occupational programs in the United States covering a work force about 90 million strong. Sherman (1977) under the auspices of the Association of Labor-Management Administrators and Consultants on Alcoholism, the national professional organization of people concerned with occupational alcoholism in the United States (and to some extent in Canada), claimed that 1,500 such programs existed in 1977, having increased from 300 in 1971.

Clearly, no simple answer can be given to the question, how many EAPs are there? The question can be answered only in reference to a specific definition of EAP and in relation to specific types of organizations. Regrettably, inquiries to date (except Roman's) have failed to provide these parameters. It would be helpful if future studies addressed themselves to the relationship between types of programs and types of organizations.

Studies in Canada

The Province of Ontario

We conducted a limited study of EAP in Ontario at the request of the Addiction Research Foundation (ARF) of that province. The ARF has a long record of industrial, commercial, and business involvement through approximately fifty consultants who are distributed throughout Ontario. The purpose of this involvement has been principally to bring EAP to the employers of Ontario, though it was recognized that various forms of the policy were advocated by different consultants. Nonetheless, the typical message to employers was that they should adopt a written policy statement about alcoholism and drug abuse which emphasized the rehabilitative alternative to dismissal through clear procedures of problem identification, documentation of job-performance levels, constructive coercion, and the treatment-discipline choice. Joint policy development, issue and implementation with unions, was advocated where relevant as were various other elements of program management such as training supervisors, the need for adequate insurance coverage, confidentiality, and a thorough follow-up capacity. The consultants involved in this dissemination and implementation process (both full and part time) were all interviewed by us. Prior to the interview they were asked to contact employers in their areas who had policies in effect which incorporated constructive coercion. They were asked to record the level of activity in the use of coercion and to document the number of resultant referrals. As a measure of program activity, referral rates leave much to be desired. They tend to obscure the relationship between mandatory and voluntary referrals and are probably a better reflection of the former than the latter which are often unreported. Some claim that an organization is doing very well if it can avoid making referrals to outside treatment agencies (dealing with problems internally), though this viewpoint is not an element of the ideal-model approach. Nonetheless, referral rates are one of the more readily accessible indicators of program activity and so they were used in this study.

Extent of Program Activity. The interview process resulted in the identification of 348 organizations in Ontario known to the ARF consultants as employers who utilized constructive coercion in 1975. This is certainly an underestimate of ultradisciplinary practices by Ontario employers as our subsequent studies will demonstrate. The present study is best seen as a report on the extent of EAP among those organizations with whom the ARF had working relationships at that time and who had expressed interest in this approach.

Characteristics of These Organizations. The size of the work force employed by the 348 organizations was 365,642, or approximately 8 percent of Ontario's work force in 1975. This bears an interesting similarity to the NIAAA's estimate of 7 percent of the U.S. work force covered by such programs. The interested group included privately as well as publicly owned organizations. Interest came primarily from the private sector; 71 percent of the organizations were privately owned. The three levels of government represented 29 percent of the 348 employers. The largest single group of organizations (44.8 percent) fell into the 100 to 500 employee category (table 4-1). Very few organizations employed less than 100 people (8.1 percent). The remainder were large organizations with over 500 employees, 2.4 percent having over 5,000.

Eighty-six percent of the organizations were partly or totally unionized. Unions took an active role in the development and implementation of the rehabilitation policy in 127 (42.4 percent) organizations. It is of interest to determine the extent to which the 348 organizations were representative of the industrial divisions in Ontario. Table 4-2 summarizes the relationship between the distribution of the EAP group (the "interest" group) and that of Ontario's employing organizations as a whole.

Table 4-1
Distribution of Organizations by the Size of the Work Force

Number of Employees	*Percent of Organizations in This Category (n=348)*
100 or less	8.1
101-500	44.8
501-1,000	22.5
1,001-5,000	22.2
5,001-10,000	1.5
10,001+	0.9

Table 4-2
Distribution of Organizations by Industrial Divisions

	Percent in This Category		
Industrial Division	*Ontario*	*Interested Group (n=348)*	*High Referring (n=53)*
Agriculture	6.9	0.0	0.0
Forestry	0.3	0.6	0.0
Fishing and trapping	0.1	0.0	0.0
Mines, quarries, oil	0.3	4.0	13.3
Manufacturing	7.6	48.0	40.1
Construction	17.9	0.6	2.2
Transportation, communication, and utilities	1.3	9.2	11.1
Trade	24.6	1.3	0.0
Finance	8.1	1.3	0.0
Community business and personal service industries	31.7	8.2	6.6
Public administration and defense	0.7	25.3	26.6

Source: Ontario Statistical Centre Classifications.

Note that table 4-2 refers to percentages of organizations, not to percentages of work forces employed by those organizations. For example, manufacturers represent about 7.7 percent of employing organizations (Ontario Statistical Centre) but account for 25.6 percent of the work force (Kirkham 1977). Obviously, manufacturers employ a disproportionately large percentage of the work force. On the other hand, community business and personal service industries (including education, health and welfare, religious organizations, amusement and recreation, and accommodation and food services) account for 31.7 percent of employing organizations but 26.4 percent of the work force.

Table 4-2 shows that among the 348 organizations there were a disproportionate number of manufacturers relative to the distribution for Ontario as a whole. In terms of ARF's consultant efficiency this is probably an advantage in that it makes sense to devote limited resources to areas in which maximum impact could be expected. The relatively small number of manufacturing organizations employ a disproportionately large number of employees, making them an excellent target for EAP intervention. However, the proportions represented from various industrial divisions in table 4-2 are not necessarily a result of selective pressures from outside agencies, such as ARF. Such agencies are often simply responsive to requests from industry where interest originated in some other fashion. Clearly, the manufacturing industry in Ontario is both more interested and easier to motivate than other industries where EAP-like practices are underrepresented. Such underrepresentation occurred in the divisions of agriculture, construction, trade, and finance, and community, business, and personal service industries. Overrepresentation occurred in manufacturing, mining, transportation, communication, and utilities, and public administration and defense. The qualification in the manufacturing industry that its overrepresentation was a product both of employer motivation and ARF consultant's selective intervention applies equally to these observations. Overrepresentation and underrepresentation of industries relative to the overall distribution may be a function of employer motivation in interaction with consultant (interventionist) effort.

We were able to look closely at areas of high employer interest by inspecting subgroups within major industrial categories. Within the manufacturing division (table 4-3) the major groups were food and beverage companies, paper and related products companies, metal fabricators, and makers of transportation vehicles. These groups were proportionately represented among the EAP organizations save that transportation was underrepresented while food and beverage was overrepresented.

A similar comparison can be conducted in the division of transportation, communication, and utilities (table 4-4). Evidently, a disproportionate amount of activity occurred in utility (electricity, gas, and water) and communications companies, but less than expected in transportation and storage. In the mining division (table 4-5) metal mines are dramatically overrepresented among the EAP-oriented organizations while all other concerns are underrepresented. In the community and personal services division (table 4-6) health, welfare, and educational services are boldly overrepresented, while the rest are underrepresented to the point of absence in religious organizations, personal service, and amusement and recreation concerns.

Referral Rates. We must further note that the prevalence of alcoholism and other problem conditions varies from one industry to another and even within industries. Therefore interest in or response to EAP might vary according to

Table 4-3
Major Industries in the Manufacturing Division

	Percent in This Category	
Major Groups	*Interested Group (n=148)*	*Ontario*
Food and beverage	9.4	11.0
Tobacco products	0.6	0.0
Rubber and plastics	6.7	3.0
Leather	0.6	1.1
Textile	2.0	2.6
Knitting mills	0.0	0.5
Clothing	1.3	3.4
Wood	2.0	6.7
Furniture and fixtures	0.6	7.3
Paper and allied industry	12.8	13.7
Printing	2.0	1.7
Primary metal	5.4	1.9
Metal fabricating	18.3	17.2
Machinery	6.7	5.1
Transportation	15.5	3.6
Electrical products	5.4	3.8
Nonmetal mineral products	2.7	3.8
Petroleum and coal products	0.6	0.2
Chemical and chemical products	6.7	3.6
Miscellaneous manufacturing industry	0.0	9.0

Source: Ontario Statistical Centre Classifications.

Table 4-4
Program Representation in Transportation, Communication, and Utilities

	Percent in This Category	
Major Groups	*Interested Group*	*Ontario*
Transportation	50.0	69.0
Storage	0.0	20.2
Communication	14.2	4.2
Electric power, gas, and water utilities	35.7	6.3
Total	100.00	100.00

Source: Ontario Statistical Centre Classifications.

Table 4-5
Program Representation in Mining

	Percent in This Category	
Major Groups	*Interested Group*	*Ontario*
Metal mines	92.8	12.4
Mineral fuels	0.0	6.2
Nonmetál mines	0.0	0.0
Quarries and sand pits	7.1	34.9
Services incidental to mining	0.0	43.3
Total	100.00	100.00

Source: Ontario Statistical Centre Classifications.

Table 4-6
Program Representation in Community and Personal Services

	Percent in This Category	
Major Groups	*Interested Group*	*Ontario*
Education and related services	36.0	2.8
Health and welfare service	52.0	17.7
Religious organizations	0.0	8.2
Amusement and recreation	0.0	6.7
Services to business management	4.0	18.7
Personal service	0.0	11.6
Accommodation and food service	4.0	20.4
Miscellaneous services	4.0	13.5
Total	100.00	100.00

Source: Ontario Statistical Centre Classifications.

the perceived need for it. This subject is taken up in detail in chapter 7. Similarly, variations in prevalence might be reflected (directly or indirectly) in referral rates. However, there are some limits in the use of referral rate as an indicator of program activity. Variations in prevalence compound the difficulties of using this rate.

The overall rate of referral or the number of persons referred per hundred employees annually by the 348 organizations was 0.33 percent in 1975. Of the 348 organizations, 97 did not refer participants during this period at all. The rate of referral among the active 72.1 percent ranged from 0.01 to 10.0 percent with the mean at 0.77 percent. Over 60 percent of the referring companies maintained rates below 0.5 percent. Somewhat less than one in every five organizations had referral rates in the 0.5-0.99 percent range (table 4-7). Fifty-three

Table 4-7
Pattern of Referrals from Organizations Involved with the Addiction Research Foundation in 1975

Range of Referral Rate	*Frequency in Percent (n=243)*	*Cumulative Frequency*
0.01-0.10	9.6	9.6
0.11-0.50	50.6	60.2
0.51-0.99	18.3	83.7
1.00+	21.5	100.0

Note: Excludes ninety-seven organizations which made no referrals in the study year.

organizations activated referral rates of 1 percent or over. Organizations in this high-referring group were rarely large, close to 80 percent of them employing less than 500 persons. The rate of referral in this high referring group ranged from 1 to 10 percent. Approximately half of the organizations attained rates between 1 and 2 percent, 40 percent were between 2.01 and 3.00 percent, and 10 percent of this group referred 3.01 percent or over.

The present data indicate that very high referral rates (3.01 percent and over) were achieved only by very small organizations (100 or fewer employees). The fifty-three organizations in this high-referring category represented six of the eleven industrial divisions. Forty percent were engaged in manufacturing. Public administration and defense accounted for another 25 percent. The other four divisions were mining, transportation, personal business, and construction, which were responsible for 33.2 percent of the total (table 4-2).

The high-referring group resembled the interested group in industrial characteristics, save that mining was overrepresented, sending more referrals than would be expected either from their declaration of interest in EAP or their proportion of the total work organizations in Ontario. The average annual referral rate for 1975 in organizations with some form of EAP (0.33 percent) is higher than the range of referral rates reported by Hitchcock and Sanders (1976) in their review of the literature. When averaging the reported referrals over the reported lifespans of the programs, Hitchcock and Sanders concluded that the penetration rates were in the range 0.01-0.006 percent.

Studies of Selected Industrial Communities

The study of 348 organizations was predicated on the assumption that all those employers had some form of EAP, even though their practices may not have corresponded to the ideal-model described in chapter 1. Chapter 5 gives an account of the extent to which a sample of the high-referring group identified from among the 348 exhibited the ideal characteristics thought to be necessary to generate high levels of program activity. It soon became evident that the concept of rehabilitative management or employee assistance flourished in some employing organizations which had never come to the attention of ARF and did not consider that they had a program or indeed a policy. It was apparent, too, that the 348 organizations known to ARF in 1975 were usually not the result of systematic evaluation of community needs. With these considerations, we decided to seek out and take advantage of opportunities to conduct surveys of industrial communities. Several such opportunities arose as a result of ARF consultants' interest in serving their communities more effectively through establishing a broader base of activities in the industrial, commercial, business, and public sectors to control alcoholism and drug abuse. We report three surveys of this type in the form of case studies.

Case Study Number One

The data were collected in a community in northwest Ontario, with a population slightly in excess of 5,000. The majority of the inhabitants are French Canadians. The sample included all organizations employing more than ten persons, forty-seven in all. The majority (76 percent) employed less than fifty persons and only 2.4 percent were in the larger category employing over 500 (table 4-8). All organizations in public administration employed less than fifty-five people. The organizations represented eight industrial categories. Approximately 25 percent were in public administration, 23 percent in trade, and 11.9 percent in manufacturing. The others were distributed in the remaining five divisions (table 4-9). Forty-two percent of the organizations were partly or totally unionized.

The study utilized a questionnaire, and a personal interview with the chief executive of the organization. Of the forty-seven asked, forty-two or 90 percent completed the interview; the others were not available. During the interview the participants were asked to communicate their knowledge and opinions about their own work environments in three areas. The first area dealt with prevalence rates. The second area focused on the methods the organization used to manage problems created by drug- and alcohol-abusing employees. The third area involved taking an inventory of how many problem employees were identified, referred, or dealt with internally. Also the size of the unidentified problem population and the reasons for not reaching them were explored. We now describe the results.

Reported Prevalence. In response to questions about the prevalence rates of alcoholism and drug abuse among the work force at their plant or office,

Table 4-8
Distribution of Organizations by Size

Number of Employees in Organization	*Frequency*	*Percent*
Less than 20	15	35.7
20-49	17	40.5
50-99	4	9.5
100-199	3	7.1
200-299	2	4.8
500+	1	2.4
Total	42	100.0

Table 4-9
Distribution of Organizations by Industrial Division

Division	*Percent*
Agriculture	2.4
Manufacturing	11.9
Construction	2.4
Transportation	7.1
Finance	4.8
Community business	7.1
Public administration	28.6
Trade	23.8
Missing	11.9
Total	100.0

Source: Ontario Statistical Centre Classifications.

40 percent of the respondents believed there were no employees on staff who abused alcohol or drugs. In approximately 30 percent of the organizations the size of the work force impaired due to alcohol abuse was estimated to be between 1 and 5 percent. A further 14 percent estimated that alcoholism affected in excess of 5 percent of their work force, in some cases as much as 13 percent. Some of the participants were not familiar with the subject and were not able to comment on prevalence rates (table 4-10).

Basically, drug abuse was not seen as a problem by the majority of the participants. Two-thirds of the organizations reported no past experience with employees whose job performance was affected as a result of drug abuse. One in four did not know if there were employees on their payroll who could be classified in this category. Only 4.8 percent felt that drug abuse affected a portion of their work force (table 4-11).

Table 4-10
Alcoholism Prevalence as Estimated by Employers

Estimated Prevalence Rate (%)	*Percent of Respondents*
0.0	40.5
0.1-4.9	16.8
5.0	11.9
5.1-7.0	4.8
7.1-13.0	9.2
Do not know	16.8
Total	100.0

Table 4-11
Drug Abuse Prevalence as Estimated by Employers

Estimated Prevalence Rate (%)	*Percent of Respondents*
0	66.6
2	2.4
5	2.4
Do not know	26.2
Missing	2.4
Total	100.0

Reported Methods. Although a large number of employers reported no current problems with alcoholic employees, all were familiar with the problem through some earlier experience. All the organizations had a method for dealing with such employees. The mechanisms differed somewhat from organization to organization but could generally be classified into one of four categories (table 4-12).

1. Personnel policies to guide the management of problem employees in a uniform way had been developed by one-third of the organizations. Of these, half had a formalized, written policy while the others used past precedents and hence could be regarded as following a procedure. Those guided by a written policy were all government organizations whose guidelines had been developed by their respective ministries.

2. The majority of employers in this area dealt with each problem case individually. Since the symptoms of alcoholism varied, the employer set up a flexible system in which such factors as age, skills, and seniority were taken into consideration.

Table 4-12
Approaches Followed by Different Organizations with Problem Employees

Management Approach	*Organizations Following This Approach (%)*
Written policy	16.7
Procedure	16.7
Case by case	61.8
Fire them	2.4
Other	2.4
Total	100.0

3. Though emphasizing the merits of written personnel policies in other areas, some considered management of substance-abusing employees did not create a serious enough problem to warrant a specific formalized policy.
4. One organization fired employees with addiction problems.

Identification and Referral. Reported identification rates for the twelve-month period prior to the interview ranged from zero to 7.4 percent. About 47 percent of the organizations did not identify alcoholic cases, 38 percent identified less than 1 percent, and 7.2 percent between 1 and 2 percent. The identification rate was over 2 percent in one organization (table 4-13). Only one organization had to deal with drug-related performance problems. The opinion of the respondents on the penetration rate (based on identification) showed a high level of confidence in their respective systems. Fifty percent reported no unidentified alcoholics among their work force. One in four believed a few were unidentified. Only 8 percent felt that the size of the unidentified group was large and 20 percent did not know (table 4-14).

The group which indicated potential candidates for identification believed that such people had not yet been reached because either their drinking had not yet affected their job performance in a noticeable way or the employees had been able to cover up their unsatisfactory job performance (table 4-15). Although approximately half the organizations made identifications of alcoholics, only 12 percent made referrals to outside treatment agencies (table 4-16).

It is conceivable that the difference between the total number of organizations which made identifications (47.6 percent) and the number which made referrals (12 percent) is an expression of the degree to which most identified cases were dealt with internally. There is little to suggest from the data whether either internal or external management was effective in restoring employees to a level of job performance satisfactory to their employers. However, the presence of a written policy was not related to whether identifications were made (table 4-17). On the limited evidence available, it appears that referrals were less likely to be made from organizations with written policies (table 4-18).

Table 4-13
Identification Rates for Alcoholics

Rate in Percent	*Percent of Respondents*
0.0	47.6
0.1-0.9	38.1
1.0-1.9	7.2
2.0+	2.3
Do not know	4.8
Total	100.0

Table 4-14
Employers' Estimates of Size of Unidentified Problem-Employee Population

Estimated Percent of Unidentified Group	*Percent of Respondents*
5 percent	4.8
All unidentified	2.4
Some unidentified	23.8
None unidentified	50.0
Do not know	19.0
Total	100.0

Table 4-15
Perceived Barriers to Identification of Problem Employees

Perceived Barriers	*Percent of Respondents*
Alcoholic hides problems successfully	7.1
Job not yet affected	23.8
Not applicable	69.1
Total	100.0

Table 4-16
Referral Rate of Alcoholics

Rate in Percent	*Percent of Respondents*
0.0	85.6
0.1-0.9	7.2
1.0-1.9	2.4
2.0+	2.4
Do not know	2.4
Total	100.0

Table 4-17
Organizations Identifying Alcoholic Employees

Identification Method	*Percent in This Category (n=40)*[a]	*Percent Who Identified Alcoholic Employees (n=22)*
Written policy	17.5	15.0
Procedure	17.5	20.0
Case by case	65.8	65.0
Total	100.0	100.0

[a]One could not answer; one fired all alcoholics.

Table 4-18
Identification Methods of Referring Organizations

Identification Method	*Percent in This Category (n=40)*[a]	*Percent Who Referred (n=6)*
Written policy	17.5	0.0
Procedure	17.5	16.6
Case by case	65.8	83.4
Total	100.0	100.0

[a]One could not answer; one fired all alcoholics.

However, all organizations with formal written policies were agencies of the government. In addition, the organizations in this sample were small. Consequently, generalizations are not in order. Nonetheless, the results raise questions about any simple relationship between the existence of a written policy and actual identification and referral activity. They suggest further that employers of smaller work forces are able to control alcoholism by means other than formal policies at least to some extent. Chapter 6 explores the case of the small businessman in greater detail.

Case Study Number Two

This study was conducted in an area of northern Ontario bordering on Lake Superior and served by a regional office of the ARF. The area for which this office is responsible included, in 1978, about 60,000 people in the work force. This figure grew from approximately 45,000 in 1968. About 40 percent of the work force were employed by fifty organizations, three-quarters of which had more than 100 workers. The data for the study are derived from records maintained by the ARF center director. These records were in the form of completed questionnaires sent out annually to forty-eight of the organizations. This group of employers received considerable attention from the ARF center between 1971 and 1977 since they represented the most efficient target for the limited resources of the agency. Generally, the efforts of the ARF were directed toward the dissemination of the ideal model of EAP. It must be stressed that the data collected were intended primarily for use by the interventionist (the ARF center director) in monitoring the activities of the client organizations and in determining their needs: they are not suited to the task of evaluation, and are not presented in that context. The information is of value to a wider audience, however, because it provides an example of the manner in which the EAP ideal model *can* be disseminated, even though much data on this process is not available. Thus, even though it is not possible to attribute a known effect to the work of the ARF interventionist, by 1977 over three-quarters of the forty-eight organizations had developed a written policy. The remainder had some type of procedure in effect for the management of problem employees. Among those with policies over half had a broad-brush approach: that is, assistance was available for a variety of problem conditions beyond alcoholism and drug abuse (table 4-19).

Over 66 percent of the organizations were private, 87.5 percent were unionized, and nearly 80 percent employed more than 100 people, though only 8.2 percent employed between 1,501 and 2,500 (table 4-20). Nearly half the organizations employed between 100 and 500 people. Whether or not the prevalence of EAP in this group of employers is due to the interventionists' actions, clearly it is an unusual situation judging from the literature on the extent of EAP reviewed earlier in this chapter. It is evident, too, that the trend toward greater use of EAP among these organizations was progressive, at least between 1971 and 1975 at which point a leveling off and even a decline may be detected (table 4-21). The dropoff which can be seen in table 4-21 may be more marked than the 1977 figure would suggest since the latter includes a certain number of repeaters—employees referred more than once. It was not always possible to determine whether referrals were repeaters or not because of the uneven quality of record keeping.

The value of record keeping by organizations on identified problem employees has been for years a controversial issue. There are two sides to the debate: (1) if the company does not keep records, there cannot be an adequate followup and so an effective course of rehabilitation cannot be maintained; (2) if a person becomes labeled as an alcoholic, in the long run he may suffer through loss of promotion opportunities. Also references needed for another job might include the treatment record.

The short-term record-keeping practice of these forty-eight organizations was known to the center because the yearly questionnaire included the number of referrals. It was not known if the organizations kept accurate records on their own referrals. As part of the 1977 survey we asked the employer for this

Table 4-19
Type of Organizational Policy for Problem Employees

Policy Scope	*Frequency*	*Percent*
Alcoholism only	11	29.7
Alcoholism and drug abuse	6	16.2
All problems (broad brush)	20	54.1
Total	37	100.0

Table 4-20
Distribution of Organizations by Size of Work Force

Employees	*Number of Organizations*	*Percent of Organizations*
100 or less	10	21.3
101-200	5	10.6
201-300	5	10.6
301-500	12	25.5
501-1,000	9	19.1
1,001-1,500	2	4.2
1,501-2,500	4	8.2
Unknown	1	2.1
Total	48	100.0

Table 4-21
Long-Term Referral Practices of Participating Organizations

Year	*Number of Referrals*	*Number of Mandatory Referrals*	*Mandatory Referrals as Percent of Total Referrals*
1971	19	No information	–
1972	68	29	42.6
1973	62	31	50.0
1974	118	49	41.5
1975	140	49	35.0
1976	141	68	48.2
1977	110	No information	–

information and compared it with the yearly reports. Of the forty-eight organizations, forty-four responded to this question and thirty-eight reported long-term record keeping.

A comparison of the number of referrals reported yearly to ARF and those cumulative figures for 1977 showed that the majority of employers who keep long-term records, underreport the number of referrals. That is, the majority of employers keep long-term records only on certain problem employees, resulting in underestimation of referrals over the long run.

It was also evident from the data that there is more than one pattern in the referral behavior of each organization when dealing with the alcoholic employee. Some refer each problem employee only once; others give a number of chances. Of the thirty-one who kept records and made referrals, fourteen gave the problem employee only one chance. The total referral by these organizations was fifty-nine in 1977. A somewhat larger group of employers (seventeen of the thirty-one) was willing to give more than one chance to alcoholic employees. Between 1972 and 1977 the 17 organizations referred 191 of which 84 were repeaters.

Organizations which refer their employees more than once for alcoholism treatment reported higher recovery rates than those which gave only one chance. The latter group indicated that 28.8 percent were fired within the first twelve months after treatment, the same size group quit, and 42.9 percent were on staff twelve months or longer after treatment. Recovery rates reported by individual organizations varied and ranged from 13.5 to 100 percent. Organizations which allowed more than one chance to their employees reported that at the end of the twelve-month followup 10.5 percent were fired, 12.4 percent quit, and 76.7 percent were still employed. The reported recovery rate by individual companies again demonstrated wide variation. Some saw 100 percent success while others perceived very little.

Another area of concern was the method the employer used to identify the problem employee. At one time, signs and symptoms of alcoholism were considered good indicators. Later on, advocates of the ideal-model approach emphasized that the supervisors' strength lies in the area of job-performance evaluation rather than diagnosis. This point of view was and is based on the belief that job performance will suffer as a result of substance abuse and will be the best and earliest signaling device of developing problems. In spite of this belief it is not clear to what extent employers follow the job-performance-alone approach in identifying problem employees. The results of our study indicate that 62.2 percent of employers do not use job performance exclusively for identifying the alcohol-abusing employee but depend on other aspects such as signs, symptoms, and reports from co-workers, family, and plant nurse.

Although beset with problems of interpretation, it is worth noting the referral rates reported by forty-three employers whose records were sufficiently complete and accurate to warrant a computation (table 4-22). Over a three-year period the majority of organizations referred in the range of 0.01 to 1.0 percent of their employees. Some referred over 1 percent while others referred none. The number of voluntary referrals bore an uneven relationship to the number of mandatory referrals over the total study period (table 4-21). The proportion of mandatory referrals reached a high in 1973 (50 percent) and a low in 1975 (35 percent). No overall trend toward more voluntary referrals

Table 4-22
Average Rate of Referral for a Three-Year Period in Forty-Three Organizations

Average Annual Rate of Referral	*Number of Organizations in This Category*	*Percent*
0.00	10	23.2
0.01-0.10	4	9.3
0.11-0.50	15	34.9
0.51-1.00	9	20.9
1.01-1.50	1	2.4
1.51-2.00	4	9.3
Total	43	100.0

is discernible. The noted variations may be as much a function of variations in reporting practices as in actual practice. On the whole, however, referrals from this sample of organizations occur at rates that are higher than those reported by Hitchcock and Sanders (1976) as being typical of EAP.

Case Study Number Three

This study was conducted in an industrial sector of the southwest corner of Ontario. It is a small, isolated industrial island surrounded by predominantly agricultural sections. This area is often referred to as the petroleum capital of Ontario. Large segments of the work force are employed by the petroleum and its support industries. The ARF serves this area through a regional office. During its early days the staff of this office formed liaisons with local and provincial health care delivery agencies to develop treatment facilities for industrial referrals within the community.

The limited resources of the center allowed only a passive, responsive type of promotion of industrial programs. Service to industry was in the form of support for those who needed assessment, counseling, or supervisory training. Later changes in ARF's organizational objectives necessitated a more aggressive role toward local industry. To carry out this mandate the center wanted to assess the present state of occupational programs among local employers. To achieve this aim the present survey was conducted, involving all the organizations in the area employing more than forty workers, a total of forty-six. These organizations employed approximately two-thirds of the total work force or close to 19,000 people.

The aim of the survey was to assess the perceived seriousness of alcohol- and drug-related problems among various work forces, to document the types of program developed by different organizations to cope with these problems, and to see what impact such interventions made in terms of identifying and referring substance abusers. The method used in this study was identical to that described in case study number one. We now describe the results.

Participating Organizations. The majority of these organizations employed less than 300 persons (table 4-23) and were privately owned (69.6 percent). The largest subgroup among the private organizations was the petrochemical and affiliated manufacturers (table 4-24). Three-quarters of the organizations were unionized.

Perceived Size of Alcohol- and Drug-Abusing Groups. Approximately 30 percent of the respondents estimated the size of the alcohol-abusing population in their own work force to be less than 1 percent, somewhat more than one-third estimated it to be between 2 and 7 percent, and 33.3 percent did not know. The majority (70 percent) of the participants claimed no knowledge of the size of the work force abusing drugs. About 19 percent estimated that drug abuse affected between 1 and 5 percent of their work force.

Types of Intervention. Only 4.3 percent of employers still practice dismissal for alcoholism. The others had adopted a rehabilitative approach to deal with the problem employee. As many employers (41.3 percent) opted for a written policy for the regulation of these matters as opted for a case-by-case approach.

Table 4-23
Sizes of Organizations

Sizes	*Frequency*	*Percent*
Less than 100	8	18.2
100-299	10	40.9
300-499	15	15.9
500-999	6	11.3
1000-1999	2	4.6
2000+	3	6.9
Total	46	100.0

Table 4-24
Types of Industry in Participating Organizations

Industrial Classification	*Percent*
Agriculture	2.2
Manufacturing	39.1
Construction	13.0
Transportation	2.2
Community business and personal service	13.0
Government	30.4
Total	100.0

Source: Ontario Statistical Centre Classifications.

About 6.5 percent had a procedure, that is, a uniform way of managing problem employees which respected precedents but was not formalized. Over half of the employers (56.5 percent) offered assistance only to those with alcohol-related problems, though nearly one-third (28.3 percent) afforded aid to all employees with any problem that affected job performance in an adverse manner.

Because of the concern for maximizing rehabilitation opportunities for employed substance abusers, it was of interest to know why some organizations decided not to develop a more formalized method for handling problem employees. While the reasons varied, most fell into one of three categories: (1) it was not a sufficiently serious or recurrent problem to warrant a more elaborate administrative method (13 percent); (2) each problem case manifested itself in a different way and needed unique handling (13 percent), so that a blanket policy would not be flexible enough to fulfill these needs; and (3) the present method met the organization's requirements, and until new needs arose any change in this practice would be premature (6.5 percent). Another 8.7 percent used all three arguments to support their lack of a formalized policy.

Indicators of Deteriorating Job Performance. The majority of the employers (80 percent) used job-performance-related indicators only, while the remainder used signs and symptoms of alcoholism as an additional part of the identification process. The most commonly used job-performance-related indicator was absenteeism. This was used exclusively by 26.1 percent of the organizations, but the majority used a more holistic approach and considered the employee's attendance as only part of his total performance. Other indicators were day-to-day performance, behavior on the job, lateness, and safety records. Some employers combined job-related indicators and the putative signs and symptoms of alcoholism such as blurry eyes, shaky hands, and so forth to make the identification (table 4-25).

The group responsible for the identification of substance-abusing employees varied. In 65.2 percent of organizations the supervisor was responsible for identification, though the medical department was usually supportive. In seven organizations supervisors took no part in identification. This responsibility was taken over by personnel officers, superintendents, or others. Although nearly two-thirds of the organizations reported that supervisors were responsible for identifying problem employees, only one-third provided supervisory training, and only one-tenth indicated that at least 80 percent of the supervisors were trained.

Program Impact. Without accurate data on the prevalence of substance abuse in specific work forces, it is difficult to judge the effectiveness of the procedures described so far in terms of identification and referral rates. However, an attempt was made to estimate effectiveness by using two different approaches. The first was through the participants' own perception. Employers were asked

Table 4-25
Indicators of Deteriorating Job Performance

Indicators	*Percent*
Absenteeism	26.1
Absenteeism, job performance	13.1
Absenteeism, behavior	6.5
Absenteeism, behavior, safety	2.2
Absenteeism, behavior, job performance	8.7
Absenteeism, behavior, lateness	4.3
Absenteeism, signs, symptoms	4.4
Absenteeism, signs, symptoms, behavior	2.2
Absenteeism, signs, symptoms, behavior, lateness	2.2
Absenteeism, signs, symptoms, behavior, job performance	2.2
Safety	2.2
Job performance	6.5
Behavior	4.3
Signs, job performance	2.2
Signs, attitude, job performance	2.2
Do not know	6.6

to indicate whether in their knowledge or judgment there were alcohol or drug abusers not yet involved in their rehabilitative programs. Six percent believed that their program identified all the alcoholics. Nineteen percent did not know. Approximately 70 percent believed there were active alcoholics in their work forces not yet involved in the program. Several reasons were given for this. The most commonly held view was that job performance is the last thing to suffer, and that intervention before job deterioration appears is not feasible. Also in some work situations close supervision was not possible. This would be typical for plants where relatively few specialists maintained equipment distributed throughout large areas. Also mentioned were factors such as coverup and union interference (table 4-26).

The second approach was to document the number of alcoholics each organization identified between 1970 and 1977 and compare the identification rate with an estimated prevalence rate. Only thirty-five organizations (76 percent) were involved, since the others did not keep records (tables 4-27 and 4-28). The thirty-five organizations identified 127 substance abusers of whom 114 were alcoholics and 13 were dependent on drugs (table 4-29).

Using the number of identified abusers, a crude estimate of the system's effectiveness can be calculated for alcoholism. No such estimate can be attempted for drug abuse. The impact of the alcoholism control policies can be calculated by relating the known rate of identification to an estimate of the prevalence of alcoholism. One of our recent estimates of the latter in the industrial setting, reviewed in chapter 7, places the population at risk in the range of 1.8 to 2.6 percent, which means a population at risk of between 283 and 426 (based on

Table 4-26
Reasons for Failure to Identify Problems

Reasons	*Percent*
Alcoholics hide their problems	8.7
Job not yet affected	30.4
Job not affected; coverup	6.6
Job not affected; lack of supervision	2.2
Job not affected; voluntary referrals	8.7
Coverup	4.3
Lack of supervision	10.9
Union interference	2.2
Do not know	2.2
No problems	4.3
Missing	19.6
Total	100.0

Table 4-27
Status of Record Keeping in Participating Organizations

Record-Keeping	*Percent of Organizations in This Category*	*Number of Employees in Organization*
Yes	76.1	17,077
No	23.9	2,663
Total	100.0	19,740

Table 4-28
Organizational Referring Pattern

Referral Activity	*Number of Organizations in This Category*	*Number of Employees in Organization*
Alcoholics identified	32	15,762
Alcoholics not identified	3	1,315
Total	35	17,077

Table 4-29
Identified Substance Abusers, 1970-1975

Dependence	*Number Identified*	*Frequency in Percent*
Alcohol	114	89.7
Drugs	13	10.3
Total	127	100.0

tables 4-28 and 4-29) in the present area. This estimate is based on survey use of the Mortimer-Filkins questionnaire (1973) in industrial settings and is thought to be conservative. This survey device defines three groups: the high-risk or alcoholic group; the presumptive problem drinkers or medium-risk group; and the normal or nondrinking group. For present purposes discussion of the medium-risk group is omitted. When attention is focused solely on the high-risk group, a maximum of one in three alcoholics is identified through the industrial identification system in this area. The chances of identification vary depending on the organization for which the employee-at-risk works.

What happens to identified problem employees varies. Two organizations fire them. The others provide rehabilitative opportunities, either by referring the alcoholic employee to outside agencies or by providing internal counseling. Some use both rehabilitative methods, depending on which alternative is thought to be most beneficial for the employee (table 4-30). Naturally, one of the first steps in any program is an effective identification procedure. While identification may be successful, it can be meaningful only if linked with proper treatment and followup. Employers can contribute a great deal to success by providing followup programs for their returning employees. Although employers recognize the importance of this phase, only 15 percent of the organizations included followup in their rehabilitation program.

Organizational Size and Employer Practices. Our recent study (chapter 9) suggests that organizational size is an important influence on the type of substance abuse policy, procedure, or practice in industrial settings. The present study appears to bear out this relationship, though there are only four large (1,000 or more) organizations so that no statistical inferences can be made about the apparent trends in tables 4-31 to 4-35. It is evident, nonetheless, that larger companies tend to have written policies (table 4-31), while smaller firms (200 or less) tend to subscribe to case-by-case management of problem employees, emphasizing discretion and expedience rather than consistency and uniformity of practice.

Table 4-30
Organizational Procedure When Dealing with Alcohol-Abusing Employees

Procedures	*Percent in This Category*
Refer to outside agency	50.0
Refer some; handle the rest internally	21.9
Handle internally	18.6
Missing	9.5
Total	100.0

Table 4-31
Size of Organization and Type of Intervention

	Organizations			
Type of Intervention	*Small (≤ 200)*	*Medium (201-999)*	*Large (≥ 1,000)*	*n*
Written policy	33.3	46.2	75.0	18
Procedure	3.7	15.4	0.0	3
Case by case	44.4	38.5	25.0	18
Fire them	7.4	0.0	0.0	2
Other	3.7	0.0	0.0	1
Missing	7.4	0.0	0.0	2
n	27	13	4	44

Table 4-32
Size of Organization and Percentage of Population Estimated to Be Abusing Alcohol (on Payroll)

	Organizations		
Population, Percent	*Small*	*Medium*	*Large*
Less than 1	7.7	8.3	0.0
1-5	46.2	41.7	100.0
5+	7.7	16.7	0.0
Do not know	38.5	33.3	6.0
n	27	13	4

Table 4-33
Training for Supervisors and Size of Organization

	Organizations		
Size of Organization	*Training*	*No Training*	*n*
Small (≤ 200)	9 (42.9)	12 (57.1)	21 (58.3)
Medium (201-1,000)	5 (45.5)	6 (54.5)	11 (30.6)
Large (≥ 1,000)	4 (100.0)	0	4 (11.1)
n	18 (50.0)	18 (50.0)	36 (100.0)

Note: Figures in parentheses are percentages.

Table 4-34
Speculation about Existence of Unidentified Alcoholics on the Payroll and Size of Organization

	Organizations		
Unidentified Alcoholics	*Small*	*Medium*	*Large*
Some	72.0	84.6	75.0
None	8.0	7.7	0.0
Do not know	20.0	7.7	25.0
n	27	13	4

Table 4-35
Followup Program and Size of Organization
(percent)

Followup Program	*Small*	*Medium*	*Large*
Yes	22.2	66.7	33.3
No	77.8	33.3	66.7
n	27	13	4

The four largest companies estimated the size of their alcohol-abusing population to be between 1 and 5 percent. Although this estimate is common among other industries, too (table 4-32) many small-sized and medium-sized firms would not or could not estimate the percentage of alcoholics on the payroll. While both medium-sized and small-sized organizations reported similar rates of supervisor training programs (slightly less than half having carried out some such training), all firms with over 1,000 employees had this type of training (table 4-33). Medium-sized organizations were somewhat more likely to report the existence of unidentified alcoholics on their work force than either small or large organizations (table 4-34).

Although not too much should be read into this observation, it is consistent with a finding of our study in which medium-sized organizations (500 to 1,000 employees) emerged as having the greatest difficulty with control of alcoholism (see chapter 5). This observation must be juxtaposed with the finding of the present study which says that medium-sized organizations are *more* likely to have a followup program than either their larger or smaller counterparts (table 4-35). It might appear that although medium-sized organizations try hard, they still experience more dissatisfaction with the results of their efforts than larger firms (perhaps with better *formal* control) or smaller firms (perhaps with more effective *informal* control over employee job performance).

Union and Employer Practices. Eleven of the forty-six organizations were not unionized, providing an opportunity to look at the role of unions in program development. The size distribution of unionized and nonunionized firms was almost identical, making a comparison between them more meaningful.

The existence of unions was not associated with written policies as opposed to case-by-case methods of problem management. No association was found between unionization and the tendency to report unidentified alcoholics in the work force in question. Unionized companies seemed somewhat less likely to have followup programs for referred problem employees on return to work (30 percent) than nonunionized firms (50 percent). There was only a slight tendency for unionized companies to have provided more supervisory training than nonunionized concerns (55 percent as opposed to 45 percent) and no difference between them at all with respect to keeping records on their alcoholic or drug-dependent employees.

5 Hypothetical Key Elements

The concept of an ideal model of employee-assistance programs (EAPs) was discussed at length in chapter 1. Numerous theoretical and logical arguments were put forward to suggest that such a model might be of limited usefulness in the long-term task of developing and implementing assistance programs for more than a small minority of employees. Chapter 4 showed that employers often practice some form of rehabilitative management with problem employees but the particular requirements of an ideal-model EAP are rarely met. Even though 8 percent or less of all employees were covered by EAP in something resembling the ideal-model form both in the United States and Ontario, the majority of employers used ultradisciplinary means to cope with problem employees. We suggested earlier that EAP may be too rigid for the needs and capacities of many employing organizations and that the very idea of a fixed program might be dysfunctional. However, theory and logic are best put to empirical trial, since the concepts involved in organizational functioning are complex. Potentially important variables can be left out of the abstract reasoning process unless care is taken to test the mettle of the latter in the field and modify the theory accordingly. We decided, therefore, to investigate the putative role of "key elements" in the development and implementation of EAPs. These key elements were outlined in chapter 1, drawn from various accounts of the essential components of EAP. Useful summaries of these components may be found in Follman (1976) and Hitchcock and Sanders (1976). Hardly any field tests of the assumptions underlying these accounts have been attempted. The work of Roman (1977) is one of the few examples of such field tests. While Roman tried to identify the reasons for policy adoption, nonadoption, and use and nonuse among major American corporations, he listed a series of essential EAP components according to their level of importance as perceived by company executives. In general, executives attached more importance to the need for program confidentiality and health insurance coverage for inpatient treatment of alcoholism than to orientation sessions for management, education of employees about the program, or supervisory training. These concerns may be unique to the positions held by Roman's respondents: they were all highly placed officers in their organizations. However, their responses raise the issue of relativity in key elements and suggest that a full picture of EAP functioning can be achieved only through multirespondent sampling within organizations. This form of sampling was undertaken in our study.

Method of the Study

In this study we converted the hypothetical key elements into the form of questions incorporated within an interview guide which was administered to senior executives, managers, and union officials in a sample of organizations selected from those with some form of EAP in Ontario. The eighteen organizations had referred 1 percent or more of their employees for treatment of alcoholism in 1975.

The criterion of referral rate, based on the percentage of the work force which has treatment, is open to question. The study raised major doubts about the usefulness of this rate as an index of program success. Similarly, recovery rates were not useful as indicators of success. We used this criterion in making our selection because the literature on evaluation of such programs invariably includes the penetration rate as an indicator of program success or at least program activity (Hitchcock and Sanders 1976, Williams and Tramontana 1977, Edwards 1975). We decided to allow the criterion to stand the test of our study rather than shelve it prematurely.

Hypothesis

We expected that uniformity in the organizational characteristics and procedures found among the eighteen industries would tend to confirm the validity of the assumptions on which EAP goals and imperatives are based. Notable variation in these organizational characteristics and procedures would suggest that employee-assistance activity is related to variables other than those implied or explicit in the assumptions.

Selection of Respondents

We interviewed respondents from key areas in the selected organizations. We wished to talk not only to informants who were responsible for the program but also to respondents from production, medical, and personnel departments, and to union officials. We aimed to move beyond the viewpoints which emerged from studies such as those of Schlenger, Hallan, and Hayward (1976) of "selected occupational programs" and of Erfurt and Foote (1977) which are based on reports of program functioning by those responsible for the programs. The bias in such reports limits their usefulness in understanding how organizations manage problem employees. Having once decided to draw on a wider variety of opinion, however, the problems of data analysis were quite severe. While the objective of multiinformant sampling is to obtain a more comprehensive picture of organizational functioning, it is difficult to compose an integrated picture of these organizations in such a way that they can be compared. The difficulty arises from the tendency of informants to be inconsistent among themselves, requiring the use of a device to describe the various levels of consistency as well as the content of agreements and disagreements. A further confounding reality is the fact that not everyone we wanted to talk to was available, for reasons both practical and political. The end result of this selection procedure was that the initial sample of eighteen organizations was reduced to twelve for multirespondent comparisons. Consequently, though data are available on the other organizations from single informant sources, our report is based on the twelve organizations for which multi-informant data are present. A total of forty-six respondents provided information in the eighteen organizations.

Characteristics of the Sample Organizations

The sample was selected in a purposive manner according to the criterion of high activity based on penetration rates. Employers in both public (n = 3) and private (n = 9) sectors were included. The tasks of these organizations varied from national defense to foodstuff manufacture, to mining and heavy industry. The size of the organizations was from 115 to 2,500. However, some employers were part of larger parent companies or organizations. In those cases it might have been expected that the existence of a master policy, governing alcoholism control throughout the organization, would have a major influence on the shape and functioning of specific programs under its auspices. This turned out to be the case in only very broad terms. Master policies appeared to be less important than adaptations and specific applications developed in response to local conditions.

The Interview Questionnaire and Procedure

The principal data-collecting device was an interview questionnaire administered to two or more respondents in each organization. Informants were always seen alone, even though this request sometimes raised anxieties. The interviews were invariably carried out by one of two researchers (the authors). The questionnaire consisted of sixty-five sets of questions most of which had unstructured or partly structured response possibilities (see appendix B). The origin of the items used in the interview was principally the framework represented in table 1-1.

In addition to questions based on the hypothetical key elements, other items inquired about overall organizational functioning and characteristics: size, ownership, extent of unionization, type of management style, and type of work done. Particularly important was a set of questions about the type

Table 5-1
Employee Health Services

Type of Service	*Percent of Respondents*
No medical department	14.6
Physician on staff	18.8
Nursing station	41.7
First aid	14.6
Do not know	10.4

Table 5-2
Employee Health Care

Medicals	*Percent of Respondents*
None	14.6
Routine	10.4
Required	29.2
Preemployment	25.0
Do not know	20.8

and quality of control which respondents perceived their organizations to have over management of human resources in their workplace. Consequently, these items are referred to as "organizational control items." The remainder of the items used in the interview are referred to as "organizational perception and program items."

Before discussing whether or not key elements were discernible from the data gathered, we will first describe some basic characteristics of the organizations. The responses of all forty-six respondents are used.

Results of the Study

General Data

The respondents reported that 80 percent of the participating organizations were privately owned. The organizations employed between 115 and 2,500 persons. Respondents were distributed among these organizations as follows: sixteen respondents in small firms (115-500 employees); fifteen in medium (50-1,000); and fifteen in large (1,001-2,500). Eighty percent were unionized. Union membership was high, ranging from 80 to 95 percent of the respective work forces. The privately owned companies were either in mining (16 percent) or manufacturing (62 percent). Employee health services were established in 75 percent of the organizations. The scope of these services differed between organizations; some were offered by physicians, others by nurses, still others by first-aid personnel (table 5-1). The type of health care also varied. Employees infrequently received routine medical checkups. Preemployment examinations were reported by one out of four respondents (table 5-2).

Perceived Seriousness of Substance Abuse. Participants' perception of the seriousness of alcohol or drug abuse among their own work force varied: 35 percent believed that alcoholism was either a serious problem or was disrupting production; 38 percent thought it was not serious; and 25 percent could give no opinion. However, 23 percent of the respondents estimated that between 5 and 10 percent of their work force were abusing alcohol to the point at which it affected their job performance, and 8 percent estimated that the problem affected an even larger proportion of their employees (table 5-3). Nearly 30 percent were unable or unwilling to make an estimate of alcohol abuse. Well over half of the respondents would not or could not estimate the percentage of their work force affected by drug abuse so that it interfered with job performance (table 5-4). However, those who made an estimate considered drug abuse less prevalent than alcoholism insofar as it affected job performance.

Perceived Level of Organizational Control. The participants' perception of their organization's control system was a central concern of this study. Recall that all the selected organizations had high-referral rates. It was assumed that in order to achieve these high-referral rates, the program had to be fully implemented. An organizational framework that allowed a high degree of efficiency must have a high level of control over employee job performance: that is, an environment in which the majority of jobs were supervisable, quality supervision enabled quick perception of job deterioration, and documentation of other job indicators (such as absenteeism) helped to identify and process a referral efficiently. The results did not bear out these assumptions. Sixty percent of the participants reported that the control system of their organization was functioning at a less than satisfactory level (table 5-5).

The reasons for this varied. In some cases loose management practices or large spans of control were cited. In others the production system simply did not permit day-to-day control. An example of the latter state of affairs is a production system dispersed over wide geographic areas such as might be found in forest industries. Another case is minimally supervised night shifts.

A third of our respondents could not give a clear answer concerning the capacity of their organization's record-keeping system to identify deteriorating job performance within a reasonable period of time. Another third felt that their record-keeping system had the capacity; still another third believed their

Table 5-3
Proportion of Respondent's Work Force Estimated to Be Abusing Alcohol

Estimated Percent of Work Force	*Percent of Respondents*
0	12.5
0.1-0.9	12.5
1.0-4.9	14.7
5.0-9.9	23.0
10+	8.4
Do not know	29.2

Table 5-4
Proportion of Respondent's Work Force Estimated to Be Abusing Drugs

Estimated Percent of Work Force	*Percent of Respondents*
0	29.2
0.1-0.9	2.1
1.0-4.9	10.5
5+	4.2
Do not know	56.2

Table 5-5
Reported Satisfaction with Job-Performance Control

Job-Performance Control	*Percent of Respondents*
Not satisfactory	42.1
Partly satisfactory	18.4
Satisfactory	39.5

Table 5-6
Record-Keeping Capacity for Identifying Job Deterioration in a Reasonable Time Period

Response	*Percent of Respondents*
Depends on the job, but does not take long	35.5
Yes, but not acted upon	16.7
No	14.2
Do not know	33.3

record-keeping may or may not have had the capacity but even if it did the information was not always acted upon (table 5-6).

Development of Documentation Methods. In theory, documentation of a problem employee's job deterioration and the action taken to correct the behavior is a major factor in, if not a prerequisite for, effective implementation of a program. From the participant's practical viewpoint less emphasis was given to this issue. Only 27.1 percent reported that documentation of this kind was well developed. An additional 12.5 percent said that they had a limited kind of documentation. Half the respondents, however, were unable to comment on this matter.

Types of Procedures and Policies. About 61.4 percent of participants reported that their organizations had a written policy to handle employees with addiction problems; 12.5 percent reported procedures; and 18.8 percent followed a case-by-case method. Only 35.4 percent of the participants considered that their alcoholism policy or procedure fitted well with other standard organizational policies and procedures. Over 40 percent could not make this judgment.

Age of Programs. Remarkably, 25 percent of the respondents did not know the age of the program in their organization. About 31 percent said the program evolved over time; 10.5 percent declared their organizations had been practicing a form of EAP for three to six years, and 12.5 percent for 7 years or more. Another 20 percent said their programs were two years old or less. Evidently the majority of these organizations had policies, procedures, or practices which had been in existence for some time.

Program Promotion. A variety of program promotion methods were reported by participants. In some organizations the policy with a covering letter was sent to the employees' home, in the hope that the family might act as a first line of defense against developing problems. The family, in particular the spouse, was seen as a potential ally in getting the abuser into treatment, perhaps even as a voluntary referral. Other organizations confined program promotion to the work environment and posted the policy on bulletin boards. In a limited number of cases, the union was actively involved in policy promotion and the discussion of the program was placed on the union meetings' agenda. Often organizations took a less aggressive approach and did not arrange a policy announcement. In these companies if problem employees required treatment, the employee was given the opportunity to obtain it. Recovered employees later on became the program promoters (table 5-7).

Supervisory Training. Over half the participants indicated that supervisors had been sent to training programs in order to help them cope with problem

Table 5-7
Method for Informing Employees of Existence of Program

Promotion Method	*Percent of Respondents*
No promotion	20.8
Word of mouth	20.8
Policy sent to all homes and posted on bulletin boards	12.5
Posted on bulletin boards	8.3
Union meetings	4.2
Other	6.1
Do not know	27.1

employees. Twenty percent indicated clearly that this had not occurred, while about the same number did not know.

Responsibility for Program. Responsibility for the EAP lay most frequently in the personnel department (39 percent). In only one case was the medical department exclusively responsible for the program in spite of the fact that several organizations had such departments. Some 14 percent of respondents claimed unions had primary responsibility; 16 percent said a committee (not necessarily a joint committee) fulfilled this role. However, 20 percent of the respondents were not clear where the responsibility lay.

The infrequency with which medical departments are exclusively responsible for EAPs among organizations large enough to have such facilities (over 500 employees) is a phenomenon noted also by Erfurt and Foote (1977) in their study of EAP in the Greater Detroit area. The personnel department, the industrial or labor relations unit, the union, and other special departments played a much more significant role in the operation of EAP than the medical department. This difference was not accounted for by the size of the organization: that is, companies large enough to have medical departments did not always or even usually assign responsibility for EAP to these units. A higher proportion of organizations had medical departments in charge of programs in a study by Schlenger, Hallan, and Hayward concerning the characteristics of selected occupational programs (1976). Here, seven of the fifteen organizations studied were reported as having the medical department in charge of the EAP.

Evidently, there is considerable variation in program location. Although no clear evidence exists, it might be hypothesized that program location depends on an interaction between several factors: (1) the orientation of management and to some extent union toward alcoholism: do they consider it a disease amenable to medical intervention, or is it more a psychosocial or behavioral problem requiring appropriate intervention; (2) the available resources or functions in an organization: locating the program in the medical department is not an option if no such department exists; (3) the type of organizational structure that preexisted the program's introduction: the existence of a functional management control system suggests different alternatives for EAP location than a strictly hierarchical control system; (4) the decision of management and union whether to approach alcoholism, however defined, from a specific or broad-brush direction; and (5) the degree to which alcoholism control is seen to be an integrated part of employee job-performance control or a separate problem.

Implementation. Respondents were asked whether the EAP in their organization was fully implemented. This was interpreted to mean whether the policy or procedure was actively used or available for use throughout the organization. Over 52 percent of respondents replied affirmatively, 20 percent could not speak for the whole organization, and another 20 percent felt the program was not fully implemented.

Program Structure. The importance of active union involvement in program implementation is often emphasized. In our study the cooperative partnership concept between management and union when developing, implementing, and managing the program (specifically, joint policy development, joint policy issue, and a joint committee) did not materialize. The majority of participants perceived the policy development issue and program implementation as management's responsibility. Only in a very few cases was the union involved. After the program was developed the managing aspect was sometimes delegated to a committee. At this level union involvement was more frequent (table 5-8).

Responsibility for Identification and Confrontation. There was a general agreement on program procedures. If an employee's job performance needed improvement, he would first be admonished. If improvement did not follow this confrontation, a written warning was issued. Suspension followed the written

Table 5-8
Structure of Program

Structure	*Percent of Respondents*
Formal joint committee	10.4
Informal joint committee	6.3
Formal committee (management)	8.3
Not unionized, no committee	8.4
No committee, but unionized	56.3
Joint development and issue	6.3
Joint development	10.4

warning with the threat of eventual dismissal. About 37 percent believed it was the supervisor's job alone to identify problem employees; 27 percent, a cooperative effort with supervisor, a superintendent, the head of personnel, or the medical department. Confrontation was perceived as the manager's responsibility. Only 17 percent reported that confrontation was also left to the supervisor, and again only one person mentioned mutual responsibility between management and union. Indeed, the role of committees, whether formal, informal, joint, or not, appears to be relatively insignificant. Participants did not consider them as either a source for identification or as the groups who eventually deal with the problem employee. Although 16 percent said that the committee was responsible for the program and 25 percent reported the existence of a committee, only 10 percent believed that the committee was involved in the development and use of the program, and none saw the committee as the channel through which the program was implemented.

Indicators of Problem Development. Part of the ideal model of EAP is the stipulation that procedures for identification of problem development should be based on signs of deteriorating job performance. Consequently, respondents were asked to describe the cues which warned them that a problem existed or was developing. As table 5-9 shows, job performance occurred frequently as a problem indicator but usually in conjunction with such others as social behavior, absenteeism, and the signs and symptoms of drinking: hangovers, blurry eyes, shaking hands, and so forth. The latter are considered by many experts in the field to be so ambiguous that they should not be used as problem indicators for EAP unless they directly affect job performance. Even then, it is easy to mistake the results of heavy drinking for other conditions. The problem identifier is not a diagnostician.

Table 5-9
Indicative Signals of a Problem Employee

Indicators	*Percent of Respondents*
Job performance	14.6
Job performance, social behavior	18.6
Job performance, absenteeism	12.5
Job performance, absenteeism, social behavior	4.2
Job performance, absenteeism, signs, symptoms	4.2
Absenteeism	6.3
Absenteeism, social behavior	4.2
Absenteeism, signs, symptoms, social behavior	6.3
Job performance, absenteeism, signs, symptoms	4.2
Signs, symptoms	2.1
Do not know, no answer	22.9

Absenteeism is itself an aspect of job performance but respondents referred to it separately and often used it alone and in conjunction with other indicators without reference to job performance as such. This may reflect a reality of problem employees, namely, that they often choose to absent themselves from work if they judge that the risk of making mistakes, having an accident, or otherwise coming to their employers' attention is too great. In summary, job performance was mentioned as the sole indicator in only 14.6 percent of responses (with 22.9 percent not responding at all to this question), but it was mentioned as the prime indicator in conjunction with others in a total of 58.3 percent of all cases. Similarly, though absenteeism is mentioned as the sole indicator in only 6.3 percent of all cases, it can be found together with other indicators in a total of 37.7 percent of the responses.

Insurance Coverage. The financial survival of the identified employee and his family causes anxiety not only for the problem employee but also for his supervisor. The status of the substance abuser's insurance claims for lost wages during the treatment period is obviously an important issue, but unfortunately a very unclear one. On the basis of this study insurance covering wage losses treats alcoholism as an illness and covers the employee's wages for the treatment period (52 percent), but 33 percent did not know whether this was the case or not. Again nearly half of those participants who reported alcoholism being included in the wage loss coverage were unable to identify the terms of the policy. The reported policy coverage varied. In some cases it covered 100 percent of the wages and paid from the first day. Others had a waiting period, and some paid only part of the insured wage (table 5-10). About 42 percent of respondents did not know whether wage losses for drug-dependent employees seeking treatment were covered, but 44 percent said such coverage existed. Few of the latter knew details (table 5-11).

Followup. Employees returning to work after treatment for alcoholism or drug addiction need a supportive environment. The employer can provide this in the form of followup. The participants were asked about the followup system their organization included in the program: 27.1 percent saw the usual job performance evaluation as the best check on the individual's progress; 14.6 percent reported a formal followup program involving meetings with the employee on a regular basis sometimes in conjunction with an Antabuse program; 16.7 percent said there was no followup program; and 41.9 percent did not know whether any followup system was provided.

Origin of Program. Participants were asked what motivated their organizations in the development of a rehabilitation program. The most commonly held view was that the program evolved over time and it was not prompted by one specific factor or issue. Some felt that alcoholism affected production and the program

Table 5-10
Type of Coverage for Alcohol Abusers

Coverage	*Percent of Respondents*
Waiting period	25.0
100 percent first day	10.4
Less than 100 percent first day	6.3
Less than 1)0 percent, waiting period	6.3
Not applicable	8.3
Do not know	43.8

Table 5-11
Type of Coverage for Drug Abusers

Coverage	*Percent of Respondents*
100 percent first day	19.0
Less than 100 percent first day	14.3
Less than 100 percent, waiting period	14.3
Do not know, waiting period	52.4

Table 5-12
Origin of Program Development

Response	*Percent of Respondents*
Key people developed alcoholism	4.2
Alcoholism affected production	29.1
No one reason, gradual development	39.6
Outside pressure, public opinion	10.5
Education	6.3
Organization looks after its employees	20.1
Organization's desire to control accidents and absenteeism	6.3
Decrease retraining costs	2.0
Head office	8.3

development basically was a corrective measure. Twenty percent indicated that their organizations "looked after" their employees: the substance abuse program was just one part of their personnel policy which included all problems their employees might have to deal with. Other reasons such as pressure from outside agencies, financial reasons, or desire to control absenteeism were also mentioned but only by very few (table 5-12).

Discipline or Rehabilitation. Guidelines by which problem employees who are to be managed on a primarily disciplinary basis can be differentiated from those who are to be treated on a primarily rehabilitative basis were expected to characterize the procedures of the organizations studied. Such differentiation was thought to lie at the root of any well-functioning program for identification and referral of employees with problems beyond their ability to control. Clearly, rehabilitative methods are not intended for management of employees who simply do not care to work or otherwise fulfill their bargain with the employer of wages for a good day's work.

However, few such guidelines existed. This situation tends to throw supervisors back on their own resources when trying to determine whether the rehabilitation policy should be activitated. Frequently, this appears to involve the use of information from outside the workplace: a phone call from the employee's wife or rumors about the employee's drinking habits.

Accountability. The identifier, though entrusted with the identification of those whose job performance has fallen below normal, is not expected by management to do this job according to set standards. Only 16.7 percent of the participants reported that the identifiers' job evaluation included the management of employees with lower performance than average and 14.6 percent indicated that although supervisors are expected in theory to be responsible for the management of problem employees, in practice they were not and problems relating to this aspect of their own job performance did not affect their evaluation. Surprisingly, one-third of the respondents were not familiar with the policy or the practice.

Exclusion. Rehabilitative programs are generally intended to apply without discrimination to all employees, both white collar and blue collar, supervisory and nonsupervisory. In our sample, over half the respondents indicated that this was the case, but 29.2 percent did not know, or were not prepared to comment, while 14.6 percent felt that white-collar employees were sheltered from the policy—a practice which is not necessarily in their best interests.

Confidentiality. Confidentiality is often considered to be a program component which is essential for effective implementation. In practice, however, it was not so easy to achieve. Organizations located in more isolated areas or smaller communities found confidentiality difficult to maintain, especially in alcohol-related cases. Often coworkers knew about the source of the employee's problem long before it affected job performance requiring the employer to take corrective steps. Confidentiality is also a problem area for smaller organizations, especially when the work force is stable. Employees get to know each other on a personal basis and again the problem is known among coworkers often before corrective measures by the employer become relevant (table 5-13).

Career Promotion. A question which arises frequently for employees considering the treatment option is whether their chances of promotion within the organization are affected by a decision to seek help, thereby admitting to

Table 5-13
Confidentiality Component of Program

Confidentiality	*Percent of Respondents*
Emphasized	22.9
Difficult to achieve	25.0
No special precautions	14.6
Do not know, no answer	37.5

certain problems. According to 47 percent of our respondents, their chances would not be affected. Some in this group even suggested that a recovered alcoholic might have a better chance since he had proved his ability to cope with difficult situations. However, in certain careers a record of alcoholism could mean the end of the person's professional future, as reported by approximately 10 percent of the participants. Over one-third did not know what would be the effect of a history of alcohol abuse on the individual's opportunities, even if it could be demonstrated that the condition was under control.

Early Identification. The employer often knows about an employee's problem before job performance shows any deterioration. If the problem is alcohol-related, the employee's chance for recovery is thought to increase when referred to treatment at an early stage. From a social and also a private cost point of view, therefore, it might be desirable to have an EAP set up in such a way that it would function at a secondary prevention level and would have a built-in referring mechanism for those who have a problem but are not yet impaired at the job-performance level. Although the importance of focusing on this group was evident to some of the participants (12.6 percent), the majority either did not know whether it would be advantageous for their organization to emphasize early identification (42 percent) or thought that under the present ethical and legal guidelines of their organization it would be impossible to interfere with an employee on anything other than a job-related basis (35 percent).

How Could the Program Be Improved? Over a third of our respondents were unable to offer an opinion on this subject, while 27 percent felt that the program was working well. Suggested improvements included (1) more education for supervisors and the whole work force (10 percent), (2) more structure for the program such as is provided by a policy or full-time coordinator (10 percent), and (3) change in attitudes within the organization so all problem drinkers would be referred to outside help (8 percent).

Key Elements

The primary goal of data analysis was to find whether high alcohol-control program activity was associated with uniformity of management practices across all the organizations studied. This meant that a measure of uniformity had to be derived to consider both intraorganizational and interorganizational consistency. These measures had to reflect both the amount of agreement among respondents and what the agreement was about within and between organizations.

After we analyzed and coded the interview responses we developed a scoring method which ascribed a consistency score to every item for every organization. The score was based simply on how many respondents in a given organization answered a question in the same manner. Since all the organizations provided three respondents, we gave a maximum score of 3 for complete agreement on any item, 2 for two out of three, and 0 for no agreement. Building on scores for individual items, we derived a total consistency score for every organization. These scores, in table 5-14, range from 54 to 153, a considerable variation. A further breakdown of these scores is shown in table 5-15 where consistency scores for organizational control items (size, ownership, degree of control over job performance, and so on) and organizational perception and program items are shown separately. In this table, an actual score and a relative score are shown for both sets of items.

The relationship between the relative scores on both organizational control items and organizational perception and program items is shown in table 5-16. Although most organizations scored high on the organizational control items, their scores on organizational perception and program items were quite scattered. This suggests that there is little overall relationship between the manner in which organizations perceive and report their *general* functioning, as seen through the control items, and the manner in which they perceive and report the functioning of their rehabilitative programs.

The pursuit of the key-elements hypothesis required that we investigate whether common elements could be found among organizations reporting the same high level of program activity. Table 5-14 shows that some organizations were able to generate a high level of referral activity with remarkably little consistency to back them up; see, for example, organizations 11 and 15. The question remains, however, whether some of the items for which consistency scores were generated are more important than others and whether a subset can be found that is common to all or a majority of the organizations studied. However, the eighteen items associated with the organization demonstrating the lowest overall consistency in table 5-14 were not a common set.

Another approach to identifying key elements was to rank order all the interview variables according to their mean consistency. This was computed

Table 5-14
Organizational Consistency Scores

Organization Code	*Consistency Score*[a]	*Number of Consistent Control Items*	*Number of Consistent Perception and Program Items*
1	104	7	48
2	102	7	31
3	94	7	30
4	106	7	34
11	54	4	21
12	109	6	37
13	144	7	48
15	57	5	18
16	66	6	24
17	153	7	46
18	132	7	45
20	113	7	41

[a]Maximum score: 180.

Table 5-15
Relative Organizational Consistency Scores

	Organizational Consistency Control Scores		*Organizational Consistency Perception and Program Scores*	
Organization	*Actual (occs)*[a]	*Relative (roccs)*[b]	*Actual (ocpps)*[c]	*Relative (rocpps)*[d]
1	21	1.0	83	.53
2	21	1.0	81	.51
3	21	1.0	73	.46
4	21	1.0	85	.54
11	10	0.5	44	.28
12	18	0.8	86	.54
13	19	0.9	125	.79
15	15	0.7	42	.26
16	17	0.8	49	.31
17	21	1.0	131	.82
18	21	1.0	111	.70
20	21	1.0	71	.45

[a]occs = organizational consistency control scores.

[b]roccs = relative organizational consistency control scores.

[c]ocpps = organizational consistency perception and program scores.

[d]rocpps = relative organizational consistency perception and program scores.

Table 5-16
Relationship between Consistency of Organizational Control and Consistency of Organizational Perception and Program Items

	rocpps[a]									
roccs[b]	*1*	*0.9*	*0.8*	*0.7*	*0.6*	*0.5*	*0.4*	*0.3*	*0.2*	*0.1*
1						12	20			
0.9			17[c]	18		2 4	3	1		
0.8			13							
0.7								16		
0.6								15		
0.5										
0.4									11	
0.3										
0.2										
0.1										

[a]Relative organizational consistency perception and program scores from table 5-15.

[b]Relative organizational consistency control scores from table 5-15.

[c]Organization code numbers.

by totaling consistency scores for every item across organizations and dividing by twelve, the number of organizations. The rank order of consistent items is shown in table 5-17. This method, however, conceals the possibility that a high consistency score could be based on agreement *within* organizations but disagreement *between* organizations. If an item in the interview has four categories of coded responses, it could occur that all respondents from company X were united in their subscription to value 1 of the item while all respondents from company Y were united in the adoption of value 2. This would still indicate the item's *importance* across organizations but it would not define a key element. A key element would be expected to reveal itself by universal subscription of all respondents in all organizations to the *same* value of the interview item.

To determine which items possessed such homogeneity of response as would indicate the presence of a key element, the following computation was performed. First, for every item, the *number* of consistent responses across organizations, irrespective of what the agreement was about, was computed as in table 5-17. Second, the category of the item which drew the highest frequency of response was identified. The actual frequency of response in this category was then *added* to the cross-organizational consistency score already computed in the first step. Third, the number of other categories of the item which also drew responses was counted and *subtracted* from the total of the

Table 5-17
Mean Consistency Scores of Interview Variables

Item Code	*Frequency (orgs.)*	*Sum of Consistency Scores (across organizations)*	*Mean Consistency Scores*
5	12	36	3.0
6	12	36	3.0
7	12	35	2.9
8	12	35	2.9
9	12	36	3.0
10	12	35	2.9
11	10	28	2.3
12	8	22	1.8
13	8	18	1.5
14	7	16	1.3
15	5	10	0.8
16	9	23	1.9
17	8	23	1.9
18	8	19	1.5
19	11	30	2.5
20	9	22	1.8
21	8	21	1.7
22	10	26	2.1
23	9	22	2.1
24	3	8	0.6
25	9	21	1.7
26	11	30	2.5
27	9	25	2.1
28	11	29	2.4
29	9	22	1.8
30	9	20	1.6
31	7	15	1.2
32	7	15	1.2
33	2	4	0.3
34	10	21	1.7
35	7	16	1.3
36	5	13	1.1
37	7	18	1.5
38	12[a]	28	2.3
39	11	25	2.1
40	12[a]	31	2.5
41	12[a]	34	2.8
42	12[a]	23	1.9
43	11	35	2.9
44	10	29	2.4
45	7	15	1.2
46	8	19	1.6
47	8	21	1.7
48	8	17	1.4
49	9	24	2.0
50	8	20	1.6
51	5	12	1.0
52	7	16	1.3
53	6	11	0.9
54	10	25	2.1

Table 5-17 continued

Item Code	*Frequency (orgs.)*	*Sum of Consistency Scores (across organizations)*	*Mean Consistency Scores*
55	7	17	1.4
56	5	12	1.0
57	7	18	1.5
58	6	15	1.2
59	7	18	1.5
60	7	18	1.5
61	10	26	2.2
62	9	22	1.8
63	6	13	1.1
65	3	6	0.5

[a]Agreement on category, "I do not know." These items are excluded from analysis in table 5-18.

first and second steps. The maximum score attainable in this exercise was 24: twelve organizations with internally consistent responses plus twelve cases in which the same category of the item was universally checked. The actual scores are shown in table 5-18. The highest score is 16, with only 22 percent of all scores falling above 10. On the whole, this suggests little homogeneity of the kind expected for confirmation of key elements.

In summary, we have two sets of data which must be seen together in order that the key-elements hypothesis be tested—at least to the extent that it can be given the constraints of the present study. First, the rank ordering of the mean consistency scores for all items gives a picture of those variables which are of *importance* to all the studied organizations. These scores do not tell us what *values* of these variables are important. Second, the rank ordering of homogeneity scores gives us a picture of those variables which are also *important in the same way* to all of them. Table 5-18 demonstrates immediately that few variables present themselves as being important in the same way to all the studied organizations. The highest scores are not very high (16 out of 24). Nonetheless, a juxtaposing of those variables which are relatively high on homogeneity and those which are high on mean consistency is instructive in that it shows whether a relationship exists between the two sets of scores. It might be expected, for example, that the variables which are high on homogeneity are a subset of items which are high on mean consistency. As table 5-19 shows, this is not the case to any marked extent.

In fact, the situation revealed by this comparison is that although there is a good deal of consistency *within* organizations, as shown by high mean consistency scores, there is relatively little consistency *between* organizations, as shown by the low scores on homogeneity. However, the fact that a group of variables can be found which are given the same values by respondents from

Table 5-18
Homogeneity of Items across Organizations

Score	*Group*	*Frequency (items)*	*Percent in This Category*
0	Low	1	26.0
1		1	
2		0	
3		5	
4		5	
5	Average	4	52.0
6		5	
7		4	
8		1	
9		3	
10		7	
11	High	3	22.0
12		2	
13		1	
14		1	
15		1	
16		2	
Total		46	100.0

several organizations (those items high on homogeneity) should not be ignored even if this group is remarkable for neither its size nor its content. The important point is that these organizations are not associated with any higher referral rates than the others since the premise of this study was that *all* the studied organizations had high referral rates (greater than 1 percent).

Organizational Size and Its Effects. The approach so far has been based on the search for relationships among groups of organizational variables in an attempt to define items of sufficient consistency and homogeneity that they would qualify as key elements. A more conventional approach was taken in order to ascertain whether certain major organizational factors were affecting the search for key elements. This approach was based on cross-tabulation of such important organizational variables with the other variables discussed in this chapter. The candidates for major organizational factors were size (number of employees), the type of alcohol-control policy used (written, case by case, or procedural), the perceived seriousness of alcoholism in the respondents' workplace, and the extent of management control over employee job performance. It would have been most desirable to analyze variations according to the type of work done by the organizations but the size of the sample (twelve) and the variability within it in terms of activities (manufacturers of various products, mines, heavy steel producers, and national defense organizations

Table 5-19
Items According to High or Low Scores on Homogeneity and Mean Consistency

High on homogeneity and mean consistency
Designation of department responsible for program
Report of program implementation
Report of keeping followup records
Reported success of referrals.
High on homogeneity[a]
Report of wage coverage while in treatment
Report of grievance activity in alcohol cases
Reported effect of referral on career
Type of reporting system designated
Reported policy on exclusion of certain people from program coverage
High on mean consistency[b]
Designation of type of policy/procedure
Reported activity level of committee
Reported guidelines for distinguishing discipline and rehabilitation cases
Rationale for program development
Perceived level of job-performance control
Use of nonwork-related information about drinking in identification process
Reported proportion of wage coverage in treatment referrals
Perceived percentage of employees using drugs at problem levels
Reported extensiveness of policy (alcohol, drugs, or more)
Effect of alcohol on job performance cited as impetus to program development
Reasons for policy not being fully implemented
Designation of person responsible for identification
Reported training of identifiers
Reported worthwhileness of early-identification efforts

[a]Highest is only 16/24 from table 5-18.

[b]Greater or equal to 9, table 5-17.

were all included) made such comparisons virtually meaningless. It is, however, worth reiterating the point raised in chapters 1, 2, and 3 that the type of work done by an organization exerts powerful influences over management practices. Consequently, we recommend that future studies of this type be conducted with controls built in for the type of work carried out by the selected organizations.

In this study the only variable which appeared to exercise any important influence on the variation in the data was organizational size. It was related to the following characteristics of organizations: the perceived seriousness of alcohol abuse; the type of alcohol-control policy in effect (written or otherwise); the extent of management control exercised over job performance; the consistency of problem employee management; the age of the alcohol-control policy; the extent of policy promotion; the degree to which line supervisors are held accountable for management of problem employees; the capacity of the system to identify problem employees quickly; and the extent to which insurance coverage is provided for lost wages. These findings are shown in tables 5-20 through 5-28.

A summary of the differences among organizations, according to these characteristics, as influenced by size is as follows.

Larger Organizations (1,001 or more employees). They have had alcohol-control policies in existence longer; promote their programs in a formal manner; hold their supervisors accountable for the management of problem employees; have written alcohol-control policies; have well-developed systems for the control of employee job performance; and have a consistent method for dealing with their problem employees.

Table 5-20
Size of Organization and Perceived Seriousness of Alcohol Abuse

	Perceived Seriousness	
Size of Organization	*Yes*	*No*
Small	23.1	76.9
Medium	75.0	25.0
Large	45.5	54.5

Table 5-21
Size of Organization and Type of Policy

	Policy Type	
Size of Organization	*Written*	*Other Methods*
Small	40.0	60.0
Medium	61.5	38.5
Large	92.9	7.1

Table 5-22
Size of Organization and Control System

	Control System (%)	
Size of Organization	*Not Well Developed*	*Well Developed*
Small	57.8	46.2
Medium	92.3	7.7
Large	33.3	66.7

Table 5-23
Size of Organization and Program-Implementation System

	Discipline System	
Size of Organization	*Consistent*	*Case by Case*
Small	42.9	57.1
Medium	27.3	72.7
Large	100.0	0.0

Table 5-24
Age of Program and Size of Organization

	Age of Program			
Size of Organization	*Less than 1 Year*	*1-5 Years*	*5+ Years*	*Evolved Over Time*
Small	38.5	15.4	7.7	38.5
Medium	0.0	41.7	8.3	50.0
Large	0.0	9.1	54.5	36.4

Table 5-25
Program Promotion and Size of Organization

	Program Promotion	
Size of Organization	*No*	*Yes*
Small	50.0	50.0
Medium	36.4	63.6
Large	0.0	100.0

Table 5-26
Size of Organization and Supervisor's Responsibility for Management of Problem Employees

	Supervisor's Responsibility		
Size of Organization	*Some*	*No*	*Yes*
Small	36.4	63.6	0.0
Medium	27.3	63.6	9.1
Large	20.0	10.0	70.0

Table 5-27
Size of Organization and the System's Ability to Identify Problem Employees in a Short Time Period

	Identification Ability	
Size of Organization	*Yes*	*No*
Small	63.6	36.4
Medium	30.8	69.2
Large	83.3	16.7

Table 5-28
Wage Coverage and Size of Organization

	Wage Coverage	
Size of Organization	*Yes*	*No*
Small	37.5	62.5
Medium	100.0	0.0
Large	100.0	0.0

Medium-Size Organizations (501-1,000 employees). They report the greatest difficulty in identifying problem employees quickly; report the most serious alcoholism problems in their work forces; are least likely to have a well-developed system for the control of job performance; and are most likely to follow a case-by-case approach to the management of problem employees, rather than a consistent policy.

Small Organizations (500 or less employees). They report the least amount of problems with alcoholism; are least likely to have insurance coverage for payment of lost wages while in treatment; are more likely than medium-sized but less likely than large organizations to have a well-developed control system; and favor case-by-case management of problem employees as opposed to a consistent policy.

Many of the noted differences relate to the degree of formality in the management-control system of the organizations. The degree of formality in the overall management of employee job performance is likely to be reflected in the management of problem employees. This process of formalism is most likely to be evidenced in the greater appearance of written communications, standardized procedures, and an emphasis on consistency of practice (Weber 1946). The need for formalism, however, is not exclusively related to the size of the organization as sometimes smaller concerns are formalized while sometimes larger ones are not. Other factors clearly influence formalism, many of which are related to the task of the organization, such as its technology, or its type of business. Consequently, the physical requirements and location of the job, the kind of work force, the type and amount of supervision feasible, and the amount of competition in the market, all interact to influence the degree of formalism in an organization. Nonetheless, the smallness or largeness factor tends to urge management in certain directions. In general, largeness is associated with formalism, smallness is not.

Although organizations above and below certain sizes tend to exhibit a steady state in management systems, medium-sized organizations in our sample do not. Representatives of these concerns reported problems both in overall job-performance control and in problem employee management. However, all the organizations in this sample had reported a problem employee referral rate of 1 percent or more. Indeed, this was the criterion for their inclusion in the sample. Consequently, whatever dissatisfaction is registered by the respondents from the medium-sized organizations must be interpreted in that context. Nonetheless, this group of organizations is obviously faced with more acute difficulties according to its representatives. Without other types of evidence, one cannot know whether or not these perceptions are grounded in a different objective reality. Perhaps as an organization outgrows the size where informal control mechanisms are adequate, or as technological or environmental changes compel management changes, it suffers a period of transition in which new ways are still undefined and old ways will not work. At such a stage one might expect the greatest expressions of discomfort. If control over job performance does not keep abreast of growth, job-performance deterioration might become more prevalent (at least in the short run) and its causes (alcoholism among them) might become more visible if less amenable to control.

Diffusion of Policies, Procedures, and Practices

In presenting our data from the key-elements study, we pointed out that frequently our respondents could not venture an opinion on topics about which they might have been expected to have some knowledge if the policies, procedures, or practices of their organizations with respect to the management of alcoholism and drug abuse were well disseminated and implemented. The extent of nonresponse is an approximate measure of the degree to which those policies, procedures, or practices were disseminated and sometimes implemented.

In general, production managers provided the most complete information. On the average their completion rate was 80 percent for all the items combined. Personnel directors achieved a corresponding rate of 69 percent; coordinators and medical directors, 67 percent; and union presidents or their delegates, 53 percent. The rank order of items from the interview questionnaire according to their rate of completion is shown in table 5-29.

Table 5-29
Completion Rates for All Participants Combined on Key-Elements Interview Questionnaire

Rank Order	*Percent*	*Key-Element Items*
1	97.9	Type of business of organization
2	97.5	Type of program adopted by organization
3	89.6	Medical facilities at workplace
4	91.6	Type of coverage program offers
5	87.5	Followup record-keeping practice
6	79.2	Extent of medical care offered by company
7	79.2	Adequacy of organizational control system
8	79.2	Department responsible for program
9	77.1	Existence of committee to manage alcoholism program
10	77.1	Signs of problem employees
11	77.1	Training for identifiers of problem employees
12	77.1	Person responsible for identification
13	75.0	Record keeping adequate for quick identification
14	75.0	Age of program
15	76.0	Seriousness of alcohol abuse in respective work force
16	72.9	Extent of program implementation
17	72.9	Promotion of program
18	70.8	Program discrimination
19	70.8	Percent of work force abusing alcohol
20	70.8	Type of reporting system
21	66.7	Accountability for management of problem employees
22	66.7	Insurance for wage loss due to alcoholism
23	64.6	Program improvement
24	62.5	Frequency of absenteeism monitoring
25	62.5	Alcohol-related grievances
26	62.5	Effect of program participation on career path
27	62.5	Program confidentiality
28	62.5	Followup record-keeping practice
29	60.4	Person responsible for followup
30	60.4	Type of followup
31	60.4	Insurance for wage loss due to drug abuse
32	60.4	Consistent system of discipline
33	60.4	Program outcome
34	58.3	Terms of insurance policy
35	58.3	Progressive discipline
36	56.3	Term of insurance policy: alcohol
37	56.3	Desirability of early identification
38	56.3	Guidelines for identification of problem cases
39	54.2	Person responsible for discipline of problem employees
40	54.2	Person responsible for confrontation of problem employees
41	54.2	Seriousness of drug abuse
42	50.0	Documentation of deteriorating job performance
43	48.0	Degree of fit between program and organizational structure
44	47.9	Reason for program development
45	43.8	Action taken to improve discipline
46	43.8	Percent of population abusing drugs
47	37.5	Absenteeism rate

The average completion rates conceal a wide variation, ranging from 97.9 percent on one item to a low of 37.5 percent on another. When the response rates of professional groups on individual items (table 5-29) were compared, their rank order was notably similar in every case. That is, certain concerns or topics were not more salient for production managers than personnel managers or union presidents, at least in terms of the questions raised in the interview. Union men might have tended to be more forthcoming and knowledgeable about grievance activities related to alcohol abuse; the terms of insurance coverage for alcoholism treatment; outcomes of referrals made to treatment agencies; protection of confidentiality and the identified problem employee's job; and the possibility of discriminatory use of the policy or procedure. Further, we expected that union presidents or their delegates would have a keener eye for the principles governing the relationship between disciplinary and treatment issues; but this was not so. Union people were in fact less able to answer questions in these areas than any of the other groups. When their responses were rank ordered in terms of completeness, these issues were no more salient (close to the top of the list) than in the other groups. This suggests very strongly that no professional group in this sample had parochial concerns in relation to alcoholism control. On the other hand, the policies, procedures, and practices associated with alcoholism control were severely underdiffused in relation to union people and poorly diffused in relation to personnel departments and even coordinators who were not informed on some matters essential to the proper execution of their responsibilities. The best informed group were the production managers who have the most intense firsthand experience of alcoholism and drug use. In only one instance were personnel managers significantly more knowledgeable than production managers, namely, the guidelines governing identification of problem employees. In this case, production managers may have been less than usually forthcoming because this is an area in which the sensitive issue of job-performance indicators of developing problems arises. Since in practice multiple indicators are used (not all related to work), perhaps production managers were not keen to skate on such thin ice with extraorganizational interviewers.

The underdiffusion of the policies, procedures, and practices considered in this study raises serious doubts about the degree to which they were implemented in some cases, if implementation means these methods are both well known and used. The fact that all these organizations reported high-referral rates during one year is no proper basis for classifying them as the "same" for any practical purpose: the prevalence rate may have varied between organizations and probably did; the attitudes toward this prevalence rate (usually based on only a guess) varied considerably so that a 5 percent rate represented a problem in some settings and none at all in others. Consequently, if all the policies, procedures, and practices among the studied organizations had been fully implemented (as judged by diffusion), the level of program activity may have been quite different. On the other hand, the essential thing about the use of any procedure is that its effectiveness must be judged primarily, though not exclusively, in relation to the employers' goals for the organization and its control as an entity. If the employer is pleased with the procedures in a partly implemented form, it is idle to argue that they could be put to better use. It may be true but it is an academic point.

6 Smaller-Business and Corporate Executives

The typical host for employee-assistance programs (EAPs) has been the larger corporation with upward of a thousand employees, often many thousands. Such organizations frequently operate on the basis of formal control of employee work behavior (chapter 5). Formal-control mechanisms are often compatible with the recommended procedures of EAPs and consequently there is little difficulty in locating them in corporate units, provided that the executive and management group are persuaded of their value. Indeed, it is in large corporate structures that EAP appears to be most at home simply because its philosophy, theory, and practice are tailored to the conditions most likely to be encountered in such organizations. In spite of this compatibility, EAP appears to be used most frequently in relation to blue-collar employees (Schlenger, Hallan, and Hayward 1976; Trice and Beyer 1977). The Task Force on Employee-Assistance Programs (1978) of the Addiction Research Foundation (ARF) of Ontario concluded that EAP in its full panoply was not registering much if any success with corporate executives or indeed with a large proportion of white-collar workers in the private sector. They reached this conclusion after extensive consultation with 152 individuals and 60 organizations directly involved in doing something about alcoholism in the workplace both in the United States and Canada, including such agencies as the National Institute on Alcohol Abuse and Alcoholism (NIAAA), the National Council on Alcoholism, and the Association of Labor-Management Administrators and Consultants on Alcoholism.

They further recognized that EAP in its ideal form was not likely to be of much use to employers of small work forces. The term *small* is not without ambiguity. In the literature it refers to organizations with as few as 10 people as well as to those with as many as 500. Even so, little information exists about the needs of employers within this whole range. Based on the investigations reported in chapters 4 and 5, there is considerable doubt concerning the need of these employers for EAP at least in its ideal form.

This chapter reports on certain studies and makes certain observations concerning the needs of both executives and small-work-force employers. Various proposals for meeting these needs are explored and where possible data presented on the usefulness of such proposals.

Needs of Smaller-Work-Force Employers

Employers of smaller work forces have been something of an embarassment to the advocates of EAP since the assistance program does not adapt readily to the needs of such employers. It is assumed, however, that such employers feel the need for some intervention to alleviate their problems with employees who are alcoholics or drug abusers. To our best knowledge, no study exists which tests this assumption in a methodical way. Consequently, when we received a request from an ARF consultant to help in conducting a survey of small business needs, we designed a study incorporating such a test.

A Study of Small Businesses in Metropolitan Toronto

An area was selected in the northeastern sector of metropolitan Toronto in which all manufacturing firms employing between 15 and 150 people were contacted for purposes of conducting an interview with one or more of the senior managers or executives. The ARF consultant conducted all the interviews with the aid of an interview questionnaire which was an adaptation of the one used in the key-elements study reported in chapter 5. Cooperation was obtained in forty-five companies, all manufacturers in the private sector. This represented a response rate of 63 percent in relation to an eligible total of seventy-one. Forty-one companies were autonomous, two were branches of larger firms, and two were not classified. In 47 percent of the interviews, the president of the company was the sole respondent; in 34 percent the respondent was another senior executive; and in 18 percent there was more than one respondent. The basic characteristics of these organizations were as follows.

Size. The mean was forty-eight employees, the median, thirty-four employees. The organizations were later grouped for comparative purposes according to size: smallest, 15-25 employees (n = 13); smaller2, 26-35 (n = 12); smaller1, 36-55 (n = 9); and small, 56-150 (n = 11).

Sex Distribution. Males had a mean of thirty employees, and a median of twenty-three; while females had a mean of thirteen employees, and a median of seven.

Unionization. Forty of the companies (89 percent) were not unionized.

Medical Services. Forty-three had no such service, while one had a first-aid post and trained attendants, and another had a nursing station. No routine medical examinations were conducted on employees except in one company.

Policies, Practices, and Procedures with Respect to Alcoholism. Only two of the organizations in this sample had no policy, practice, or procedure. Ninety-three percent pursued some form of case-by-case management of problem employees. In one case, respondents claimed they had an unwritten policy for handling such people. There was a committee structure in only one case.

Responsibility for Problem-Employee Identification. The president was involved in identification directly in thirteen cases, appeared not to be involved at all in another thirteen firms, and might have been appealed to as a last resort in nineteen cases. In the last-resort situation, identification procedures followed the hierarchy of command, so basically the supervisor at the line level was the initiator of such a process. The difference in procedure is associated with the size of the organization, as will be shown later.

Responsibility for Confrontation of Problem Employees. The responsibilities for identification and confrontation fell in much the same areas. The president was personally involved in confrontations in 31 percent of the firms, not involved in 29 percent, and involved as a last resort in 40 percent. In neither identification nor confrontation were supervisors or others specially trained for these purposes.

Indicators of Developing Problems (Alcoholism). The most commonly mentioned indicators of developing problems in alcoholism were job-performance deterioration in general (77 percent), absenteeism (70 percent), and lateness (66 percent). The actual signs of drinking were not mentioned, while insubordination received scant attention (4 percent).

Procedures Mentioned. In the EAP ideal model, certain components of a process leading up to a point where the problem employee may have to choose between discipline and treatment are stressed. These components are documentation of deteriorating job performance, mentioned by three respondents in this sample; warnings, mentioned by thirty-two; confrontation, mentioned by twenty-nine; referral for treatment, mentioned by one; and followup, mentioned by no one. The relative absence of documentation as a stressed component in the identification procedure may be a reflection of several related factors which tend to be characteristics of small firms. First, documentation of a written type is associated with larger organizations where control of employee behavior is conducted along bureaucratic lines. Middle managers often require written reports about the activities of their subordinates who in turn are accountable for the activities of their own subordinates. Careful documentation of job performance, therefore, is as much a protective device for the supervisor as it is a quality control mechanism for the organization. In smaller organizations more reliance can be placed on verbal reports, and the whole work situation is often literally visible to supervisors at all levels. This physical situation makes informal control a viable proposition in small plants.

Second, documentation is associated with building a case for rehabilitation rather than discipline, though the presence of a vigilant union tends to dictate its use under both circumstances. In situations where the employees are aware that their supervisors do not see the products of their labor on an hourly, daily, or weekly basis, documentation of performance over time can help to build credibility for any assertion made about fluctuations in the quality or quantity of work done. This credibility is important from several viewpoints: for the employee challenging the supervisor's recall of events; and for the supervisor building a case for the employee and his own superiors for a disciplinary or rehabilitative intervention where work performance has dropped off. Furthermore, it is important to the union representative who needs to know whether the employee's rights have been acknowledged and proper procedures have been followed. In this sample, organizations were small and mostly non-unionized, which would probably account for the absence of documentation.

Employers placed most reliance on a system of warning and confrontation. There was little or no reliance on referral for treatment, though most respondents (69 percent) knew of some resource in the community which dealt with alcoholics. The likelihood of employees being referred for treatment was very low. No company reported having insurance coverage for payment of wages or treatment costs while employees were undergoing treatment for alcoholism.

Number of Cases Seen. One factor which may be a determinant of many practices with respect to problem employee management and which in turn is related to the size of organizations in this sample, is the infrequency with which problems due to alcoholism are likely to occur in small work forces. During the whole period from January 1974 to mid-1978, 31 percent of employers had seen no cases of alcoholism, 26 percent had seen only one, 29 percent had seen two, and 13 percent had seen three or more. Only seven respondents claimed to have encountered drug-dependent employees during this period. In five of these cases, only one such employee had been seen. These facts provide some context for the absence of any formal or written policies or even of any standard procedures for the management of alcoholic and drug-dependent employees in organizations of the size considered here.

Perceived Seriousness of Alcoholism and Responsibility for Treatment. Notwithstanding the infrequency with which the phenomenon was observed, employers usually reported some sense of obligation toward helping alcoholic or drug-dependent employees (55 percent). Some stated they were responsible with little reservation (29 percent), a few said they would be highly selective about those they helped (7 percent), and others that the alleviation of the problem was the joint responsibility of the employer and employee (9 percent). Only four respondents said that alcoholism was a serious problem in their work force. While acknowledging it was a problem, 44 percent claimed it was not serious; 40 percent said it was not a problem at all.

Perceived Relationship between Drinking and Safety Problems. The majority of employers either saw some relationship (53 percent) or emphasized the relationship (29 percent) between problem drinking (on or off the job) and safety hazards. Only seven respondents felt there was no real relationship, while one was not sure.

Willingness to Band Together to Provide Treatment Services. Because of the popularity of the consortium in which several employers band together in order to spread the burden of providing treatment for problem employees (alcoholics and drug abusers in particular) through the development of a third-party service, employers in this survey were asked whether they would be willing to support such an idea. Most respondents (76 percent) said they would not be willing to do so; others (20 percent) said they were not prepared to think about it at present. Only one firm expressed interest in the idea. Sixty-four percent of these companies were members of a trade association. That is, they do not reject banding together for certain purposes.

Variation of Practice among Small Businesses

The size of an organization plays an influential part in determining the kind of policy, procedure, or practice for control of alcoholism. Even in this sample of small businesses variations in practice occur, so firms employing between 56 and 150 people exhibited somewhat different characteristics from firms employing fewer people. The important point about the variation noted here is that we must be careful to specify what is meant by "small" when discussing the needs of employers in this category. Evidently subclassifications aid in the process of conceptualizing needs and possible ways of dealing with them. On the other hand, there is no clear dividing line between the four subgroups of organizations used in this analysis. Consequently, very small organizations are sometimes run like larger organizations (though still employing less than 150) and vice versa.

Tables 6-1 and 6-2 show that firms employing more than fifty-six people were more likely than smaller companies to follow hierarchical procedures in the identification and confrontation of problem employees. That is, companies above this size began to manifest signs of more formal control, less often being run on the "family" model, where the head of the organization knows everything that goes on in a direct way. Further evidence of increasing formalism of control can be seen in table 6-3; supervisors tend to be held accountable for problem employees more among the larger firms. The term *not applicable* refers to the fact that the very small firms often had not encountered problems of substance abuse in the recent past.

Table 6-1
Responsibility for Identification of Problem Employees and Size of Organization

	Identification			
Size	*President Involved*	*President Not Involved*	*Hierarchical Procedure*	*n*
Smallest	3 (23.1)	5 (38.5)	5 (38.5)	13 (28.9)
Smaller 2	6 (50.0)	2 (16.7)	4 (33.3)	12 (26.7)
Smaller 1	3 (33.3)	3 (33.3)	3 (33.3)	9 (20.0)
Small	1 (9.1)	3 (27.3)	7 (63.6)	11 (24.4)
n	13 (28.9)	13 (28.9)	19 (42.2)	45 (100.0)

Note: Numbers in parentheses are percentages.

Table 6-2
Responsibility for Confrontation of Problem Employees and Size of Organization

	Confrontation			
Size	*President Involved*	*President Not Involved*	*Hierarchical Procedure*	*n*
Smallest	3 (23.1)	6 (46.2)	4 (30.8)	13 (28.9)
Smaller 2	7 (58.3)	1 (8.3)	4 (33.3)	12 (26.7)
Smaller 1	3 (33.3)	3 (33.3)	3 (33.3)	9 (20.0)
Small	1 (9.1)	3 (27.3)	7 (63.6)	11 (24.4)
n	14 (31.1)	13 (28.9)	18 (40.0)	45 (100.0)

Note: Numbers in parentheses are percentages.

Table 6-3
Accountability of Supervisors for Problem Employees and Size of Organization

	Accountability				
Size	*Formal*	*Informal*	*None*	*Not Applicable*	*n*
Smallest	1 (7.7)	3 (23.1)	5 (38.5)	4 (30.8)	13 (29.5)
Smaller 2	1 (8.3)	4 (33.3)	5 (41.7)	2 (16.7)	12 (27.3)
Smaller 1	0	4 (50.0)	4 (50.0)	0	8 (18.2)
Small	3 (27.3)	6 (54.5)	2 (18.2)	0	11 (25.0)
n	5 (11.4)	17 (38.6)	16 (36.4)	2 (13.6)	44 (100.0)

Note: Numbers in parentheses are percentages.

Table 6-4 suggests that as the size of an organization increases, its executives are more likely to report that early identification of problem employees is worth the effort. Again this may be related to the greater experience of the larger companies with problem employees, especially alcoholics and drug abusers. Though it cannot be substantiated, larger organizations may allow more leeway for the development of alcoholism and for its coverup for a longer time. Thus early identification may be a more real issue for larger firms. It was pointed out in chapter 5 that medium-sized organizations (those employing between 500 and 1,000) tended to experience the greatest difficulty with the control of alcoholism, possibly because such companies represent the no-man's-land between successful informal control systems and effective formal control systems.

Further evidence of the manner in which experience with alcoholism affects perception is in table 6-5; larger companies were more inclined to report that alcoholism was a problem, even though not a serious one. The smaller firms were more likely to dismiss alcoholism as a problem. Similarly, respondents in larger companies were more likely to know about the availability of alcoholism treatment resources in the community than the smallest firms (table 6-6). Respondents in the smallest organizations were most likely to be negative about pooling resources for provision of a third-party service for alcoholic and otherwise dependent employees (table 6-7) and were least likely to belong to trade associations (table 6-8).

Table 6-4
Worthwhileness of Early Identification of Problem Employees and Size of Organization

	Worthwhileness of Early Identification				
Size	*Yes*	*Perhaps*	*No*	*Not Sure*	*n*
Smallest	4 (30.8)	3 (23.1)	5 (38.5)	1 (7.7)	13 (28.9)
Smaller 2	3 (25.0)	6 (50.0)	3 (25.0)	0	12 (26.7)
Smaller 1	2 (22.2)	5 (55.6)	2 (22.2)	0	9 (20.0)
Small	5 (45.5)	4 (36.4)	0	2 (18.2)	11 (24.4)
n	14 (31.1)	18 (40.0)	10 (22.2)	3 (6.7)	45 (100.0)

Note: Numbers in parentheses are percentages.

Table 6-5
Perceived Seriousness of Alcoholism in Respondents' Work Force and Size of Organization

	Perceived Seriousness of Alcoholism				
Size	*Not Serious*	*No Problem*	*Problem*	*Rare but Disruptive*	*n*
Smallest	2 (18.2)	9 (81.8)	0	0	11 (26.1)
Smaller 2	5 (41.7)	5 (41.7)	1 (8.3)	1 (8.3)	12 (28.5)
Smaller 1	5 (55.6)	2 (22.2)	2 (22.2)	0	9 (21.4)
Small	8 (80.0)	2 (20.0)	0	0	10 (23.8)
n	20 (47.6)	18 (42.8)	3 (7.1)	1 (2.3)	42 (100.0)

Note: Numbers in parentheses are percentages.

Table 6-6
Knowledge of Treatment Resources in Community and Size of Organization

	Reported Knowledge		
Size	*Some*	*None*	*n*
Smallest	6 (46.2)	7 (53.8)	13 (28.9)
Smaller 2	8 (66.7)	4 (33.3)	12 (26.7)
Smaller 1	6 (66.7)	3 (33.3)	9 (20.0)
Small	11 (100.0)	0	11 (24.4)
n	31 (68.9)	14 (31.1)	45 (100.0)

Note: Numbers in parentheses are percentages.

Table 6-7
Willingness to Pool Resources for Treatment of Problem Employees and Size of Organization

	Willingness to Pool Resources				
Size	*Yes*	*Not Now*	*No*	*Do Not Know*	*n*
Smallest	0	0	13 (100.0)	0	13 (28.9)
Smaller 2	0	3 (25.0)	8 (66.7)	1 (8.3)	12 (26.7)
Smaller 1	1 (11.1)	2 (22.2)	6 (66.7)	0	9 (20.0)
Small	0	4 (36.4)	7 (63.6)	0	11 (24.4)
n	1 (2.2)	9 (20.0)	34 (75.6)	1 (2.2)	45 (100.0)

Note: Numbers in parentheses are percentages.

Table 6-8
Membership of Trade Associations and Size of Organization

	Membership of Trade Association		
Size	*Yes*	*No*	*n*
Smallest	5 (38.5)	8 (61.5)	13 (28.9)
Smaller 2	8 (66.7)	4 (33.3)	12 (26.7)
Smaller 1	6 (66.7)	3 (33.3)	9 (20.0)
Small	10 (90.0)	1 (9.1)	11 (24.4)
n	29 (64.4)	16 (35.6)	45 (100.0)

Note: Numbers in parentheses are percentages.

Table 6-9
Proportion of Females in Work Force and Employers' Report of Problems with Employee Alcoholism

	Alcoholism Problems		
Proportion of Females	*Yes*	*No*	*n*
Less than one-third female	17 (65.3)	9 (34.7)	26 (65.0)
More than one-third female	6 (42.8)	8 (57.2)	14 (35.0)
n	23 (57.2)	17 (42.7)	40 (100.0)

Note: Numbers in parentheses are percentages.

Females and Alcoholism-Related Problems

It is sometimes claimed that female employees cause less difficulty to their employers in terms of the incidence of job-related drinking problems. However, the incidence of such work-related problems may not be an accurate reflection of the prevalence of alcoholism among female employees since they may maintain an outward appearance of normalcy longer than males. This study afforded an opportunity to consider the relationship between the proportion of females in various work forces (albeit small ones) and employers' likelihood of reporting that alcoholism was a notable problem in their work force (table 6-9). If more than one-third of the work force consisted of females, there was a greater likelihood that the employer would report no problem with alcoholism among his employees. About 57 percent of such employers reported no problem with alcoholism in comparison with 35 percent of employers of work forces where less than one-third of employees were female.

Notwithstanding this observation, greater proportions of females were employed by larger organizations in this sample (table 6-10). The table shows that 65 percent of smaller organizations (less than fifty-five employees) had work forces in which less than one-third were female, while only 43 percent of larger organizations had so few. Since it has already been shown that employers of larger work forces tend to report more problems with alcoholism (table 6-5), it was hypothesized that the effect of larger proportions of females in such work forces would be to reduce the degree to which employers reported problems with alcoholism. To test this hypothesis a correlation was made between the size of the organizations (number of employees) and the extent to which employers indicated that they experienced problems with alcoholism among their employees. The Pearson product-moment correlation between these variables was -0.33 (p less than .02), confirming that size and perception of problems were related in a significant if not overwhelming manner. Next, a control was added to the calculation so that the effect of the presence of females in the larger work forces could be taken into account. The resulting partial correlation was -0.46 (p less than .001), confirming the hypothesis that the greater presence of females in the larger work forces tends to create an impression of less alcoholism-related problems in the minds of their employers.

The small manufacturing organizations were not motivated to do more than they were already doing with respect to the management of alcoholic and drug-dependent employees. They do not see themselves as having real problems and consider that most problems can be dealt with within a disciplinary

Table 6-10
Proportion of Females in the Work Force and Size of Organization

	Size of Organization		
Proportion of Females	*Smaller (≤ 55)*	*Small (≥ 56)*	*n*
Less than one-third female	19 (65.5)	10 (34.5)	29 (67.5)
More than one-third female	6 (42.8)	8 (57.2)	14 (32.5)
n	25 (58.1)	18 (41.9)	43 (100.0)

Note: Numbers in parentheses are percentages.

framework. There is a tendency for firms employing over 55 and fewer than 150 people to intimate greater willingness to think about alternate ways of dealing with problem employees, but the situation could not be described as a receptive market for EAP-like interventions. A serendipitous finding of the present survey was that employers tend to report fewer problems with alcoholism in work forces where there are larger proportions of female employees.

The Consortium Approach

The consortium approach refers to a situation in which a group of employers band together to provide a third-party service for coping with industrial referrals of alcoholics, drug abusers, and sometimes other problem employees. Because small-work-force employers are often considered to have insufficient resources for coping with such problems, the consortium approach is touted as the providential answer. Several issues are involved in such an approach, which we will now examine. First, do small employers want such a service? The second issue concerns the point at which organizations attain a sufficient size to warrant their executives even thinking about the generation of a specific service for alleviating problems of substance abuse. There is some evidence that consortia have been used by large rather than small organizations. Gavin (1978) notes that consortia have included firms that range in size between 60 and 5,000 employees and observes further that these arrangements vary considerably in such characteristics as whether or to what extent participants share fiscal and governing responsibilities; the sources of funding (self, public, or insured); scope (alcoholism only to all problems likely to affect job performance); types of participating organizations (size and type of work done); staffing (qualifications and ratio of staff to clients); and criteria for evaluation.

Gavin argues that for a durable arrangement both fiscal and governing responsibilities should be shared by all participants, each according to his means. He proposes that stability of service and satisfaction with it vary in direct relation to the fiscal and managerial commitment of participants. Further, a broad range of services should be offered to accommodate varying needs. In addition to direct service to industrially referred clients, other services may include consultations on specific clients; formal educational seminars for staff and managers; and consultation on policy, procedures, and implementation steps. The biggest problem faced by consortia, according to Gavin, is the variation in participant expectations of the service and consequently in the criteria used to evaluate success.

The Baltimore Employee Health Program

Schramm (1977*a*) describes a consortium called the employee health program (EHP) which was developed in Baltimore and lasted from 1973 to 1976 when a funding transition problem caused it to close. Essentially, the EHP was an outpatient service for twelve employing organizations. It began as a demonstration program run through the Johns Hopkins University School of Hygiene and Public Health in contract with the U.S. Department of Labor. Three directors, for treatment, administration, and research, together with a principal investigator constituted an executive committee of the EHP which reported to the central administration of Johns Hopkins University. The executive committee had an advisory board consisting of representatives of participating managements and unions, together with members of Baltimore's "alcoholism community." A separate entity, the Baltimore Area Council on Alcoholism (BACA), was under contract with the executive committee of the EHP to develop an inservice training program for personnel in participating industries and was to act as liaison with management. The Metropolitan Baltimore Council of the American Federation of Labor and Congress of Industrial Organizations (AFL-CIO) acted in the same capacity with unions in the participating industries. At its peak, the EHP had fifteen staff: counselors, physicians, liaison officers, and secretaries. Schramm reports that a chronic difficulty of this program was in reconciling objectives in the areas of demonstration (with pressures toward service expansion), research (with pressures toward service stabilization), and service (with strains toward flexibility). During the whole span of its existence the overriding goal of the EHP was financial and managerial self-sustenance. Eventually, the objective became one of transferring the management of the program to AFL-CIO's Community Service Agency, which turned out to be the group with the greatest motivation to continue the service.

Clearly, the history of this project is of a highly political nature. Schramm details the juggling act that needed to be done in order to balance the interests of all the groups involved in the future of the EHP. Almost as a warning to others who might try to launch such a project, he lists these groups as follows: two government funding agencies (NIAAA followed by the Department of Labor); employers, unions, the Joint Commission on Accreditation (which could give or withhold legitimacy for the EHP as an alcoholism treatment service); the insurance carrier, which held the main chance of financial viability; and the medical and alcoholism establishment in the community whose endorsement (given very slowly) was necessary for the project's survival. In this regard, Schramm speaks of "fictions" which had to be developed "for various assessors regarding their importance to the project" (1977*a*:142). Unfortunately, it is not clear why the EHP was considered to be necessary, and it is not possible to form a clear opinion about the origins of resistance from the "alcoholism industry" in relation to the project. Whatever its origins, however, Schramm's point is well taken that any new service, such as the EHP or any other consortium-generated project, is going to have to deal with the reality that in most large population centers there are existing services for the treatment of alcoholism. No matter whether these agencies are good at their job or not, they are a force to contend with. In the end, they may be a crucial force.

Changes in funding policies and philosophies of major grant-awarding agencies play an important role in service continuity. In the Baltimore case, the NIAAA pulled out its 75 percent funding because of a growing commitment to broad-brush policy development which was not shared by the EHP group who had a medical-model orientation focusing on alcoholism. The latter approach, as pointed out vigorously by Perlis (1977), is much more attractive to the AFL-CIO.

The twelve organizations involved in the EHP employed a total of 134,000 people but their characteristics beyond this are not described. It would be interesting, for example, to know what kind of work these organizations were engaged in and their respective sizes. A certain amount of data about the policy bases and referral practices of the organizations is given in Schramm, Mandell, and Archer (1978) but still the emphasis of the project description is on the kinds of people referred rather than on the sources of referral. It might be argued that a proper understanding of consortiumlike arrangements would have to be based as much on knowledge about the characteristics of the referring organizations as about the third-party service itself. From January 1974 to July 1975 the EHP saw 328 patients for a total of 5,486 visits. It is almost certain that during the earlier part of this time employers were also referring some employees to other treatment services as well as EHP. This natural tendency on the part of employers unfortunately dogs attempts at evaluation of consortium arrangements. Unless the evaluator knows exactly where the participating employers are sending all their referrals, it is impossible to determine trends in the use of the consortium-generated service. The exclusive use of consortium service depends on the degree to which the employer is getting from it what he needs and expects. Certainly, the more options an employer has the less financially secure the third-party service will be unless it is supported by fixed subscriptions independent of the number of referrals or other service requests. Though probably unusual, this type of funding arrangement is one variation on three models of financing mentioned by Schramm, the other two being fee for service and third-party reimbursement (insurance). The last alternative was chosen for the EHP though it failed to develop in time to save the program. Insurance arrangements for outpatient care of alcoholism are not common, at least in the United States, as Schramm (1977*a*) and Follman (1976) point out.

To our knowledge, no followup of EHP patients was conducted. Schramm, Mandell, and Archer (1978) note that a common criterion of program failure (getting fired on return to work) has as much to do with variations in company policies as with employee characteristics. This observation relates to the need for understanding the dynamics of referring organizations before a meaningful evaluation of a consortium arrangement can be made. Schramm et al. intimate this problem in describing the different identification and referral practices found among the twelve participating organizations. Five distinct practices were found: (1) equilateral power shared by the medical and personnel departments: this was the most common arrangement in which either department could initiate a referral; (2) personnel department dominant, determining whether referrals were made or not; (3) medical department dominant, as in the case of personnel; (4) an employee counseling department (part of the personnel department) through which referrals were channeled: only one example of this type was found; and (5) a joint union-management committee (only in one case) took responsibility for making referrals. Only two of the twelve guiding policies were broad-brush EAPs. The others were alcoholism specific. Schramm et al. argue that referrals were more frequent from organizations where one person was designated to coordinate such activities, even though in other organizations top management was committed to their program. This is tantalizing information but unfortunately it is not conclusive because no data are given on the major characteristics of the organizations in which these variations are found. One would like to know whether the presence of a coordinator was influenced by company size, the type of control system used, the kind of work done, and so forth. However, the auspices of identication and referral probably bear a relationship to the type of followup practices found among different organizations and this in turn influences the chance of success in any given case where a referral to a treatment program is made.

Unions as Auspice for Consortium Development

In reviewing the various auspices under which the consortium model may be viable, Schramm et al. conclude that the most solid support is likely to come from unions. They state their rationale as, "it would seem that there already exists an infrastructure for the diffusion of industrial treatment programs that can act independently of criteria of cost-effectiveness" (p. 113). Consequently, they recommend "that policymakers encourage and assist organized labor in its interest in promoting alcoholism treatment for membership." Whether or not this is a default recommendation based more on EHP employers' notably tepid attitude toward collaboration on a continuous basis is unclear.

The willingness of unions to accept such a mandate varies considerably within the movement. Until recently clear differences existed between the positions adopted by the AFL-CIO in the United States and the Canadian Labor Congress (CLC). Both are large umbrella organizations: the AFL-CIO represents about 14.5 million organized workers through 110 unions and 60,000 locals; the CLC has about 2.3 million members distributed through a number of unions and locals. While the AFL-CIO seems ready to accept a direct-service mandate, and indeed actively seeks opportunities to have more input into community service delivery and planning (Schramm 1977*a*), the CLC until 1978 made it clear that their responsibility was focussed on the encouragement, development, and implementation of treatment programs, occupational programs, and preventive education programs by other agencies, government included (Dunbar 1978). The AFL-CIO recommended, according to Perlis (1977), that alcoholism control procedures be spelled out clearly in the collective agreement. The CLC used to resist this approach, urging its members to enter into cooperative programs with employers outside the context of the collective agreement (Groeneveld, Simon, and Shain 1978). Recently, however, the CLC has shifted its position at the national committee level so that all troubled employees, alcoholics included, would be covered by a policy negotiated under the auspices of the collective agreement. This position has yet to receive endorsement at the local level. The CLC still maintains that formal identification of troubled employees should be tagged to deteriorating job performance. Perlis, although wary of disguising alcoholics as troubled employees argues that it is desirable to identify them before they manifest problems on the job and that a broad health and welfare policy should be negotiated through the collective agreement which would enable alcoholics to be treated like any other sick person (1977:73).

In conclusion, the Schramm et al. recommendation that unions accept a mandate to promote alcoholism treatment for their membership may be received in different ways in the United States and Canada. Indeed, there may well be differences within the labor movement in both countries. In the end, much will depend on the manner in which the respective resolutions of the AFL-CIO and CLC are interpreted and put into effect.

Union-Made Consortiums in Toronto

An example of the variation in union perceptions of what they should be doing is provided by the Lifeline Foundation in Toronto, Ontario. This organization was initiated by the United Steelworkers of America (USWA) in Toronto in response to a need for an alcoholism service for its members. (A full account of how this organization operates is given in Groeneveld, Simon and Shain (1978). In addition to Lifeline, the Alberta Civil Service Union and the Canadian Airline Pilots Association have union-initiated programs for problem members.

The Lifeline Foundation does not provide treatment services but assesses employees and makes referrals to community agencies. In addition, it consults with member organizations on problems ranging from the needs of a specific client to the development of a more effective identification and followup system. Further, training sessions are provided for personnel in member organizations on identification, documentation, confrontation, and related techniques germane to an EAP.

A board of directors with equal management and union representation is elected by members and generates an executive group to serve for a year. An advisory committee, with a staff of three, is also appointed by the board to provide advice to the manager of Lifeline on counseling and education. Part of Lifeline's operating principle is the development of joint union-management committees in all member organizations. The function of these committees is to facilitate referrals to Lifeline but not to conduct assessments or make diagnoses. Lifeline Foundation is supported through the sale of memberships to client organizations, charitable donations, and government grants.

The potential market for Lifeline's services is 182 organizations, of which 75 were members at time of writing. Table 6-11 shows a tendency for smaller organizations (less than 100 employees) to be interested in the service. However, all four potential organizations with over 500 employees were members of Lifeline.

From January 1977 to approximately March 1978, eighty-six clients were seen by Lifeline for assessment. The majority of these cases were alcoholism-related (61.6 percent), then financial problems (22.1 percent) and health problems (8.1 percent). A few cases were related to family problems, housing, and drug abuse. Of the eighty-six cases, seventy-four were new clients and twelve were repeaters. These proportions are probably not stable since Lifeline went over to a broad-brush EAP approach in 1977. There has been a tendency for self-referrals to increase between 1974 and 1978. From 1974 to 1978 self-referrals accounted for 13.1 percent of the total 145 referrals, while in 1977-1978 they accounted for 21.4 percent of all seventy new referrals. The earlier figure might be higher if repeater referrals were removed from the total during that period. However, it appears that self-referrals have increased, though the evidence is not conclusive.

Perhaps the most intriguing aspect of the Lifeline experience is its contradiction of the conclusion reached in the study of small manufacturing organizations in northeast metropolitan Toronto. In that study, few organizations with between 15 and 150 employees were interested in banding together now or in the future to provide a third-party service of the consortium type. On the other hand, whether they actually made referrals or not, nearly three-quarters

Table 6-11
Size of Lifeline Member Organizations Relative to Size of Organizations in Potential Market

Number of Employees	*Member Organizations (No.)*	*(%)*	*Potential Organizations (No.)*	*(%)*	*Contact Rate (%)*
100 or less	54	72.0	108	59.3	50.0
101-200	12	16.0	45	24.8	26.6
201-300	2	2.7	16	8.8	12.5
301-400	2	2.7	6	3.3	33.3
401-500	1	1.4	3	1.6	33.3
501+	4	5.3	4	2.2	100.0
Total	75	100.0	182	100.0	–

of Lifeline's members were organizations employing less than 100 employees. Indeed, half of the potential market in this size category had been attracted to membership. However, more than 80 percent of the businesses in the northeast Toronto sample were not unionized and therein may lie the difference. The work forces of all Lifeline's member organizations belong to the USWA. Union pressure and awareness of such problems as alcoholism make certain alternatives available to unionized firms that are not viable for nonunionized companies. However, this is a speculative conclusion. Other variables may be the differences in the kind of work done by the organizations in the Lifeline group (all steelworking companies). It cannot be assumed that the prevalence of alcoholism or the incidence of problems due to it are the same among both groups.

The most significant point about the noted differences, however, is simply that they exist. Evidently, the needs of small work-force employers are quite complex and variable, ranging from no need to considerable need for alcoholism services. Where such a need exists, the consortium approach is a possible way of meeting it, but no assumptions should be made about the existence of the need itself. In addition, consortia can suffer from many problems among which are continuity of managerial and fiscal responsibility, particularly where a variety of employer expectations exist. Possibly the Lifeline Foundation will be a more stable arrangement because its constituency is more homogeneous (all steelworkers), expectations may be consequently more uniform, and conflicts of need less disruptive. Furthermore, Lifeline reflects the recommendation of Schramm based on the Baltimore experience which says that unions are the auspice under which consortia are most likely to endure.

Needs of Executives

There is a substantial body of opinion which holds that EAP does not reach corporate executives or indeed a major portion of white-collar, highly skilled employees. Certainly, the ideal model dictates that EAP should be applicable and available to all employees, male and female, high and low status (see chapter 1). It is claimed on occasion (Schlenger, Hallan, and Hayward 1976) that the broad-brush approach of EAP may be facilitating the attraction of more females into helping programs than the alcoholism-specific approaches. However, the methods used to derive these suggestions do not take into account the complicated interactions between the percentage of females at risk in given work forces, the type of work done by the organizations, the size of the organizations, and the likelihood of having either an alcoholism-specific policy/procedure or a broad-brush type. Few would argue that either type of policy or procedure reaches executives. Trice and Beyer (1977) reported a study of federal civil service installations in the Northeastern United States, in which executives and highly skilled employees were less often approached by supervisors with a view to activation of the EAP. The authors advanced several explanations for this phenomenon, summarized as follows:

1. Executives and other upper-echelon employees may simply have less alcohol-related problems than their lower-echelon counterparts. Trice and Beyer draw on Cahalan and Room's data (1974) on drinking practices among American males for this explanation, though they suggest that the differences noted by Cahalan and Room may have been exaggerated because their sample was based on households and included the unemployed. In addition, there may be less openness among higher-status people concerning their drinking practices. It is argued that perhaps alcohol-related problems are not as manifest among the executive group because they do not drink as much as their less exalted counterparts. According to Trice and Beyer, the commonly used indicators of problem drinking are less useful for identification of at-risk executives since their absenteeism is the on-the-job type (they are there but do little) and the opportunity for on-the-job accidents rarely presents itself.

2. It is difficult to assess job performance at the executive level. The problem is usually described in terms of the low visibility of executive job performance. This means executive accountability is rendered on a less frequent basis than it is among, say, assembly-line workers and detection of problems on a day-to-day basis is more difficult. Executive errors may cost millions, as may an error on the assembly line, but the odds of detection are greater in the latter case than in the former. Also executive accountability may vary among organizations. No doubt in some companies and other workplaces, executive performance is monitored more closely than in others.

3. Trice and Beyer report that a compounding difficulty is that sometimes the executive's coverup of drinking problems may be aided and abetted by an unscrupulous subordinate who maintains the superior's image while grooming himself for the takeover. Such calculative maneuvers occasionally occur.

4. Perhaps one of the greatest difficulties in getting executives who drink too much into helping programs is the frequent absence of a supervisor with sufficient status to do the necessary confrontation, assuming that an identification of the problem has been made. Though to some extent a function of low visibility, it is also a problem of too great an affinity between supervisor and supervised at the executive and highly skilled level. Trice and Beyer point out that where supervisors perceive greater social distance (and more difference generally) between themselves and their subordinates, they are more willing to invoke an alcoholism policy. At the executive level, however, there appears to be less chance of such social distance occurring. Often, both supervisor and supervised have the same sociocultural background and education and have had similar work experience, with perhaps one having worked longer than the other. They may belong to the same social groups as may their spouses. While this situation may well occur among blue-collar workers, it probably occurs less often in such a "binding" way. Indeed, blue-collar supervisors may

find it easier to put the required distance between themselves and their subordinates. It may be that at this level there is a greater distance between two steps of the ladder than at the executive level.

5. Supervisors of executives and the highly skilled may be taking a greater risk and be courting less reward than supervisors at blue-collar levels when attempting to activate an EAP or alcoholism policy. Trice and Beyer report that the executive supervisor may see himself as responsible for allowing a situation to develop in which a subordinate has a drinking problem. It makes him look bad; it may indicate poor selection procedures, poor supervision, and poor management. The reputation of the whole organization may suffer as a result of its being known that a key executive is a problem drinker.

6. Finally, the attitude of the executive may be a problem. He may perceive the freedom to drink as he pleases as an earned benefit. This is somewhat different from the attitudinal problem encountered generally among alcoholics, namely, that they do not have a problem at all.

Trice and Beyer suggest alternate approaches for reaching the alcoholic executive. These suggestions include special training for executive supervisors to facilitate putting social distance between themselves and their subordinates, and provision of specially tailored treatment services. Both suggestions appear to be based on the view that EAPs can be tailored in some fashion to accommodate the needs of executives.

The Health and Lifestyle Approach

Many reasons advanced for the current shortfall of EAP for executives are underpinned by lack of constraint or coercive measures. Consequently, the ultimate sanction of EAP—the loss of one's livelihood—is often mitigated and sometimes removed in the case of senior executives. The normal basis for identification and confrontation is structurally weakened by the absence of such a sanction and of anyone to apply it. Executives must therefore rely on themselves and only occasionally on the good offices of a colleague to generate the required motivation to find help.

This formulation of the problem suggests a possible solution, whose prototype has existed for approximately thirty years and which appears to be replicating itself in various forms across the continent, namely, the health and lifestyle approach to the prevention and amelioration of physical and mental problems among executives. In common with EAP, the health and lifestyle approach covers a variety of more specific interventions, ranging from provision of a few exercise machines in the basement of corporate headquarters to elaborate gymnasiums and sports facilities. These facilities may be linked up with a program of use by all or some employees, though the emphasis has been so far on activities for executives. Sometimes an external firm provides a service which includes courses and seminars on a variety of topics, such as stress, exercise, weight control, diet, drugs, alcohol, smoking, blood pressure, heart disease, cancer, and sugar. Vicary (1978) describes a process in which a personal risk diagnosis generates an actuarial statement of life expectancy, then a modified statement based on recommended changes in lifestyle.

It is impossible to evaluate the potential of such approaches for identifying executives who are either in trouble with alcohol and drugs or are about to be. In cases where all executives are required to take a screening test leading to individualized health development programs, problems may come to light more readily than in cases where the health program was provided but not pushed. To the extent that such a program is pushed, coercion is reintroduced, which was just noted as being dysfunctional when applied to executives because it could not be enforced. There is, however, a difference between the goals of the coercion in the two cases and in the ways in which it may be applied. In the case of EAP, coercion is supposed to be applied in relation to a known or suspected problem: alcoholism, for example. Further, it is coercion that must be applied primarily by a superior. In the case of the health and lifestyle approach, coercion relates to positive goals: improvement of health, fitness, and well-being. Moreover, it is coercion that can be brought to bear not only by superiors but also through informal, collegial pressure.

For the executive group, it may be easier to develop an organizational culture which emphasizes health, fitness, well-being, and consequent efficiency than a culture which emphasizes moderate drinking. Vicary (1978) points out that the essential difference between EAP and the health and lifestyle approach is one emphasizes the minimization of further loss while the other emphasizes the maximization of potential gain. Of course, these are differences of emphasis and EAP contains elements of prevention (particularly in relation to its early identification and voluntary, self-referral components) while the health and lifestyle approach has elements of loss minimization. Nonetheless, the latter approach may be more attractive to executives because of its avoidance of problem labeling and its reliance on the development of inner, personal controls rather than external coercion. If attention can be brought to bear on hazardous drinking practices in the context of a health development program, it may have more credibility and impact than if drinking is separated out for unique treatment.

While the health and lifestyle approach has a tempting rationale for intervention with executive problem drinkers, it may have a more useful future in preventing such problems. In neither case, however, has there been any research in which the value of the health development approach has been evaluated with regard to its effect on drinking practices. This remains to be done, and the value of such an approach to be explored with respect to all levels of employees. Insofar as such an approach may be applicable to the entire work force as it pertains to primary prevention of problems due to drinking and drug use, it will be further explored in chapter 9.

7 Alcoholism and Drug Use in Workplaces

The Importance of Prevalence Estimates

Although numerous efforts have been made to estimate the prevalence of alcoholism in general populations, few attempts have essayed it in specific workplaces. Consequently most prevalence estimates of workplaces are simply informed guesses (Hayward, Schlenger, and Hallan 1975). As pointed out in chapter 3, chances are high that prevalence rates will vary between organizations, particularly if they engage in different kinds of work, employ people with different skills and educational levels, and are located in different social, cultural, and economic environments. Although it may make little difference to the man in the street whether the overall national prevalence rate for alcoholism is 3, 6, or 10 percent, it makes a great deal of difference if these figures hold for three separate work organizations in which an EAP is in operation. Unless the extent of alcoholism is known (usually given by the prevalence rate), it is impossible to determine objectively the effectiveness of the program in terms of its ability to identify the population at risk. The problem is clear: if a company reports that it has achieved a penetration rate of 1.5 percent, it means one thing in relation to a prevalence rate of 3 percent and another to a rate of 6 percent. The trouble is that we rarely know which is the case. Employers in the key-elements study tended to use national prevalence estimates as their basis for estimating the amount of alcoholism in their work force, adding or subtracting a couple of percentage points depending on whether they thought their situation was worse or better than in either the country as a whole or in the area best known to them.

Of course, there are grounds for questioning the very use of penetration rates even when the prevalence of alcoholism is known in a given work situation. The problem is one of appropriate criteria for evaluating alcoholism control or employee-assistance programs (EAPs). Chapters 3 and 5 note that employers often use criteria that are quite different from those used by organizational consultants or interventionists, particularly those with public health interests in mind. Employers seem content to achieve a stable state in their organizations whether all or most alcoholics have been identified, particularly if their job performance is not affected. However, interventionists and perhaps unions need to know the basic prevalence rate of alcoholism in specific work forces. Employers may take a more active interest in their alcoholism control programs or EAPs if they have an objective referent against which they can measure their impact, even if other dimensions may be just as important for evaluating their outcome. Interventionists must first gather basic information on the prevailing problem. In the case of alcoholism, this means more than an inventory of such obvious problems as high accident rate, absenteeism, or poor morale, all of which may be aggravated by excessive drinking. In fact, these indicators are more a reflection of the incidence of alcoholism (the rate at which new cases manifest themselves in some visible manner) than a measure of prevalence, which is the extent to which a given problem affects a population at risk in varying degrees. No obvious manifestations of the problem need be apparent in the case of prevalence: though drinking at hazardous levels and therefore part of the population at risk, the person may never have sought help for an unrecognized problem and indeed little or no physical, mental, or social signs have yet emerged to warrant diagnosis as alcoholism. Nonetheless according to public health criteria, continued consumption at a hazardous level will probably lead to physical, mental, and social consequences. The occurrence of these consequences is referred to as the incidence of alcoholism if records of them are kept by medical, psychiatric, or social agencies. Frequently, then, it is the incidence of alcoholism that employers encounter. Conditions in certain workplaces may conspire to accelerate the incidence of problems due to alcoholism and reduce it in others, while the prevalence rate may be much the same in both situations. It is therefore important to understand the rate at which new manifestations of problems are likely to occur. Furthermore, the effects of long-term consumption of hazardous amounts of alcohol may lower the overall efficiency of the employee but not to the point at which any employer intervention can be justified. If this situation is prevalent, it can serve to lower the overall productivity of an organization even though manifestations of problem drinking are infrequent. Consequently, it behooves both the employer and the consultant to conduct a survey of prevalence wherever possible. The balance of this chapter reports on ways in which we have attempted to introduce the concept of prevalence surveys as a forerunner to further efforts to evaluate EAPs and other substance-abuse-control policies. In three cases, surveys were done as a prerequisite to further negotiations between the client organizations, a third-party consultant (the Addiction Research Foundation of Ontario), and the relevant union with respect to making changes (if needed) in the terms or operation of their EAPs.

General Method for Measuring Prevalence

The basic instrument used to measure prevalence in all three cases was the Mortimer-Filkins questionnaire, which is a fifty-eight-item inventory with yes-no, true-false responses. The questionnaire is actually part of a well-researched test which was introduced under the title *Court Procedures for*

Identifying Problem Drinkers (Kerlans et al. 1971). The performance of the whole test and its constituent parts was reviewed by Ennis (1977) as it applies to use with individuals charged with "driving while intoxicated" and "driving under the influence of liquor." The questionnaire part of the Mortimer-Filkins test had never been used for survey purposes prior to this occasion. However, Mortimer thought the questionnaire might well be suitable for survey purposes in industrial situations (Mortimer 1977). In addition, Jacobsen (1975) suggested this application. Notwithstanding this encouragement, use of the questionnaire for prevalence survey purposes is clearly experimental.

The Mortimer-Filkins questionnaire yields an overall score which is used to classify respondents into one of three categories: problem drinker, presumptive problem drinker, and nonproblem drinker. These categories should be considered as classifications in terms of probability. However, the cutting points recommended for the questionnaire scores where these are the *only* estimate of problem drinking are conservative so that it is more likely that false negatives will be encountered than false positives.

The questionnaire has quite low "face validity" in that it does not look like an alcoholic involvement inventory. Such items as "are your relatives upset with the way you live?; my judgment is better than it ever was; and I have trouble sleeping" appear with greater frequency than items such as "drinking seems to ease personal problems." However, responses on all nondrinking items are highly correlated with drinking behavior, at least among impaired drinker populations. In the following reports based on Mortimer-Filkins questionnaire results the term *at risk* is used to describe people who, by virtue of moderately high and very high scores, are considered likely or very likely to experience adverse physical, mental, or social consequences as a result of continued excessive drinking. However, no assumption is made concerning how and when these consequences may occur or indeed whether they actually will occur. It would be idle to argue that all today's excessive drinkers will be tomorrow's alcoholics since to do so would fly in the face of accumulating evidence about spontaneous remission. This effect occurs when, without formal treatment intervention, excessive drinkers decrease their consumption and thereby reduce some of the adverse consequences. This effect contaminates the study of treatment outcomes (see chapter 3). Reasonable estimates of its occurrence vary between 15 and 40 percent among untreated alcoholics (Roizen, Cahalan, and Shanks 1978). Behavioral remission, however, should not be confused with remission of predisposing conditions which put the individuals at risk for problem drinking in the first place. Examples of the latter phenomenon are demonstrated in one of these studies. In the case of military personnel, certain current members of the high-risk group had not been drinkers for the last twelve months, according to their own report. This result is consistent with the function of the Mortimer-Filkins test as presently understood: it measures the psychosocial correlates of excessive drinking rather than drinking itself.

In addition to the items in the questionnaire, other items included age, sex, marital status, and cohabitation status. Occupation was not included because of ministry/union concern over the political dangers and perceived threat to civil liberties involved in collecting such information, especially since the questionnaire had not been used in such circumstances before. The three cases are estimates of problem drinking in specific samples: public employees, psychiatric hospital employees, and military personnel.

Public Employees

This study took place in northern Ontario among the employees of a provincial ministry. The total work force in the selected operating zone was 543, including all levels of employees. The ministry had a functioning EAP but neither management nor union were satisfied with the way in which it was being used. Typically, the union felt obliged to adopt an adversary posture when problem drinking cases occurred, because proper procedures (warnings, documentation, and so forth) had not been followed and discipline had been applied prematurely. In this atmosphere it took a full year of negotiations before the local Addiction Research Foundation (ARF) consultants were satisfied that a commitment existed on the part of both management and union to bury the hatchet and to approach the subject of problem drinking from a fresh perspective. This new phase was ushered in with an agreement to conduct a prevalence survey. On the basis of the results of this survey, a decision would be made about further program development, including joint management-union committee formation, employee education, staff training, and general dissemination.

For survey purposes, all ministry staff were scheduled to attend one of eleven sessions which were arranged for a week during the spring of 1977. All sessions were held in the auditorium of a local high school in order to remove as much "management pressure to respond" as possible. Each survey session was attended by the regional director for the ministry, the area representative for the union, and the ARF center director, all of whom made brief introductory statements as to the importance and validity of the study; their support for it; its anonymity; and its voluntary nature. Considerable attention was paid to ensuring confidentiality throughout the conduct of the survey.

The survey yielded 382 complete returns from an eligible total of 543 (70.4 percent). Because of uncertainties in attendance records it is unclear how many people were sick, on vacation, or otherwise absent from work on the three test occasions. Among those who did appear on the appointed days, however, there were only four refusals.

The necessary qualifications in attempting to deduce prevalence statistics from a 70 percent return rate apply equally to a return of 80 to 90 percent. One can never be sure whether all or no problem drinkers were among the absentees. Statements of prevalence, therefore, must be couched in terms of those who did attend the test sessions. For attendees the results were: nonproblem drinkers or abstainers, 89 percent; presumptive problem drinkers, 9.2 percent, and problem drinkers, 1.8 percent. The picture was modified somewhat when sex differences were introduced, as in table 7-1.

All the problem drinkers in this sample were males. The figure of greater importance, however, relates to the presumptive problem drinker category in which females were proportionately represented. If the population at risk is defined as the combination of the problem drinker and presumptive problem drinker, slightly more than 9 percent of this sample could be thus described. For public health purposes, this would represent a conservative estimate of the target in relation to which EAP impact could be assessed.

No statistical differences were found between Mortimer-Filkins group and age, but all save 17.2 percent of the presumptive problem drinker group were under age 45. Thus on the average, they were somewhat younger than the nonproblem drinkers, which may be relevant to goal setting in early identification programs. Most of the problem drinkers were under 45 years of age in this population, which is much the same as for the nonproblem drinker group (table 7-2).

Psychiatric-Hospital Employees

This study was conducted in the same area of northern Ontario as the previous survey. This was a psychiatric hospital with 434 employees at all levels (medical, nursing, support, and administrative). The union in the ministry survey also represented employees in this survey. A similar history of adversary relations had characterized the dealings between management and union with respect to problem drinking in this setting. The prevalence survey had much the same status in the history of these relations as in the ministry. It was to mark the beginning of a more cooperative approach toward the management of problem drinking and alcoholism and provide the basis for goal setting relative to the penetration of the EAP into the population at risk. The same general procedures were followed in the administration of the Mortimer-Filkins questionnaire as in the ministry case.

The survey yielded 310 complete and usable returns from an eligible total of 434 (71.4 percent). In the hospital, the following classifications were made according to the Mortimer-Filkins groupings: nonproblem drinkers, 87.4 percent; presumptive problem drinkers, 9.7 percent; and problem drinkers, 2.9 percent. In this case, the sex differentiation was more marked than in the ministry, as shown in table 7-3.

Males scored higher than females in this sample, and overall there appeared to be more problem drinkers than in the ministry sample. Unfortunately, we

Table 7-1
Sex and Mortimer-Filkins Scores in a Sample of Public Employees

Mortimer-Filkins Grouping	*Male*	*Female*	*n*
Nonproblem drinkers	289 (89.2)	38 (90.5)	327 (89.3)
Presumptive problem drinkers	28 (8.6)	4 (9.5)	32 (8.7)
Problem drinkers	7 (2.2)	0	7 (1.9)
n	324 (88.5)	42 (11.5)	366[a] (100.0)

Source: M. Kerlans, R. Mortimer, B. Mudge, and L. Filkins, *Court Procedures for Identifying Problem Drinkers*, vol. 1: Manual, N.H.T.S.A. Report #DOT-HS-800-632, Highway Safety Research Institute, University of Michigan, June 1971.

Note: Numbers in parentheses are percentages.

[a]16 missing observations.

Table 7-2
Age and Mortimer-Filkins Scores in a Sample of Public Employees

	Age					
Mortimer-Filkins Grouping	*Under 26*	*26-35*	*36-45*	*46-55*	*56 & Over*	*n*
Nonproblem drinkers	59 (17.3)	96 (28.2)	88 (25.9)	62 (18.2)	35 (10.3)	340 (89.0)
Presumptive problem drinkers	7 (17.2)	13 (37.1)	10 (28.6)	5 (14.3)	1 (2.9)	35 (9.2)
Problem drinkers	0	2 (28.6)	3 (42.9)	2 (28.6)	0	7 (1.8)
n	65 (17.1)	111 (29.1)	101 (26.4)	69 (18.1)	36 (9.4)	382 (100.0)

Source: M. Kerlans, R. Mortimer, B. Mudge, and L. Filkins, *Court Procedures for Identifying Problem Drinkers,* vol. 1: Manual, N.H.T.S.A. Report #DOT-HS-800-632, Highway Safety Research Institute, University of Michigan, June 1971.

Note: Numbers in parentheses are percentages.

were not permitted to gather data on occupation so that there is no way of ascertaining which if any occupational subgroups accounted for the higher rates. Overall, it would appear that the population at risk for purposes of employee-assistance programming was somewhat in excess of 12 percent in this sample. Such figures must be taken strictly as approximations given the nature of the sampling and the characteristics of the questionnaire used. Even so, we would argue that the combined characteristics of a reputedly conservative

Table 7-3
Sex and Mortimer-Filkins Scores in a Sample of Psychiatric-Hospital Employees

Mortimer-Filkins Grouping	*Male*	*Female*	*n*
Nonproblem drinkers	89 (80.9)	166 (90.7)	255 (87.0)
Presumptive problem drinkers	15 (13.6)	14 (7.7)	29 (9.9)
Problem drinkers	6 (5.5)	3 (1.6)	9 (3.1)
n	110 (37.5)	183 (62.5)	293[a] (100.0)

Source: M. Kerlans, R. Mortimer, B. Mudge, and L. Filkins, *Court Procedures for Identifying Problem Drinkers*, vol. 1: Manual, N.H.T.S.A. Report #DOT-HS-800-632, Highway Safety Research Institute, University of Michigan, June 1971.
Note: Numbers in parentheses are percentages.
[a]17 missing observations.

measuring device and a compliant sample of employees conspire to suggest that the resulting estimates of prevalence are themselves low. At all events, the same limitations probably apply across organizations, making the *comparative* use of the Mortimer-Filkins of more value than its absolute use. Used in a comparative manner, the results demonstrate the differences that can exist in prevalence even between two samples of public employees doing different kinds of work. Though much more work has to be done on analyzing the variation in prevalence between occupational subgroups, the results so far indicate a clear need to abandon the notion that penetration rates can be compared with one another in the absence of objective information about prevalence rates.

The psychiatric hospital staff sample bore a similarity to the ministry group in that the presumptive problem drinkers appeared to be clustered in the 26-35 age range, 58.6 percent of them belonging there. In the hospital employee population as a whole only 32.5 percent belonged in that category (table 7-4). The concentration of presumptive problem drinkers in the 26-35 age range appeared not to be sex related. That is, as many male as female drinkers in this category belonged to that age group.

Military Personnel

This study was carried out at the request of a military base in Ontario. The eligible sample consisted of 3,983 military personnel; some were permanent staff and some were trainees. Although the numbers were larger in this case

Table 7-4
Age and Mortimer-Filkins Scores in a Sample of Psychiatric-Hospital Employees

	Age				
Mortimer-Filkins Grouping	*Under 25*	*26-35*	*36-45*	*Over 46*	*n*
Nonproblem drinkers	43 (16.9)	75 (29.5)	57 (22.4)	79 (31.1)	254 (87.0)
Presumptive problem drinkers	5 (17.2)	17 (58.6)	3 (10.3)	4 (13.7)	29 (9.9)
Problem drinkers	2 (22.2)	3 (33.3)	1 (11.1)	3 (33.3)	9 (3.1)
n	50 (17.1)	95 (32.5)	61 (20.9)	86 (29.5)	292[a] (100.0)

Source: M. Kerlans, R. Mortimer, B. Mudge, and L. Filkins, *Court Procedures for Identifying Problem Drinkers*, vol. 1: Manual, N.H.T.S.A. Report #DOT-HS-800-632, Highway Safety Research Institute, University of Michigan, June 1971.

Note: Numbers in parentheses are percentages.

[a]18 missing observations.

than in the previous examples, the response rate was lower: 2,549 returns or 63.6 percent were eventually found to be usable. Many had to be rejected because of incompleteness or other irregularities. Unfortunately, because of the nature of the environment, we were not permitted to conduct the survey ourselves, a situation which may have resulted in less control of its administration than theoretically possible. It appeared that within the base there was variable commitment to doing the survey even though the base commander had endorsed it. The impetus for the survey had originated with the captain in charge of drug and alcohol education on the base. This officer was also the head of the base military police. It seems likely that he was not sufficiently able to transfer "ownership" of the survey to the administrative head of the base as a whole in order to make the research more credible and perhaps less resented. At all events, the community development workup was less thorough than in the previous projects which is reflected in the return rate.

It is, however, a good example of the difficulties intrinsic in any basic information-gathering exercise and the need to prepare the ground thoroughly before undertaking such an activity. Argyris (chapter 3) notes that an organization must be *committed* to the acquisition of information, must be persuaded of its value in advance, and must have a reasonable idea of how it will be used once obtained. These conditions appear not to have been fully met in this case. The information resulting from the survey, then, is of unknown value as an indication of problem drinking on the base as a whole, since a sampling bias may have been introduced, particularly through the variable efforts of unit and section heads in having their personnel complete the questionnaires. Nevertheless, the data illustrate some important variations within the obtained sample. These will be presented not with a view to generalization to the base population as a whole but rather in order to demonstrate the need for specifying target groups within particular work forces which habit may have led us to consider as homogeneous entities for purposes of EAP development.

Consistent with this intention, the results of this survey will be presented so that the Mortimer-Filkins "risk groups" are broken down according to the following descriptive characteristics which show the variation within the sample as a whole.

Staff-Trainee Status

Table 7-5 indicates that the higher-risk groups are overrepresented among trainees. Here 1.7 percent of the permanent staff were classified as problem drinkers in comparison with 3.8 percent of the trainees. Similarly, 12.3 percent of the permanent staff as opposed to 17 percent of the trainees were classified as presumptive problem drinkers.

Rank

To avoid identification because of their smaller numbers, females were grouped simply into officers and other ranks (table 7-6). Two points are worthy of note here. First, there were fewer than average female personnel in the two higher-risk categories. This is summarized for females: nonproblem drinkers, 88.4 percent; presumptive problem drinkers, 10.1 percent; and problem drinkers, 1.4 percent. The summary for the base as a whole is: nonproblem drinkers, 82.3 percent; presumptive problem drinkers, 15.1 percent; and problem drinkers, 2.6 percent.

Second, there is little difference between officers and other ranks as a whole among females in the problem-drinker category (1.3 percent and 1.5 percent, respectively). Among the presumptive problem drinkers there is somewhat more variation: officers, 7.8 percent; other ranks, 10.7 percent.

Males are divided into senior and junior officers and senior and junior NCOs (table 7-7). Among the most senior ranks there were only a few cases in either the presumptive problem or problem drinker group. However, small numbers can be unreliable. The case of one senior officer classified as a problem drinker, for example, accounted for 2.1 percent of that subgroup. Whether this proportion would be maintained among a larger sample of senior officers is questionable. It is evident, however, that among both senior and junior officers

Table 7-5
Staff-Trainee Status and Mortimer-Filkins Scores

	Status		
Mortimer-Filkins Grouping	*Permanent*	*Trainee*	*Totals*
Nonproblem drinkers	673 (86.1)	663 (79.2)	1,336 (82.5)
Presumptive problem drinkers	96 (12.3)	142 (17.0)	238 (14.8)
Problem drinkers	13 (1.7)	32 (3.8)	45 (2.8)
Totals	782 (48.3)	837 (51.7)	1,619[a] (100.0)

Source: M. Kerlans, R. Mortimer, B. Mudge, and L. Filkins, *Court Procedures for Identifying Problem Drinkers*, vol. 1: Manual, N.H.T.S.A. Report #DOT-HS-800-632, Highway Safety Research Institute, University of Michigan, June 1971.

Note: Numbers in parentheses are percentages.

[a]In tables 7-5 to 7-18 grand totals vary according to the amount of data that could be retrieved for a given analysis.

Table 7-6
Mortimer-Filkins Scores and Rank for Females

	Rank		
Mortimer-Filkins Grouping	*Officers*	*Other Ranks*	*Totals*
Nonproblem drinkers	70 (90.9)	296 (87.8)	366 (88.4)
Presumptive problem drinkers	6 (7.8)	36 (10.7)	42 (10.1)
Problem drinkers	1 (1.3)	5 (1.5)	6 (1.4)
Totals	77 (18.6)	337 (81.4)	414 (100.0)

Source: M. Kerlans, R. Mortimer, B. Mudge, and L. Filkins, *Court Procedures for Identifying Problem Drinkers*, vol. 1: Manual, N.H.T.S.A. Report #DOT-HS-800-632, Highway Safety Research Institute, University of Michigan, June 1971.

Note: Numbers in parentheses are percentages.

Table 7-7
Mortimer-Filkins Scores and Rank for Males

	Rank				
Mortimer-Filkins Grouping	*Senior Officer*	*Junior Officer*	*Senior NCO*	*Junior NCO*	*Totals*
Nonproblem drinkers	44 (91.7)	274 (92.6)	342 (88.1)	1,011 (75.9)	1,671 (81.0)
Presumptive problem drinkers	3 (6.3)	21 (7.1)	38 (9.8)	272 (20.4)	334 (16.2)
Problem drinkers	1 (2.1)	1 (0.3)	8 (2.1)	49 (3.7)	59 (2.9)
Totals	48 (2.3)	296 (14.3)	388 (18.8)	1,332 (64.5)	2,064 (100.0)

Source: M. Kerlans, R. Mortimer, B. Mudge, and L. Filkins. *Court Procedures for Identifying Problem Drinkers*, vol. 1: Manual, N.H.T.S.A. Report #DOT-HS-800-632, Highway Safety Research Institute, University of Michigan, June 1971.

Note: Numbers in parentheses are percentages.

a higher than average proportion of respondents was found among the normal drinkers (which includes nondrinkers). In this sample the likelihood of belonging to one or other of the higher-risk groups was greatest among the NCOs, in particular the junior NCOs group in which 20.4 percent were classified as presumptive problem drinkers and 3.7 percent as problem drinkers.

Living Accommodation

Those living in single quarters were most likely to be in the higher-risk categories: 17.4 percent presumptive problem drinkers and 3.7 percent problem drinkers. Those who lived off base or in married quarters on base manifested much the same lower scores: 12.6 percent presumptive problem drinkers and 1.5 percent problem drinkers (table 7-8).

Marital Status

The lowest risk levels were found among the married personnel: 12.3 percent presumptive problem drinkers and 1.3 percent problem drinkers. Single personnel manifested corresponding rates of 16.8 percent and 3.7 percent, while

Table 7-8
Mortimer-Filkins Scores and Living Accommodation

	Living Accommodation			
Mortimer-Filkins Grouping	*PMQ*	*Single Quarters*	*Off Base*	*Totals*
Nonproblem drinkers	690 (85.9)	993 (78.9)	358 (85.9)	2,041 (82.4)
Presumptive problem drinkers	100 (12.5)	219 (17.4)	53 (12.7)	372 (15.0)
Problem drinkers	13 (1.6)	46 (3.7)	6 (1.4)	65 (2.6)
Totals	803 (32.4)	1,258 (50.8)	417 (16.8)	2,478 (100.0)

Source: M. Kerlans, R. Mortimer, B. Mudge, and L. Filkins, *Court Procedures for Identifying Problem Drinkers*, vol. 1: Manual, N.H.T.S.A. Report #DOT-HS-800-632, Highway Safety Research Institute, University of Michigan, June 1971.

Note: Numbers in parentheses are percentages.

those who were divorced (29.4 percent presumptive problem drinkers and 5.9 percent problem drinkers) or separated (38.1 percent presumptive problem drinkers and 7.1 percent problem drinkers) demonstrated dramatically higher-risk levels (table 7-9).

Age

Age was one of the major correlates of risk level in this sample. Those 17-19 years old clearly had the greatest proportion of presumptive problem and problem drinker personnel (18.5 percent and 4.7 percent, respectively). There was an apparently continuous trend as age increased so that among those who were 34 years of age or above the presumptive problem group decreased to 10 percent and the high-risk group to 0.9 percent. It is not suggested, however, that age in itself accounted for all the noted differences, since in the base setting other factors were related to age such as marital status and rank (table 7-10).

Use of Professional Services.

Of the fifty-nine respondents classified in table 7-11 in the problem-drinker category, only nine had ever sought help of any kind. Little evidence was forthcoming about the source of this help, but other sources than the medical profession and social work were favored as were the clergy. Similarly, of the 372 in the presumptive problem category only 18 had ever sought help for a drinking problem. Interestingly, 1.3 percent of those classified in the lowest-risk category (twenty-six people) had at one time sought help for a drinking problem.

Table 7-9
Mortimer-Filkins Scores and Marital Status

Mortimer-Filkins Grouping	Marital Status: Single	Separated	Divorced	Widowed	Married	Totals
Nonproblem drinkers	978 (79.6)	23 (54.8)	22 (64.7)	11 (84.6)	1,024 (86.4)	2,058 (82.2)
Presumptive problem drinkers	206 (16.8)	16 (38.1)	10 (29.4)	2 (15.4)	146 (12.3)	380 (15.2)
Problem drinkers	45 (3.7)	3 (7.1)	2 (5.9)	0	15 (1.3)	65 (2.6)
Totals	1,229 (49.1)	42 (1.7)	34 (1.4)	13 (0.5)	1,185 (47.3)	2,503 (100.0)

Source: M. Kerlans, R. Mortimer, B. Mudge, and L. Filkins, *Court Procedures for Identifying Problem Drinkers*, vol. 1: Manual, N.H.T.S.A. Report #DOT-HS-800-632, Highway Safety Research Institute, University of Michigan, June 1971.

Note: Numbers in parentheses are percentages.

Table 7-10
Mortimer-Filkins Scores and Age

Mortimer-Filkins Grouping	Age: 17-19	20-23	24-33	34+	Totals
Nonproblem drinkers	422 (76.7)	504 (79.6)	521 (83.2)	563 (89.1)	2,010 (82.3)
Presumptive problem drinkers	102 (18.5)	110 (17.4)	91 (14.5)	63 (10.0)	366 (15.0)
Problem drinkers	26 (4.7)	19 (3.0)	14 (2.2)	6 (0.9)	65 (2.7)
Totals	550 (22.5)	633 (25.9)	626 (25.6)	632 (25.9)	2,441 (100.0)

Source: M. Kerlans, R. Mortimer, B. Mudge, and L. Filkins, *Court Procedures for Identifying Problem Drinkers*, vol. 1: Manual, N.H.T.S.A. Report #DOT-HS-800-632, Highway Safety Research Institute, University of Michigan, June 1971.

Note: Numbers in parentheses are percentages.

Frequency of Drinking

The device used to clasify respondents into risk categories assigns risk levels on the basis of numerous personal and social factors, only some of which are concerned directly with drinking behavior itself. Consequently, a person who has not consumed alcohol for some time (even a member of AA who has been dry for over a year) *could* still be in a high-risk category because certain personal and social factors make him a candidate for problem drinking at almost any

Table 7-11
Mortimer-Filkins Scores and Any Use of Professional Help for a Drinking Problem

	Type of Help Sought					
Mortimer-Filkins Grouping	*None*	*Clergyman*	*Social Worker*	*Physician*	*Other*	*Totals*
Nonproblem drinkers	2,015 (83.3)	10 (62.5)	1 (16.7)	3 (50.0)	12 (48.6)	2,041 (82.6)
Presumptive problem drinkers	354 (14.6)	5 (31.3)	3 (50.0)	1 (16.7)	9 (36.0)	372 (15.0)
Problem drinkers	50 (2.1)	1 (6.3)	2 (33.3)	2 (33.3)	4 (16.0)	59 (2.4)
Totals	2,419 (97.9)	16 (0.6)	6 (0.2)	6 (0.2)	25 (1.0)	2,472 (100.0)

Source: M. Kerlans, R. Mortimer, B. Mudge, and L. Filkins, *Court Procedures for Identifying Problem Drinkers,* vol. 1: Manual, N.H.T.S.A. Report #DOT-HS-800-632, Highway Safety Research Institute, University of Michigan, June 1971.

Note: Numbers in parentheses are percentages.

time if the right conditions prevail. From table 7-12, of those who had not consumed alcohol in the last twelve months, 3.1 percent were still classifiable as problem drinkers. At the other end of the scale, however, it was clear that among those who were daily drinkers, the greatest proportion of presumptive problem drinker (32.7 percent) and problem-drinker personnel (9 percent) were to be found. Conversely, only 58.3 percent of those who drank on a daily basis were classified as normal drinkers in comparison with an overall average of 82.2 percent (table 7-12).

In table 7-12 among the twenty presumptive problem drinkers or problem drinkers, seven were members of AA and two were seeking treatment elsewhere. Although no evidence for the proposition can be adduced from these data, the possibility cannot be ruled out that spontaneous remission played a part in the abstinence of at least some of the remaining eleven people who might otherwise be seen as false positives (Smart 1975-1976; Roizen, Cahalan, and Shanks 1978). The fact that these people were still at risk in terms of the Mortimer-Filkins results is consistent with the function of this test as outlined earlier in this chapter.

Membership in Alcoholics Anonymous

A total of forty-eight people reported membership in AA. Of these, twenty were classified as either presumptive problem or problem drinkers, while twenty-eight were classified as normal drinkers or nondrinkers at the time of the survey.

Table 7-12
Mortimer-Filkins Scores and Frequency of Drinking in Last Twelve Months

	Frequency of Drinking				
Mortimer-Filkins Grouping	*Never*	*Less than Weekly*	*Weekly*	*Daily*	*Totals*
Nonproblem drinkers	140 (87.5)	927 (89.5)	848 (79.3)	130 (58.3)	2,045 (82.2)
Presumptive problem drinkers	15 (9.4)	101 (9.7)	190 (17.8)	73 (32.7)	379 (15.2)
Problem drinkers	5 (3.1)	8 (0.8)	31 (2.9)	20 (9.0)	64 (2.6)
Totals	160 (6.4)	1,036 (41.6)	1,069 (43.0)	223 (9.0)	2,488 (100.0)

Source: M. Kerlans, R. Mortimer, B. Mudge, and L. Filkins, *Court Procedures for Identifying Problem Drinkers*, vol. 1: Manual, N.H.T.S.A. Report #DOT-HS-800-632, Highway Safety Research Institute, University of Michigan, June 1971.
Note: Numbers in parentheses are percentages.

The majority of all personnel on base who were presumptive problem drinkers or problem drinkers were not members of AA (table 7-13).

Convictions for Driving while Impaired

Of the total sample, 143 people reported that at some point in their lives they had been convicted of a driving while impaired offense. Among the once-convicted group there was a much higher proportion of presumptive problem and problem-drinker personnel (table 7-14).

Use of Marijuana

Over 13 percent of the total sample reported some use of marijuana or hashish in the twelve months prior to the survey (table 7-15). Constituting the 13.9 percent, 0.9 percent was reportedly daily use, 1.8 percent was weekly, and 11.1 percent less frequently. There was a strong tendency for those who used marijuana to be overrepresented in the presumptive problem and problem-drinker categories. Among daily users 56.5 percent belonged to the latter risk categories combined in comparison with 14.6 percent of nonmarijuana users. The combined proportions of presumptive problem and problem drinkers among weekly users of marijuana were similarly high, 51.1 percent. Even those who used marijuana on a less than weekly basis were more at risk in problem drinking terms (32.5 percent, combined).

Table 7-13
Mortimer-Filkins Scores and Membership in Alcoholics Anonymous

	AA Membership		
Mortimer-Filkins Grouping	*Yes*	*No*	*Totals*
Nonproblem drinkers	28 (58.3)	1,987 (82.5)	2,015 (82.0)
Presumptive problem drinkers	11 (22.9)	367 (15.2)	378 (15.4)
Problem drinkers	9 (18.8)	55 (2.3)	64 (2.6)
Totals	48 (2.0)	2,409 (98.0)	2,457 (100.0)

Source: M. Kerlans, R. Mortimer, B. Mudge, and L. Filkins, *Court Procedures for Identifying Problem Drinkers,* vol. 1: Manual, N.H.T.S.A. Report #DOT-HS-800-632, Highway Safety Research Institute, University of Michigan, June 1971.

Note: Numbers in parentheses are percentages.

Table 7-14
Mortimer-Filkins Score and Self-Report of Driving-while-Impaired Conviction

	DWI Conviction		
Mortimer-Filkins Grouping	*Yes*	*No*	*Totals*
Nonproblem drinkers	92 (64.3)	1,930 (83.2)	2,022 (82.1)
Presumptive problem drinkers	42 (29.4)	336 (14.5)	378 (15.3)
Problem drinkers	9 (6.3)	55 (2.4)	64 (2.6)
Totals	143 (5.8)	2,321 (94.1)	2,464 (100.0)

Source: M. Kerlans, R. Mortimer, B. Mudge, and L. Filkins, *Court Procedures for Identifying Problem Drinkers* vol.: 1 Manual, N.H.T.S.A. Report #DOT-HS-800-632, Highway Safety Research Institute, University of Michigan, June 1971.

Note: Numbers in parentheses are percentages.

Use of Barbiturates

Of the 3.3 percent of the total sample who reported any use of barbiturates in the twelve months prior to the survey, 2 percent said it was on a doctor's prescription, 1.3 percent without. Of those who used barbiturates on prescription, 22 percent were among presumptive problem drinkers and 6 percent among problem drinkers. This trend becomes more marked in the case of non-prescription (illicit) barbiturate use where the proportions were 25 percent presumptive problem drinkers and 25 percent problem drinkers (table 7-16).

Table 7-15
Mortimer-Filkins Scores and Use of Marijuana

	Use of Marijuana				
Mortimer-Filkins Grouping	*None*	*Less than Weekly*	*Weekly*	*Daily*	*Totals*
Nonproblem drinkers	1,836 (85.4)	187 (67.5)	22 (48.9)	10 (43.5)	2,055 (82.4)
Presumptive problem drinkers	281 (13.1)	75 (27.1)	15 (33.3)	6 (26.1)	377 (15.1)
Problem drinkers	33 (1.5)	15 (5.4)	8 (17.8)	7 (30.4)	63 (2.5)
Totals	2,150 (86.2)	277 (11.1)	45 (1.8)	23 (0.9)	2,495 (100.0)

Source: M. Kerlans, R. Mortimer, B. Mudge, and L. Filkins, *Court Procedures for Identifying Problem Drinkers*, vol. 1: Manual, N.H.T.S.A. Report #DOT-HS-800-632, Highway Safety Research Institute, University of Michigan, June 1971.

Note: Numbers in parentheses are percentages.

Use of Stimulants

Over 4 percent of the total sample reported some use of stimulants during the twelve months prior to the study. Of these, 1.3 percent used these stimulants on a doctor's prescription, 3 percent without. Again, disproportionate numbers of such users were found also to be higher risks in terms of problem drinking. Among the nonprescription (illicit) users, 17.3 percent were in the problem-drinker category, 29.3 percent in the presumptive problem-drinker group. Although none of the prescription users of stimulants were classified in the problem-drinker category, 41.9 percent were among the presumptive problem drinkers. It will be recalled that the sample average for the problem-drinker group was 2.6 percent and for the presumptive problem drinkers, 15.2 percent (table 7-17).

Use of Tranquilizers

The trend for marijuana, barbiturates, and stimulants continues as we examine the use of tranquilizers. Of the 11.8 percent who reported any use of these substances in the twelve months prior to the survey, a disproportionate number were in the two higher alcohol risk groups. Over 10 percent used tranquilizers on a doctor's prescription. Of that group, more than 21 percent were in the presumptive problem-drinker category and 6 percent in the problem-drinker category. About 1.7 percent used tranquilizers without a doctor's prescription. Among that group, 26.8 percent were in the presumptive problem-drinker category and 17.1 percent in the problem-drinker category (table 7-18).

In summary, in this sample the risk of being a problem drinker increased if personnel were trainees; male; single, separated, or divorced; or of junior

Table 7-16
Mortimer-Filkins Scores and Use of Barbiturates

	Use of Barbiturates			
Mortimer-Filkins Grouping	*None*	*With Prescription*	*Without Prescription*	*Totals*
Nonproblem drinkers	2,011 (83.0)	36 (72.0)	16 (50.0)	2,063 (82.3)
Presumptive problem drinkers	359 (14.8)	11 (22.0)	8 (25.0)	378 (15.1)
Problem drinkers	54 (2.2)	3 (6.0)	8 (25.0)	65 (2.6)
Totals	2,424 (96.7)	50 (2.0)	32 (1.3)	2,506 (100.0)

Source: M. Kerlans, R. Mortimer, B. Mudge, and L. Filkins, *Court Procedures for Identifying Problem Drinkers*, vol. 1: Manual, N.H.T.S.A. Report #DOT-HS-800-632, Highway Safety Research Institute, University of Michigan, June 1971.

Note: Numbers in parentheses are percentages.

Table 7-17
Mortimer-Filkins Scores and Use of Stimulants

	Use of Stimulants			
Mortimer-Filkins Grouping	*None*	*With Prescription*	*Without Prescription*	*Totals*
Nonproblem drinkers	1,981 (83.5)	18 (58.1)	40 (53.3)	2,039 (82.3)
Presumptive problem drinkers	342 (14.4)	13 (41.9)	22 (29.3)	377 (15.2)
Problem drinkers	50 (2.1)	0	13 (17.3)	63 (2.5)
Totals	2,373 (95.7)	31 (1.3)	75 (3.0)	2,479 (100.0)

Source: M. Kerlans, R. Mortimer, B. Mudge, and L. Filkins, *Court Procedures for Identifying Problem Drinkers*, vol. 1: Manual, N.H.T.S.A. Report #DOT-HS-800-632, Highway Safety Research Institute, University of Michigan, June 1971.

Note: Numbers in parentheses are percentages.

noncommissioned rank; living alone; between the ages of 17 and 23, particularly 17 and 19; and daily drinkers, or to some extent regular weekly drinkers.

In addition, such high-risk people were more likely to have been involved in criminal driving charges (DWI) and were not likely to have sought help for their problem.

Conversely, low-risk personnel were concentrated among permanent staff, officers, females, those who were married, those living in married quarters or

Table 7-18
Mortimer-Filkins Scores and Use of Tranquilizers

	Use of Tranquilizers			
Mortimer-Filkins Grouping	*None*	*With Prescription*	*Without Prescription*	*Totals*
Nonproblem drinkers	1,838 (83.9)	182 (72.8)	23 (56.1)	2,043 (82.3)
Presumptive problem drinkers	311 (14.2)	53 (21.2)	11 (26.8)	375 (15.1)
Problem drinkers	41 (1.9)	15 (6.0)	7 (17.1)	63 (2.5)
Totals	2,190 (88.3)	250 (10.1)	41 (1.7)	2,481 (100.0)

Source: M. Kerlans, R. Mortimer, B. Mudge, and L. Filkins, *Court Procedures for Identifying Problem Drinkers*, vol. 1: Manual, N.H.T.S.A. Report #DOT-HS-800-632, Highway Safety Research Institute, University of Michigan, June 1971.

Note: Numbers in parentheses are percentages.

off base, those above the age of 24 and particularly over 34, and those who drink on a less than weekly regular basis.

It appears also that people in the presumptive problem and problem-drinker groups were much more likely than their normal or nondrinker counterparts to use marijuana, barbiturates, stimulants, and tranquilizers, both with and without a doctor's prescription.

There is some evidence from this study that problem drinking is not a fixed phenomenon: that is, people who were drinking too much may have sought help at some point and at the time of the survey were either not drinking or drinking normally (tables 7-11 and 7-13). Further, it should not be concluded that presumptive problem drinkers will all become alcoholics: they are simply more at risk for becoming so than more moderate drinkers. These observations are consistent with those made by other authors (Cahalan and Room 1974; Smart 1976; Roizen, Cahalan, and Shanks 1978) with respect to the spontaneous remission effect in alcoholism development.

Given that we are dealing in probability and not certainty, and that it is unsafe to generalize from the present sample to the military base as a whole, it seems reasonable to assert on the basis of the present data that the population at risk with respect to problem drinking can be usefully divided into a number of more specific subgroups according to the listed dimensions. It is fairly clear, too, that these subgroups have special needs; for example, the young, unmarried, NCO trainee may be facing quite different dilemmas from the older, recently divorced senior NCO instructor who has many skills but perhaps nowhere to go in terms of career. Such characterizations of a population may be as useful as any based exclusively on occupational groupings. We recommend that future studies direct their attention to variations in the population at risk of the type just described.

8 Early Identification of Problem Employees

The Nature of the Study

One of the fundamental premises of employee-assistance programs (EAPs) is their potential for achieving early identification of problem employees. This premise can be located within a framework of principles called the ideal model of EAP, discussed in chapters 1 and 2. The evidence accumulated so far has not been encouraging with respect to the actual occurrence of early identification, judging from the low penetration rates reported in the literature. Nonetheless, it is not certain whether the relatively few identified and referred cases are all "end of the liners" or whether this referred population contains a variety of cases including examples of early identification. The latter term seems to describe the identification of employees whose behavioral problems are not yet manifest but whose work performance has dropped off sufficiently over time that an alert supervisor would recognize the development of a problem and take action. It is argued that the longer an EAP has existed, the greater its chances of turning up these early cases. Moreover, it is thought that as the EAP "matures," the frequency of mandatory referrals will decline and the frequency of voluntary referrals will increase. In that way the effective operation of the policy or procedure will cease to depend on supervisory recognition and referral, relying instead on the self-generated motivation of employees who know or suspect they are headed for trouble but are concealing the fact quite adequately from their employers, if not from their family and friends.

The theoretical formulation of the manner in which an EAP should work over time suggests a form of investigation which would put the assumptions to a test. That is, a study of employer referrals under the auspices of an EAP over a number of years should provide a practical test of the view that as policies mature, early identification becomes more common. This chapter reports on a study conducted for this very purpose.

The research was carried out by analyzing selected case files from a residential facility for the treatment of employed alcoholics located in Toronto and known as "May Street." This facility, run by the Addiction Research Foundation (ARF) of Ontario under the former direction of Ed Freedberg, takes referrals from a large number of employers. From 1972 until 1978 detailed files were kept on every client admitted into the program. The records contained a face sheet, a life history questionnaire, an inventory of alcohol consumption, problem assessment battery scores at various stages of the employee's contact with the program, a supervisor's rating form, and other miscellaneous information about problems and progress. With the permission of Freedberg, these files were accessed and coded for the present study, which was undertaken to search for and examine any existing trends in the referral of alcoholics to May Street from five selected organizations, all of which had EAPs over a four-year period. Since the data already accumulated at May Street was to be used as the source of information, certain limitations were inherent in the project. There was no control for deliberate or inadvertent variations in recruitment of clients at May Street, nor control for deliberate or patterned variation in referral activity of the organizations, though some information on these practices was available. Both of these elements could have influenced the patterns which emerged. In discussing the results we attempt to deal with ways in which these two factors may have operated. The method used is described below.

Data Sources

The choice of organizations was based on an average annual referral rate of more than five people a year to May Street between 1973 and 1976. Five organizations were eligible for the study according to these criteria: the provincial government (n = 133); a federal communications agency (n = 74); a provincial public utility company (n = 58); a railroad company (n = 56); and an automobile manufacturer (n = 23).

Several sources of information on each client were consulted. The basic client files contained a face sheet with basic descriptive materials, and a life history questionnaire which dealt with history of treatment, drinking, medical problems, legal involvement, and employment. The latter form had undergone some modifications in format and content during the four-year period of the study, and thus some difficulties arose in designing a comprehensive code book, in actually recording the information presented in the forms, and in maintaining consistency over time in some variables. Some of the more serious problems caused by this are reviewed in detail in Suurvali and Shain (1978).

Other data sources included an inventory of alcohol consumption, modified from the alcohol involvement questionnaire (Aharan 1966, Gillies et al. 1974), the Ontario problem assessment battery (Freedberg and McLatchie 1976), and a supervisor's rating form (Smart 1974).

Criteria for Earlier-Identification Hypothesis

The main purpose of this study was to look for trends over a four-year period in the type of person each organization was referring to the May Street program. In particular, we were looking for any indications that in more recent years employers were identifying and referring problem drinkers at an earlier stage in their alcoholic career than they were in the first year or two of contact with the program. For this purpose, it was necessary to establish the variables and their values that would suggest an early-identification trend.

As support for the earlier-identification hypothesis, we decided to look for, in the more recent years, higher percentages of clients in such groups as younger age; married (whose marriage had not yet collapsed because of prolonged excessive drinking); voluntary admissions (instead of mandatory or forced voluntary); no previous hospitalization or treatment for alcoholism; those who had not been in detoxication centers (detox) or in Alcoholics Anonymous (AA); those whose drinking had become a problem quite recently (the age at which drinking became a problem was not too far from the age at admission to the program); no history of blackouts or delirium tremens (DTs); and those holding one job in the past two years (stability in remaining with one job). Although being employed 100 percent of the time in the past two years was considered a desirable feature as well, there were very few subjects in the study who did not fit this category, and thus its discriminatory power was limited. Fewer reports of drinking on the job and absenteeism due to drinking were also expected to occur if earlier identification was taking place. Similarly, early referral clients should not have received warnings from their supervisors about their drinking. Other characteristics of which more evidence could be expected in recent years were no past or present drinking-related legal charges; no medical problems that could be related to excessive, long-term drinking; lower scores on the inventory of alcohol consumption; lower scores and thus less negative ratings on all the assessment battery scales (with the possible exception of coercion from self-respect on which a high score might have indicated that the patient recognized his own problem before others forced him to recognize it, rather than reflecting a deeper involvement with alcohol); and higher scores on the supervisor's rating form (work performance was less affected by drinking habits, at least as far as the supervisor could see).

The statistical analyses conducted on the data consisted primarily of calculating frequencies of values of the various variables for admissions from each organization and for each of the four years under study. These frequencies were then manipulated to allow for comparisons within organizations and between years as well as between organizations. Also Pearson product-moment correlations were computed on the alcohol involvement scale score and the three major scores of the supervisor's rating form (total score, score of subscale 1 concerning job performance, score of subscale 2 concerning the effects of drinking on the job) for each year within each organization. The research results follow.

Overall Characteristics of Employees

Table 8-1 lists the percentage frequencies for the face sheet and life history form variables for each organization, without division by year of admission in order to give an overall picture of each organization's referrals to May Street during the total four-year study period. The percentages in the table should be added down the columns, but can be compared across the rows, in order to

Table 8-1
Characteristics of Employees Referred from Five Organizations According to Face Sheet and Life-History Form (All Years Together)

Employee Characteristics	*Provincial Government n=133*	*Federal Communications Agency n=74*	*Provincial Utility Co. n=58*	*Railroad Co. n=56*	*Automobile Manufacturer n=23*
Year of Admission					
1973	36.4%	25.7%	24.1%	21.4%	34.8%
1974	29.5	36.5	19.0	33.9	30.4
1975	13.6	9.5	19.0	28.6	13.0
1976	20.5	28.4	37.9	16.1	21.7
Mean Age at Admission	47	42.2	44.4	47.5	41.9
Sex					
Male	91.7	100.0	98.3	98.2	95.7
Female	8.3	0.0	1.7	1.8	4.3
Marital Status					
Single	14.3	25.7	8.6	16.4	8.7
Separated	12.8	17.6	12.1	16.4	4.3
Widowed	5.3	5.4	1.7	5.5	0.0
Married	59.4	41.9	75.9	54.5	73.9
Divorced	8.3	9.5	1.7	7.3	13.0
Number of Children					
None	24.1	40.5	19.0	28.6	17.4
One	18.0	21.6	5.2	10.7	8.7
Two	18.0	12.2	22.4	12.5	30.4
Three or more	39.9	25.9	53.4	48.3	43.5
Grade Completed					
Less than grade 8	4.7	4.1	3.4	14.5	0.0
Grade 8	14.0	19.2	13.8	7.3	21.7
Grade 9	7.8	17.8	5.2	14.5	26.1
Grade 10	29.5	30.1	13.8	30.9	21.7
Grade 11	7.8	11.0	6.9	14.5	8.7
Grade 12 or above	36.5	17.9	56.8	18.1	11.7
Special Training					
Yes	35.3	5.4	27.6	10.7	8.7
No	64.7	94.6	72.4	89.3	91.3
Length of Time at This Job					
Less than 1 year	1.5	6.8	1.7	1.8	0.0
1 year	1.5	4.1	3.4	7.3	4.3
2 years	9.8	5.4	5.2	1.8	8.7
3 to 5 years	9.8	21.7	18.9	7.3	4.3
6 to 10 years	21.9	27.1	15.5	9.0	13.0
11 to 15 years	24.9	13.5	3.4	1.8	21.7
16 to 20 years	15.9	6.9	5.1	7.2	8.6
21 to 25 years	6.1	9.5	15.5	20.1	30.3
26 or more years	1.6	5.4	31.0	43.5	8.6
Job Classification[a]					
White collar	68.1	65.8	53.3	28.3	30.0
Blue collar	31.9	34.2	46.7	71.7	70.0
Professional	17.7	0.0	32.0	0.0	14.3
Nonprofessional	82.3	100.0	68.0	100.0	83.7

Table 8-1 continued

Employee Characteristics	*Provincial Government n=133*	*Federal Communications Agency n=74*	*Provincial Utility Co. n=58*	*Railroad Co. n=56*	*Automobile Manufacturer n=23*
Supervisory	23.4%	1.4%	23.7%	18.0%	25.0%
Nonsupervisory	76.7	98.6	76.3	82.0	75.0
Supervisory and other higher	43.3	2.7	49.1	31.7	46.4
Nonsupervisory	56.7	97.3	50.9	68.3	53.6
Type of Admission					
Mandatory	86.8	90.4	52.7	92.7	63.6
Forced voluntary	3.1	8.2	20.0	5.5	13.6
Voluntary	10.1	1.4	27.3	1.8	22.7
Has Client Been Hospitalized for Alcoholism					
Never	71.2	77.0	78.9	82.1	78.3
Once	14.4	16.2	14.0	14.3	21.7
More than once	12.9	6.9	5.3	1.8	0.0
Unknown	1.5	0.0	1.8	1.8	0.0
Has Client Been Hospitalized for Psychiatric Reasons Other than Alcoholism					
Never	89.4	89.2	89.5	94.6	91.3
Once	7.6	8.1	8.8	3.6	4.3
More than once	0.8	0.0	1.8	0.0	0.0
Unknown	2.3	2.7	0.0	1.8	4.3
Number of Times Treated for Alcoholism					
Never	43.9	54.8	56.1	60.7	47.8
Once	15.2	19.2	21.1	21.4	17.4
Twice	15.9	12.3	8.8	12.5	17.4
More than twice	10.7	6.9	7.0	5.4	13.0
Several, unspecified (more than once)	14.3	6.8	7.0	0.0	4.3
Types of Treatment for Alcoholism					
None	43.9	54.8	56.1	60.7	50.0
Detoxication center	22.0	19.2	3.5	12.5	9.1
Antabuse or Temposil	18.2	15.1	7.0	8.9	18.2
Group therapy	20.5	12.3	7.0	7.1	9.1
Residential treatment	3.8	1.4	5.3	0.0	0.0
Individual therapy	18.2	12.3	14.0	10.7	13.6
Family counseling	5.3	6.8	1.8	0.0	9.1
Alcoholics Anonymous	31.1	16.4	26.3	25.0	22.7
Family doctor	3.0	4.1	8.8	0.0	4.5
Prescribed drugs (other than Antabuse)	2.3	5.5	5.3	0.0	4.5
Relaxation therapy	5.3	0.0	1.8	1.8	0.0
Deconditioning therapy	3.0	0.0	0.0	0.0	0.0

Table 8-1 continued

Employee Characteristics	*Provincial Government n=133*	*Federal Communications Agency n=74*	*Provincial Utility Co. n=58*	*Railroad Co. n=56*	*Automobile Manufacturer n=23*
Serious Illnesses Still Affecting Client[b]:					
None	79.5%	60.8%	68.4%	82.1%	65.2%
Liver damage	1.5	0.0	0.0	0.0	0.0
Ulcer	2.3	4.1	3.5	1.8	4.3
Chronic chest condition	7.6	23.0	14.0	7.1	13.0
Diabetes	5.3	2.7	8.8	5.4	4.3
Arthritis	0.8	4.1	0.0	0.0	0.0
Cardiovascular disease	0.0	0.0	5.3	1.8	13.0
Kidney dysfunction	1.5	0.0	0.0	0.0	0.0
Nerve problems	0.0	1.4	0.0	1.8	0.0
Chronic hepatitis	0.0	1.4	1.8	0.0	0.0
Others	2.3	5.4	3.5	3.6	0.0
Age Started Drinking					
Under 15 years	2.3	4.1	0.0	0.0	0.0
Between 15 and 20	50.0	57.5	42.1	41.8	34.8
Between 20 and 25	26.2	19.2	45.6	41.8	47.8
Between 25 and 30	6.2	9.6	1.8	1.8	8.7
Between 30 and 40	6.9	8.2	8.8	7.3	8.7
Over 40	8.5	1.4	1.8	7.3	0.0
Age Drinking Became Problem					
Under 15 years	0.0	1.7	2.0	0.0	0.0
Between 15 and 20	5.8	11.9	6.0	4.1	0.0
Between 20 and 25	14.0	15.3	8.0	10.2	20.0
Between 25 and 30	8.3	13.6	4.0	10.2	25.0
Between 30 and 40	27.3	20.3	30.0	16.3	15.0
Over 40	43.0	35.6	50.0	55.1	40.0
Never	1.7	1.7	0.0	4.1	0.0
Blackouts					
Yes	57.3	59.5	69.6	40.0	73.9
No	42.7	40.5	30.4	60.0	26.1
DTs					
Yes	18.3	16.9	5.3	15.1	8.7
No	81.7	83.1	94.7	84.9	91.3
Convulsions					
Yes	5.4	12.2	5.3	7.4	4.3
No	94.6	87.8	94.7	92.6	95.7
Number of Jobs in Past Two Years					
One	93.8	91.8	94.7	98.2	95.7
Two	6.2	6.8	3.5	1.8	4.3
More than two	0.0	1.4	1.8	0.0	0.0

Table 8-1 continued

Employee Characteristics	*Provincial Government n=133*	*Federal Communications Agency n=74*	*Provincial Utility Co. n=58*	*Railroad Co. n=56*	*Automobile Manufacturer n=23*
Percent of Time Employed in Past Two Years					
100	99.2%	94.4%	100.0%	100.0%	95.7%
75	0.8	4.2	0.0	0.0	4.3
50	0.0	1.4	0.0	0.0	0.0
Does Client Drink on Job (self-report)					
Yes	28.5	57.5	21.4	57.1	43.5
No	71.5	42.5	78.6	42.9	56.5
Is Client Absent Due to Drinking (self-report)					
Yes	58.5	74.3	30.9	60.7	63.6
No	31.3	21.6	49.1	32.1	18.2
Rarely	9.9	4.1	20.0	7.1	18.2
Has Client Been Warned by Supervisor about Drinking (self-report)					
Yes	80.8	74.3	68.4	73.2	69.6
No	19.2	25.7	31.6	26.8	30.4
Alcohol-Related Legal Charges in Past Two Years					
None	76.9	75.7	71.9	83.9	78.3
One	18.5	16.2	19.3	14.3	13.0
Two	1.5	2.7	5.3	1.8	0.0
More than two	1.6	1.4	0.0	0.0	0.0
Unknown number	1.5	4.1	3.5	0.0	8.7
Alcohol-Related Legal Charges at Present					
None	93.9	97.3	91.1	92.9	95.7
One	6.1	1.4	5.4	7.1	4.3
Two	0.0	1.4	3.6	0.0	0.0
Alcohol Involvement Questionnaire Total Score (range 0-124)					
Mean score[c]	53.8	58.8	53.4	65.9	67.5
Standard deviation	22.9	22.3	23.8	23.3	20.9
Total of Other Alcohol Questions (range 0-36)					
Mean score	16.4	17.1	15.7	18.1	18.6
Standard deviation	6.2	5.9	5.9	6.0	3.9

Table 8-1 continued

Employee Characteristics	*Provincial Government n=133*	*Federal Communications Agency n=74*	*Provincial Utility Co. n=58*	*Railroad Co. n=56*	*Automobile Manufacturer n=23*
Employment Assessment Score (range 17-85)					
Mean score[d]	35.4	35.5	33.6	35.4	37.0
Standard deviation	9.9	8.7	8.5	11.4	10.0
Interpersonal Assessment Score (range 12-60)					
Mean score	27.6	27.7	27.5	27.6	29.1
Standard deviation	7.7	7.9	7.7	9.1	6.8
Marital Assessment Score: Client Re Self (range 26-130)					
Mean score	52.8	55.8	57.2	50.4	52.8
Standard deviation	16.6	14.9	17.0	13.8	19.0
Assessment of Coercion Re Friends (range 5-25)					
Mean score[e]	11.8	11.1	10.4	13.7	12.3
Standard deviation	5.6	5.6	4.8	6.0	5.7
Assessment of Coercion Re Relatives (range 5-25)					
Mean score	10.1	10.6	9.0	11.5	10.2
Standard deviation	5.2	5.3	4.7	4.8	4.6
Assessment of Coercion Re Health (range 5-25)					
Mean score	16.7	17.8	17.3	18.2	18.5
Standard deviation	5.4	5.2	5.0	5.1	4.9
Assessment of Coercion Re Job (range 5-25)					
Mean score	17.7	17.3	16.5	19.5	16.0
Standard deviation	5.0	4.8	5.6	4.3	4.8
Assessment of Coercion Re Financial Position (range 5-25)					
Mean score	13.8	16.2	13.1	16.0	14.4
Standard deviation	5.8	6.7	6.4	6.3	6.3
Assessment of Coercion Re Legal (range 5-25)					
Mean score	10.9	9.7	11.7	10.5	12.0
Standard deviation	5.8	4.9	6.5	5.1	6.4
Assessment of Coercion Re Spouse (range 5-25)					
Mean score	16.5	19.6	16.8	16.5	18.8
Standard deviation	6.0	5.2	6.3	6.3	4.8

Table 8-1 continued

Employee Characteristics	*Provincial Government n=133*	*Federal Communications Agency n=74*	*Provincial Utility Co. n=58*	*Railroad Co. n=56*	*Automobile Manufacturer n=23*
Assessment of Coercion Re Children (range 5-25)					
Mean score	14.0	15.4	14.6	15.5	15.2
Standard deviation	5.9	5.6	5.9	6.7	5.9
Assessment of Coercion Re Self-Respect (range 5-25)					
Mean score	18.0	18.2	17.7	19.1	20.2
Standard deviation	5.4	5.6	5.7	5.4	3.6
Total Supervisor's Rating Score (range 16-80)					
Mean score[f]	48.9	49.7	44.9	46.3	52.1
Standard deviation	10.4	10.2	9.7	10.8	6.7
Score for Subscale 1 of Supervisor's Rating Form: Overall Job Performance (range 11-55)					
Mean score	33.5	33.2	31.9	31.5	36.2
Standard deviation	7.3	8.0	7.4	7.9	4.4
Score of Subscale 2 of Supervisor's Rating Form: Effect of Drinking on the Job (range 3-15)					
Mean score	9.0	9.8	6.9	9.0	8.9
Standard deviation	3.7	3.3	2.8	3.4	3.6

Sources: *Face Sheet, Life History Form, and Assessment Battery*: E.J. Freedberg and B. McLatchie, "A Behaviourally Oriented Test Battery for Assessment of Clinical and Normal Populations," Substudy #807, Addiction Research Foundation of Ontario, Toronto 1976; *Supervisors' Rating Form*: R.G. Smart, "Employed Alcoholics Treated Voluntarily and under Constructive Coercion–A Followup Study, *Quarterly Journal of Studies on Alcohol* 35 (1974):196-209; and, *Alcoholic Involvement Scale*: C.H. Aharan, "The Interdependence of Personal and Cultural Variables in Alcoholism, Ph.D. thesis, University of Western Ontario, 1966.

[a] The four groups of job classifications are not mutually exclusive. These classifications were done according to our own judgment and ambiguous cases are not included in these calculations.

[b] Percentages in these tables overlap and often add up to more than 100 percent.

[c] For the alcohol involvement questionnaire, higher scores indicate more involvement with alcohol. Note that remaining figures are actual values, not percents.

[d] For the assessment battery scores, lower scores indicate less problems.

[e] For the coercion scores, lower scores indicate less coercion.

[f] For the supervisor's rating form, higher scores indicate a better rating by the supervisor.

contrast the various organizations' clients. Although there are some notable overall differences between the organizations, it is likely that they are a product not only of variations in the kinds of people sent by employers but also of variations in the recruitment and hiring practices of these employers. In particular, this applies to such factors as educational level, special training, and perhaps marital status. The nature of the most prevalent jobs within the organizations could also influence the opportunity for and therefore the frequency of drinking on the job and absenteeism.

With these reservations, the characteristics of employees from the various organizations can be summarized. The referrals from the provincial government (consisting of several departments combined for purposes of this study) appeared to have few distinctive characteristics. They were more likely than referrals from other organizations to have received special training, to have been treated for alcoholism in the past (especially with the use of detoxication, individual and group therapies, AA, and Antabuse or Temposil), to have been warned by their supervisors about their drinking, but to have received adequate reviews from them, both overall and with respect to the effects of drinking on their job. Referrals from the federal communications agency were inclined to be young and single, to have started drinking early (at less than age 20), and to have found drinking a problem by age 40. A substantial minority had chronic physical problems and of those who had had previous treatment, a fairly large proportion (relative to the other organizations) had been to detoxication centers or had received Antabuse or Temposil. A somewhat higher percentage than in the other organizations had been in their present job for less than two years. They tended to drink on the job and to be absent from work because of drinking, but they were still given relatively high ratings by their supervisors to the extent of receiving the best scores on the second subscale of the supervisor's rating form which dealt with the specific effects of alcohol on the job. In general, they experienced rather high levels of coercion to enter a treatment program, particularly from their spouses and as a result of their financial position.

Referrals from the public utility company tended to be married, to have received an education of grade twelve or more plus special training, and to have been with the company for twenty-six years or more. They were somewhat more likely to have begun drinking after age 20 and to have noticed difficulties related to their consumption after age 40. Blackouts had been experienced but not DTs. Those who had received treatment for alcoholism, tended to have been to AA but not to detoxication facilities. Absenteeism because of drinking was less of a problem than for the other organizations. Coercion for treatment from friends, relatives, finances, and self-respect was fairly low, and nearly half the referrals were classed as voluntary or forced voluntary.

Clients from the railroad company appeared to be somewhat older with considerable seniority in the company (twenty-six years or more). They tended not to have been treated previously for alcoholism, but among those who had been, AA was a common source of help. Drinking usually did not commence before age 20 and associated problems came after age 40. There were fewer blackouts or chronic physical problems. Drinking on the job was relatively frequent but the supervisors indicated that alcohol had not had too great an impact on their job performance. Involvement with alcohol and the prevalence of associated problems were high as was coercion for treatment.

Finally, the automobile manufacturer's referrals tended to be younger and married. Most had been with the company for at least six years, and over a third were classed as voluntary or forced voluntary referrals. They tended not to have begun drinking before age 20, but had received treatment for alcoholism. Blackouts had occurred but not DTs. Although the subjects claimed they drank on the job and lost time because of drinking, they received the best scores on the supervisor's rating form (as a whole) as well as good scores on the subscale dealing with the effects of alcohol on the job. Alcohol involvement and the incidence of associated problems were quite high, and coercion levels (except from the job) were also relatively substantial.

In summary, the clients who came from the federal communications agency, the railroad company, and the automobile manufacturer, regardless of their year of admission, were the most involved with alcohol. They admitted their drinking habits carried over to job time, and felt the most pressure from various sources to go into treatment.

Evidence of Early-Identification Trends

For purposes of trying to detect evidence of earlier identification over the study period, each variable hypothesized to be an indicator of an early-identification trend was analyzed by year of referral, for all five organizations, so patterned variations in frequencies could be observed. Although this procedure was carried out in a painstaking manner, very little evidence of a trend toward early identification could be detected. Of the five organizations in which between-year comparisons were made, only the railroad company showed any real sign of the trend in that a unidirectional tendency according to some variables could be seen toward less alcohol-related impairment among referrals over time. The noted differences are summarized in table 8-2.

Evidence for early identification is based mainly on a tendency for patients to have reported progressively less coercion from a variety of sources between 1973 and 1976. The less recent referrals from the railroad company experienced much more job-related pressure to go into treatment and were frequently absent from work due to drinking. They were in poorer health which increased the pressure to get help, and experienced diminishing self-respect which also acted as a spur. Similarly, legal complications appeared to act as more of an incentive to earlier than to later patients to seek help, while friends increased the pressure.

Unfortunately, the variables in table 8-2 are only those which show fairly linear trends toward a situation from which, if this were the only evidence, we might conclude that earlier identification had been achieved by the railroad company over time. Other variables appear to be inconsistent with this trend, however, showing a more erratic pattern of frequencies over the years. For example, if earlier identification was actually taking place, there might have been less reported alcohol involvement in 1976 than in 1973, according to the alcohol involvement questionnaire results. This was not the case and indeed it was the first and third years (1973 and 1975) which saw the *lowest* scores on this measure—scores which should have been gradually decreasing between 1973 and 1976 if earlier identification was taking place. The variables displaying these more erratic tendencies in the railroad company are shown in table 8-3. Although it is possible that the data in tables 8-2 and 8-3 simply conflict, it is equally plausible that an explanatory factor underlies both sets of information.

An examination of the specific variables appearing in the two patterns revealed that for the railroad company the early referral trend pertained mainly to coercive forces from outside the family: the job, health, legal problems, and self-respect. The erratic pattern included alcohol involvement levels and problems due to drinking, assessments of relationships with spouse and children as well as coercion felt to come from them, marital status, length of time at present job, and supervisor's rating scores (the last item indicated dissatisfaction on the part of supervisors in the supposedly best years). The high frequency of poor ratings of general work level by the *supervisor* in 1975 seemed out of place in a set of *client* evaluations of the job situation that placed 1975 and 1976 as the years with least difficulties. Self-reported low absenteeism rates reached their peak in 1975; they retained the same frequency in 1976. One explanation in

Table 8-2
Trends Toward Early Identification in the Railroad Company, 1973–1976

Supportive Trends	*1973*	*1974*	*1975*	*1976*
Absenteeism due to drinking (patient's report)	83.3%	73.7%	56.3%	55.6%
No chronic medical problems	58.3	84.2	93.8	88.9
High coercion from friends	41.7	42.2	37.6	22.2
High coercion because of health	75.0	100.0	56.3	55.5
High coercion because of job	90.9	78.9	37.5	22.2
High coercion because of legal entanglements	41.7	10.5	18.3	11.1
High coercion from self-respect	50.0	31.6	18.8	22.2

Source: Coercion Scales and Other Measures: E.J. Freedberg and B. McLatchie, "A Behaviourally Oriented Test Battery for Assessment of Clinical and Normal Populations, substudy #907, Addiction Research Foundation of Ontario, Toronto, 1976.

Table 8-3
Data Not Supportive of an Earlier-Identification Trend in the Railroad Company, 1973-1976

Unsupportive Trends	*1973*	*1974*	*1975*	*1976*
Married	55%	71%	44%	63%
Over 15 years at present job	82	63	88	56
Low scores on alcohol involvement questionnaire	50	5	44	22
Low scores on alcohol problems	25	0	25	11
Good scores on assessment of relationship with children	75	29	50	40
Good scores on assessment of relationship with spouse	60	18	43	20
Low scores on coercion from spouse	50	27	43	20
Low scores on coercion from children	67	27	50	40
Poor scores on subscale 1 of supervisor's rating form (general work level)	46	29	67	38
Good scores on subscale 2 of supervisor's rating form (drinking and job)	18	63	13	25

Sources: *Face Sheet, Life History Form, and Assessment Battery*: E.J. Freedberg and B. McLatchie, "A Behaviourally Oriented Test Battery for Assessment of Clinical and Normal Populations," substudy #807, Addiction Research Foundation of Ontario, Toronto, 1976; *Supervisors' Rating Form*: R.G. Smart, "Employed Alcoholics Treated Voluntarily and under Constructive Coercion–a Followup Study," *Quarterly Journal of Studies on Alcohol* 35 (1974):196-209; and *Alcoholic Involvement Scale*: C.H. Aharan, "The Interdependence of Personal and Cultural Variables in Alcoholism," Ph.D. thesis, University of Western Ontario, 1966.

this particular case might be that a great deal of denial occurred among the railroad clients in 1975 for reasons undetermined by the study. Another possibility is that supervisors were more severe that year in their assessments of referred alcoholics, perhaps because of some increased pressure to justify their referral choices. At all events, it appears that the clients' impressions of their job difficulties and the supervisors' thoughts about the same did not completely coincide and that in fact something other than actual job problems and job satisfaction were influencing the responses to the various questionnaires by the employees or supervisors, or both.

The fact that familial variables appeared in the erratic pattern (table 8-3) and nonfamilial ones followed the early referral pattern (table 8-2) suggested that even if clients did not seem as involved with alcohol in 1975 and 1976, they were only less affected in some areas of their lives. Indeed, other aspects of their lives appeared to have been less disrupted in other years: family relationships seemed not to be threatened as much in 1973 and 1975. Thus it is extremely difficult to argue that alcoholics referred in 1975 and 1976 had, in general, fewer overall problems related to their consumption than their counterparts in 1973 and 1974.

Part of the difficulty of resolving the apparent conflict in the trends noted above (a conflict which also manifested itself in statistics from the other organizations in the study, but to a lesser degree) is that the various familial, social, physical, and mental *consequences* of excessive drinking do not necessarily make their appearance at the same time or in the same order. In some cases, family life may be affected first if expectations of the incipient problem drinker are sufficiently numerous and clear that failure to meet them would be quickly noticed by spouse and children; in other cases, there may be more leeway in the drinker's family life for problems to develop beyond a point which would be tolerable in other families. On the other hand, expectations at work may be greater, leading to a situation in which a problem can be masked at home and in social situations but not on the job. Sometimes erosions in health and well-being may be the first obvious indicators of problem development. In other cases drinking-related legal and financial complications may begin to close in before the family or employer has clearly identified alcoholism as the cause of numerous other incipient problems at home and at work.

These difficulties are highlighted in the terms *voluntary* and *mandatory* referrals. In view of the foregoing observations, it may well be desirable to abandon the use of these terms in favor of language which reflects the reality that there are many sources and degrees of coercion to seek help for drinking problems. Freedberg and McLatchie (1976) went a long way toward such a position when they elaborated the various types of coercion listed in table 8-1. In this conceptual framework, a referral may be voluntary with respect to the level of coercion experienced in the work setting but may be virtually mandatory with regard to pressures from the family.

Consequently, because of the obviously complex interactions and effects of varying expectations at home and at work, no clear association should be expected between the excessive use of alcohol and the sequential emergence of specific consequences in either environment. This state of affairs, however, complicates the search for valid indicators of early problem development and confounds any simple definition of the term *early identification*. If the term's use is restricted to the work environment, any impairment in the performance of certain highly skilled tasks will be more crucial than a reduction in the efficiency of performing other less skilled tasks. For example, air-traffic controllers in large airports can afford few mistakes: many lives and much expensive equipment are at stake. On the other hand, a reduction in the number of nails driven per hour is not as crucial. The chances of early identification of performance loss in the former case are hopefully greater than in the latter case. However, there is no automatic relationship between employee skill level and the degree of supervision exercised, as Trice and Beyer (1977) pointed out. Some highly skilled employees rarely encounter their supervisors, and mistakes may not be detected for some time. This may be the case with executives. Given this situation, it might be as well to define goals for early identification specifically in relation to occupational subgroups where the principal differentiation is made in terms of skill level and the quantity of supervision.

Referral and Occupational Status

There is evidence in the present study which bears upon this issue. Detailed notes were kept of referred employees' occupations and an attempt was made to analyze these to determine whether the referring organizations had adopted any kind of policy with respect to sending certain classes of people for treatment and not others, or sending some before others. These results are outside the context of the early-identification hypothesis because trends in this dimension pertain more to the penetration of the EAP into the work force as a whole rather than to earlier identification of employees within any occupational group. Consequently, we anticipated that some organizations might begin their referral activities with the most senior and probably most valued employees, while others might begin with the most visible, easily reached employees. Such differences might be attributable more to variations in methods of implementing EAPs than to progressive trends.

Classification of job titles proved very difficult since no up-to-date scheme could be found for ranking jobs according to skill level or socioeconomic status. Job classifications often meant one thing to one organization and another thing somewhere else. Neither meaning might have been prevalent even ten years earlier. Accordingly, we opted for a judgmental mode of classification which divided employees alternatively into blue-collar and white-collar workers; supervisory or nonsupervisory staff; professional or nonprofessional. This form of analysis is admittedly crude. On occasion we were unable to fit the recorded job title into one of the three sets of categories because no information on the exact nature of the job described could be found. As a result, the noted trends must be treated with caution. They are, however, of suggestive interest, and considerable convergence can be seen in the results from the use of all three forms of classification (tables 8-4, 8-5, and 8-6).

According to the ideal model of EAP presented in chapter 1, the coverage of the policy is meant to extend to all levels of employees: white-collar and blue-collar, supervisory and nonsupervisory, professional and nonprofessional. Tables 8-4 through 8-6 show that a wide variation in referrals according to occupation prevailed. Some of this variation must be attributed to the type of work done by the different organizations. It might be expected, for example, that the provincial government and federal communications agency would have a greater proportion of white-collar workers than the other organizations. Even in these cases, however, there was a tendency for fewer white-collar employees to be referred over the four-year period. In the provincial government this trend was accompanied by the less frequent appearance of professionals

Table 8-4
White- and Blue-Collar Referrals in Five Organizations

	White Collar		*Blue Collar*	
Organizations	*Percent*	*N*	*Percent*	*N*
Provincial government				
1973	72.7	32	27.3	12
1974	77.1	27	22.9	8
1975	43.8	7	56.3	9
1976	61.9	13	38.1	8
Federal communication agency				
1973	70.0	14	30.0	6
1974	84.0	21	16.0	4
1975	42.9	3	57.1	4
1976	47.6	10	52.4	11
Provincial utility company				
1973	45.5	5	54.5	6
1974	42.9	3	57.1	4
1975	50.0	5	50.0	5
1976	64.7	11	35.3	6
Railroad company				
1973	20.0	2	80.0	8
1974	37.5	6	62.5	10
1975	30.8	4	69.2	9
1976	14.3	1	85.7	6
Automobile manufacturer				
1973	33.3	2	66.7	4
1974	33.3	2	66.7	4
1975	66.7	2	33.3	1
1976	0.0	0	100.0	5

Note: Referrals do not include unclassified occupations.

and supervisors over the same period. The federal communications agency referred no professionals at any time (according to our classification) and only one supervisor in the four years. The railroad company began and ended the study period with a preponderance of blue-collar referrals, though some white-collar workers were sent during the in-between years. No professionals were sent at any time, though some supervisors were referred every year. The numbers involved in the automobile manufacturer are small so erratic trends may be apparent. It appears on the basis of limited evidence that this organization began by referring some supervisors, professionals, and white-collar workers but ended by referring only nonsupervisory, nonprofessional, and blue-collar workers.

The provincial utility company was an exception to the tendency noted among most of the forementioned organizations to refer fewer supervisors

Table 8-5
Professional and Nonprofessional Referrals in Five Organizations

	Professional		*Nonprofessional*	
Organizations	*Percent*	*N*	*Percent*	*N*
Provincial government				
1973	21.4	6	78.6	22
1974	26.3	5	73.7	14
1975	12.5	2	87.5	14
1976	6.3	1	93.8	15
Federal communication agency				
1973	0.0	0	100.0	19
1974	0.0	0	100.0	26
1975	0.0	0	100.0	7
1976	0.0	0	100.0	21
Provincial utility company				
1973	30.8	4	69.2	9
1974	12.5	1	87.5	7
1975	20.0	2	80.0	8
1976	47.4	9	52.6	10
Railroad company				
1973	0.0	0	100.0	12
1974	0.0	0	100.0	16
1975	0.0	0	100.0	11
1976	0.0	0	100.0	9
Automobile manufacturer				
1973	14.3	1	85.7	6
1974	14.3	1	85.7	6
1975	50.0	1	50.0	1
1976	0.0	0	100.0	5

Note: Referrals do not include unclassified occupations.

and white-collar workers over time. In this case, a steady increase in the proportion of referred supervisors and white-collar workers can be observed. Professionals were well represented in the first and last years of the study. Few signs of earlier identification in the terms delineated for this study could be detected in the provincial utility company. The actual existence of such a trend might have been masked by the increase in the proportion of referrals from other sectors of the work force, such as supervisors and white-collar workers. If the policy had been applied only to blue-collar employees in nonsupervisory positions over this period, a trend toward earlier identification might have been detectable. This, of course, is speculation. In future studies, we recommend that any search for earlier-identification trends be conducted in relation to specific occupational groups in order to control for the possibility that EAPs will bring in increasingly wider slices of the work force as they "mature." The introduction

Table 8-6
Supervisory and Nonsupervisory Referrals in Five Organizations

	Supervisory		*Nonsupervisory*	
Organizations	*Percent*	*N*	*Percent*	*N*
Provincial utility				
1973	26.5	9	73.5	25
1974	29.2	7	70.8	17
1975	13.3	2	86.7	13
1976	19.0	4	81.0	17
Federal communication agency				
1973	0.0	0	100.0	19
1974	3.7	1	96.3	26
1975	0.0	0	100.0	7
1976	0.0	0	100.0	21
Provincial utility company				
1973	10.0	1	90.0	9
1974	14.3	1	85.7	6
1975	28.6	2	71.4	5
1976	35.7	5	64.3	9
Railroad company				
1973	8.3	1	91.7	11
1974	16.7	3	83.3	15
1975	28.6	4	71.4	10
1976	16.7	1	83.3	5
Automobile manufacturer				
1973	42.9	3	57.1	4
1974	16.7	1	83.3	5
1975	50.0	1	50.0	1
1976	0.0	0	100.0	5

Note: Referrals do not include unclassified occupations.

of hitherto untouched groups in the work force to EAP treatment alternatives means that over time increasing proportions of more damaged employees will constantly mask any notable trend toward earlier identification in the groups who were first exposed to the program, unless care is taken to keep these groups separate for monitoring purposes. In this study we did not have sufficient faith in the job-classification system to use it as the basis for such a control. In addition, numbers would have been unconvincingly small in some cases.

At all events, the fact that little stability existed from year to year in the occupational level of employees being referred from the five study organizations provides a useful perspective on the apparent conflict between the evidence for early identification noted in the railroad company and erratic trends not at first sight consistent with that evidence. In partial explanation of this phenomenon we suggested that the familial, social, physical, and mental consequences of excessive drinking need not emerge in the same order in every case. A complex interaction was hypothesized in which the expectations of employer, family, and friends operate at different levels in different peoples' lives. Monitoring this phenomenon is difficult enough when all the subjects are members of a particular occupational group in a particular organization. When members of different occupational groups are gradually introduced into the situation, monitoring of this kind becomes extremely difficult. The problem–from a program evaluation view point–is simply that EAPs mature along more than one dimension: they expand their coverage in some cases to include a wider cross section of the work force while at the same time they penetrate deeper into specific occupational subgroups to achieve earlier identification. It is evident that in future studies aimed at detecting the latter, the former dimension must first be identified and controlled.

Supervisors' Ratings and Alcohol Involvement

Excessive drinking can lead to adverse consequences on some jobs sooner than on others. The quality and quantity of supervision, the type of work involved, the skill level of the employee, and the pressures and demands of the work environment can all lead–alone and in interaction–to a situation in which no clear linear relationship should be expected to exist between supervisory evaluations of work performance and objectively determined alcoholic involvement. Nevertheless, an axiom of the EAP ideal model is that supervisors can detect employees who are becoming alcoholics by using job-performance indicators, implying that even in its early stages excessive drinking for all practical purposes can be expected to affect job performance in such a harmful way that supervisors will be able to take action on this basis. Given the complexity of the relationship between drinking and job impairment, such a proposition may warrant some modification. In this study an attempt was made to describe the nature of the relationship between supervisory ratings of employee job performance according to the supervisor's rating form (Smart 1974) and employee alcohol involvement according to the alcohol involvement questionnaire (Aharan 1966, Gillies et al. 1974). The scores of referred employees on both scales were subjected to Pearson product moment correlations by year and by referring organization. The results appear in table 8-7.

The majority of the correlations were negative, meaning that poor supervisory evaluations were associated with high alcohol involvement scores. However, few of these correlations were statistically significant, which suggests that although the claimed relationship exists in many cases, it does not exist in a way that implies wide practical applicability. That is, even where alcoholic involvement was pronounced, it was not necessarily or even usually reflected in negative supervisory ratings of employee job performance.

Table 8-7
Pearson Correlations of Alcohol-Involvement Scale Scores and Supervisor's Ratings

	Total Supervisor's Rating		*Subscale 1 of Supervisor's Rating*		*Subscale 2 of Supervisor's Rating*	
Organizations	*r*	*Significant (2-tailed)*	*r*	*Significant (2-tailed)*	*r*	*Significant (2-tailed)*
Provincial government						
1973	−0.20	0.19	−0.27	0.07	−0.03	0.84
1974	0.02	0.88	0.05	0.73	−0.14	0.40
1975	0.50	0.04	0.46	0.05	0.23	0.37
1976	0.25	0.21	0.27	0.18	0.29	0.15
Federal communications agency						
1973	−0.21	0.38	−0.22	0.35	0.06	0.79
1974	−0.20	0.33	−0.22	0.28	−0.04	0.82
1975	−0.06	0.89	0.10	0.81	−0.35	0.42
1976	−0.12	0.60	−0.27	0.24	0.35	0.12
Provincial utility company						
1973	−0.78	0.001	−0.74	0.002	−0.78	0.001
1974	0.27	0.41	0.02	0.94	0.26	0.42
1975	−0.59	0.05	−0.38	0.23	−0.04	0.89
1976	0.29	0.20	0.34	0.14	0.10	0.65
Railroad company						
1973	−0.47	0.14	−0.56	0.07	−0.05	0.86
1974	−0.11	0.64	−0.14	0.58	−0.03	0.90
1975	−0.38	0.15	−0.29	0.28	−0.20	0.45
1976	0.31	0.44	0.08	0.84	0.27	0.50
Automobile manufacturer						
1973	−0.61	0.10	−0.72	0.04	−0.01	0.98
1974	0.44	0.37	−0.17	0.73	0.67	0.14
1975	−0.94	0.22	−0.99	0.03	−0.40	0.73
1976	0.43	0.46	0.41	0.48	0.24	0.69
All companies						
1973	−0.32	0.001	−0.38	0.001	−0.06	0.49
1974	−0.01	0.92	−0.07	0.48	0.08	0.42
1975	−0.01	0.91	−0.01	0.88	0.03	0.82
1976	0.17	0.12	0.12	0.25	0.23	0.03

Sources: *Alcoholic Involvement Scale*: C.H. Aharan, "The Interdependence of Personal and Cultural Variables in Alcoholism," Ph.D. thesis, University of Western Ontario, 1966; and *Supervisors' Rating Scale*: R.G. Smart, "Employed Alcoholics Treated Voluntarily and under Constructive Coercion—A Followup Study, *Quarterly Journal of Studies on Alcohol* 35 (1974):196-209.

Negative correlation means high (good) scores on supervisor's rating form are related to low alcohol involvement scores.

A finding which is even less supportive of a linear relationship between these variables is the presence of *positive* correlations between them during certain years in certain organizations. The most striking example of this occurred in the provincial government in 1975 where the positive correlation was statistically significant. This means that in 1975 in the provincial government positive supervisory evaluations of the referred employees' job performance were related to nigh alcoholic involvement scores. In other words, the more an employee was involved with alcohol, the more likely he was to receive a positive supervisory evaluation. This perverse and apparently freakish finding cannot be simply dismissed: it bears some relationship to reality, however devious that might be. In an attempt to explain the phenomenon, the following observations are offered. Reference to tables 8-4 through 8-6 will remind the reader that the year in which the positive correlation occurred was also a year in which—relative to other years for the same organization—fewer supervisors and white-collar employees were referred. The differences are noteworthy but not overwhelming. It is nonetheless possible that the predominantly blue-collar, nonsupervisory work of referred employees in 1975, was such that alcohol consumption (even to excess) did not affect job performance in a negative manner. To explain the positive correlation, however, we have to argue more than that alcohol involvement had no effect on supervisor-perceived job performance; we have to argue that excessive drinking had a *positive* effect on the supervisor's evaluation of the employee's job performance. This taxes the imagination, but the finding will not go away.

Another possible explanation of the finding is that in 1975, a larger proportion of referrals from the government were classed as voluntary. In that year 24 percent of referrals were so classified as opposed to 8 percent, 5 percent, and 12 percent in 1973, 1974, and 1976, respectively. The fact that nearly a quarter of all employees referred in 1975 from the government were voluntary (and another 6 percent forced voluntary) suggests the possibility that the employees recognized their problems before their supervisors. Even so, the correlation seems too large to be accounted for by five out of seventeen employees. In addition, it must be noted that the same positive correlation did not emerge in another case where a disproportionate number of voluntary referrals presented themselves from another organization in one particular year. Although in 1975 40 percent of referrals from the public utilities company were classed as voluntary and another 40 percent as forced voluntary, the correlation between supervisory evaluation and alcoholic involvement was negative at a significant level (table 8-7). Although some variation in the use of the term *voluntary* can be expected, it is unlikely that such differences can account for the phenomenon in question here. This appears to rule out the possibility that the auspices of referral (voluntary or mandatory) were alone seriously implicated in the odd relationship found in the government referrals in 1975.

A third possible explanation for the seemingly paradoxical relationship is that supervisors knew or suggested that those employees were becoming alcoholics, even though they still valued the quality of their work which had not noticeably deteriorated. This explanation assumes that supervisors sometimes make referrals on the basis of criteria that have little to do with job performance as such, even though they may claim it does. It may be easier to "get away" with doing this when employees are of lower status. The fact that company executives often argue that job performance is the *only* criterion for referral (see chapters 4 and 5) should not exclude the possibility that in reality supervisors use other criteria and that some employees will not resist attempts to get them into treatment. Indeed, the year during which the abnormal correlation occurred in the provincial government was also one in which an unusually large proportion of referrals (67 percent) reported low coercion in relation to their jobs in distinction from other years when the corresponding rates were 31 percent, 39 percent, and 37 percent.

A final possibility is that alcohol involvement scores fell within an unusually low range among referrals from the provincial government in 1975, resulting in an almost spurious correlation with supervisory evaluations. This was not the case, however, since average alcohol involvement scores in 1975 were close to the mean for all years combined.

On the whole, some combination of these explanations may offer the best estimate of what really happened to produce this situation. It appears that in 1975 an unusually large proportion of blue-collar, nonsupervisory employees were referred from the provincial government. These employees reported considerably less coercion from their employers to enter treatment than their counterparts in other years and a sizable group volunteered to seek help for their problems. Since supervisors saw little difficulty with the job performance of these employees, it seems likely they referred them on the basis of other criteria, presumably having to do with drinking itself and not contested by the employees. The nature of the work performed by the latter was not of a type to be badly affected by the alcohol consumption levels reported by this group. This unique combination of circumstances may account for the unusual positive correlation between high alcohol involvement and favorable supervisory evaluations among employees referred from the provincial government in 1975.

Summary

The study presented here was a longitudinal analysis of referrals from five selected organizations to a residential treatment facility for employed alcoholics. A search was made for signs that as their EAPs matured, these organizations referred progressively earlier cases in terms of the level of impairment from excessive alcohol use. An effect of the type hypothesized was found in only one of the five cases and even here the evidence was ambiguous. It appeared more likely that different sorts of people were being referred by the five organizations from year to year but that the variation did not follow a continuous trend toward early identification. Several observations can be made in explanation of this phenomenon.

First, it may have been unrealistic to expect that a trend toward earlier identification would be detected because it did not occur, because no one wanted it to occur, or because its occurrence was masked by the existence of other concurrent trends. Each of these possibilities requires further attention.

It is possible that the effect may simply not have occurred even though attempts were made within the organizations to make it happen. Several factors could have contributed to this result. First, the organization might have been unable to generate the level of control over employee job performance necessary to achieve earlier identification of problems. Second, it is possible that the cases who were referred were actually examples of early identification to begin with. However, this does not seem to be a tenable point of view. If it were, we would have expected to observe that the referred employees in this study were less impaired than people referred under other auspices to more general alcoholism facilities. This is not the case. In another study where the alcohol involvement questionnaire was used, Gillies et al. (1974) reported that a group of 254 referrals to alcoholism treatment facilities of all kinds (residential and nonresidential) from all sources (with few from employers) scored in the 50 to 60 percent range on the average. Although the alcohol involvement questionnaire used here was an adaptation of that used by Gillies et al., a conversion of the former scores as an expression of the maximum possible scores resulted in the conclusion that May Street patients from the five organizations also scored in the 50 to 60 percent range on the average. That is, the May Street population was no different than a group of referrals from all community sources in terms of alcohol involvement. Since the latter referrals are generally not considered to be early, it follows that the May Street population was not early either. In addition, a comparison of the median age of patients in May Street with patients in a special alcoholism ward and with others in an acute medical ward demonstrated that there was no statistical or practical difference between them, suggesting further that the May Street people were unusual primarily because they were all employed. On the other two wards only 25 to 30 percent of patients had jobs to which they expected to return (Shain and Suurvali 1976).

It is also possible, though improbable, that the absence of early referrals was a result of the organizations' policy of dealing with early cases internally. However, if the severity of problems encountered by employers follows a sort of continuum, it is likely that some of the problem employees who were not referred would have been similar to ones who were referred. The climate of these organizations, based on information from May Street liaison personnel, was not in favor of trying to treat such cases without help from outside agencies once they were identified. The more likely explanation is that although some internal management of minor drinking problems may have been attempted, the majority of the developing cases were simply not identified.

Alternatively, the effect may not have occurred because no one wanted it to occur. The referring organizations might have been quite content to refer only employees who presented manifest problems of job performance. However, it has already been suggested that in some years in some companies employers went beyond the job-performance deterioration criterion in order to refer employees with putative drinking problems. These were employers already touching the boundaries of what might be considered ethical in terms of appropriate grounds for referral. If, in order to achieve early identification, the employer has to abandon the criterion of job-performance deterioration, the price may be considered too high. Certainly, it is a matter viewed in a dim light by many unions.

It must be remembered, too, that early identification is in many ways a goal of people outside industry for industry. It was apparent from the key-elements study in chapter 5 and the small business study in chapter 6 that many employers see early identification as remotely desirable but not of any practical significance. Furthermore, *early* may simply mean at the stage when job performance begins to be affected. As can be seen from the occasional presence of positive correlations between favorable supervisory evaluations of job performance and excessive drinking, this stage may actually be quite late by the time some jobs are affected.

Employers may be more interested in referring their most valued employees for treatment as a priority. This being the case one might observe that less damaged but highly valued employees were sent for treatment first. In this case, one would be seeing cases of early identification in the beginning of program operations.

Finally, early-identification trends may be obscured by other organizational events and trends. Some organizations send problem employees to a variety of different treatment agencies. Sometimes this happens on a haphazard basis (it may depend on which facility has an opening) and sometimes it is planned. For example, a company may send its more senior, white-collar employees to one place and its blue-collar employees to another. If these practices remain constant, the trend toward early identification, as monitored through any one of the treatment agencies involved, should not be obscured. However, if referral practices change, contamination of what might otherwise have been a trend can be expected. In this study there was some suspicion that the automobile manufacturer changed its policy over the years leading to its use of May Street only for blue-collar nonsupervisory employees, a phenomenon documented in tables 8-4 through 8-6. In the railroad company, however, it is fairly certain that its use of May Street was consistent over the study period.

Another organizational event that can obscure an early-identification trend is the gradual extension of EAP coverage to different levels of employees, resulting in a constant influx of heavily impaired workers. Further, the infusion of supervisory training with respect to management of problem employees can lead to sudden surges of referrals of both early and late varieties. Such training took place in the provincial government, the federal communications agency, and the public utility company during the study period but exact information about times and number of supervisors trained is not available.

A second observation is that certain limitations appear to be implicit in the very notion of early identification such that questions about the occurrence of this phenomenon have to be asked under severe methodological constraints to make answers meaningful. It is evident that in order to obtain a clear picture about trends toward earlier identification, we will need to know about and be able to control for (statistically or otherwise) the variety of organizational factors which can mask, distort, or detract from such an effect. In addition, we must be clear about the terms in which early identification is being evaluated. It was shown in the present study that in the one case where early-identification trends were suggested (the railroad company) the indicators tended strongly to be those which related to job performance. When other indicators were inspected, it was found that the appearance of problem indicators on the job was not related in a consistent manner to the appearance of problem indicators in the family. Consequently, where deterioration of job performance is used as the sole criterion for problem identification, the course of alcoholism can be well advanced in some cases before it is spotted. Although it seems that supervisors sometimes go beyond the job-performance criterion, as evidenced by positive correlations, this practice takes them onto thin ethical ice in spite of the fact that they may be motivated by humanitarian concerns. The difficulties with this practice are reviewed in chapter 1. A simple way out of this dilemma is to discuss the concept of early identification solely in relation to the employment situation and to argue that if job performance is not affected by alcoholism, the employer should not be concerned. It can be counterargued that if the employer does this, he may be dealing with very advanced cases of alcoholism (and other problems) for whom the chances of rehabilitation are slim, often because the employee has already suffered severe consequences in his family life, may be heavily in debt, involved with the law, and lost many old friends.

In conclusion, there is relatively little support for the existence of a simple trend toward earlier identification among the organizations studied. However, this phenomenon may be as much due to the methodological problems involved in looking for such a trend as it is to the actual infrequency of early identification in practice. In the one case where natural controls on some of the more complex organizational variables existed (the railroad company) limited evidence for a trend toward early identification was noted. The evidence in this case is largely job related. In a sense, such a trend represents a success for the operation of that organization's EAP. In future studies, however, it will be necessary to maintain stricter control over the interacting organizational variables which may have masked or distorted early-identification trends in the other organizations.

9 Auxiliary and Alternative Strategies

The framework within which the review of philosophical, theoretical, and practical issues surrounding employee-assistance programs (EAPs) has been conducted so far has been the ideal-model construct described in chapter 1. Explicit and implicit objectives in this model are quite extensive: it is expected that EAP will not only cope with the chronically alcoholic or multiproblem employee but also that it will be able to identify problem development at an early stage or create a situation in which employees with incipient difficulties will avail themselves of the program voluntarily. These are ambitious objectives indeed. It should not be surprising to conclude that the evidence to date is somewhat equivocal concerning the actual achievement of these objectives. A theoretical analysis of EAP and the general thrust of most of the studies reviewed and reported in this volume suggest that there is both considerable variation in the apparent outcomes of such programs and an outer limit to their effectiveness. In this chapter, we summarize the possible sources of these variations and limits. Then we explore the realm of possibility and probability and outline various auxiliary and alternative strategies.

Variations in Program Outcomes

It appears that EAP goes under many guises and that it is welcomed in some quarters, shunned in others. Three possible explanations of this phenomenon have been reviewed in this survey.

First, EAP is too often considered, and its results compared, as though it referred to one agreed-upon set of methods and techniques for the achievement of declared and well-known objectives (chapter 2). Unfortunately, this is not the case. Within the framework of programs reviewed as though their commonalities were more important than their differences are alcoholism-specific and broad-brush approaches; poorly implemented and fully implemented models; reactive and proactive programs; and programs based on largely short-term economic goals, on humanitarian concerns, on expedience, and on odd combinations of these features. It should not be surprising that, given the grossly different types of investment in these different approaches, outcomes vary widely in identification rates, referral rates, and reported successes.

Second, even within a certain approach, such as an economically inspired alcoholism-specific program, the expectations and intentions of the concerned interest groups (employers, unions, and interventionists) may vary widely so that what is a success to one party is a failure to another. That is, the different interest groups may use different dimensions to evaluate success and may apply different criteria in relation to these dimensions (chapter 3). Similarly, they may define the various terms used to characterize outcomes in different ways. For example, the term *alcoholism* is notorious for its ambiguity, yet identification and referral rates of alcoholics are often compared as though no such ambiguity existed. Differences in outcome can certainly be expected when one organization adheres to a tight definition of the term while another is content to subsume all manner of drinking patterns under the heading "alcoholic." The same problem of comparability arises with such apparently simple terms as absenteeism and accident.

Third, the common use of penetration rates to define program success is a practice of highly limited value where no reference is made to the prevalence of alcoholism or other disorders in the particular work force (chapters 2, 3, and 7). Nonetheless, comparisons are routinely made between programs on this basis. A bland comparison of referral rates gives very little information about relative program effectiveness unless the size of the population at risk is estimated in a convincing manner. Even then, the very concept of referral rates as a major criterion for program success has been challenged (chapter 8).

All these points relate to the basic problem implicit in any attempt to compare dissimilar classes of phenomena: it is simply meaningless. A reasonable deduction from the current state of affairs might be that if meaningful comparisons between programs are to be made, the following prerequisites should be met. First, the programs should be clearly described in terms of the approach taken and the degree to which it has been implemented. Second, the expectations and intentions of all parties concerned in the program should be recorded and converted into dimensions and criteria for the evaluation of program outcomes. Third, the terms to be used in these dimensions should be closely defined. Fourth, an estimate should be made of the prevalence of whatever problem it is to which the program is a response. The more objective this estimate is, the more reliable and useful it will be.

Limits to Program Effectiveness

The problems of comparing EAP outcomes generally mask whatever effects might be seen in well-implemented programs in which all parties wish to push the policy as far as it will go in terms of early identification. Even if such masking effects could be removed, there are substantial reasons to believe that EAP has limits to how effective it can be. These limits may be considered in terms of how widespread such programs are at present; how widespread they can hope to be; and how much impact they make or could make in specific settings where they have been adopted.

1. It has been shown that EAPs are not easily applied, if indeed they can be applied to small, particularly nonunionized work settings (chapter 6). Further, they appear to have limited value, so far, in relation to females in the work force and to executives. Perhaps even more important is the fact that EAP is a self-contained system of intervention which can be located successfully only in environments that are compatible with its mode of operation (chapters 1 and 3). The ideal model of EAP, in fact, seems most suited to large, well-functioning, bureaucratically run organizations, that is, employing more than 1,000 people in the same location (chapter 5). Although many such environments exist and are important, they are by no means the whole of reality.

2. The emphasis of the relationship between the identification of problem employees and deteriorating job performance virtually defines theoretical limits to the penetration of EAPs into the workplace. According to the ideal-model approach, problems of any kind (alcoholism included) should be identified only through documentation of deteriorating job performance. Many see any other approach as unethical, though this viewpoint has its opponents who argue that the opposite is true, namely, that concealing alcoholism control under the broad-brush approach is dishonest. In practice, it appears that sometimes supervisors may use indicators for problem development that are not related to job-performance deterioration, but even though this happens, it clearly violates a key principle of EAP which is that supervisors should not be diagnosticians (chapter 8).

Further, though in theory EAP is meant to achieve earlier intervention through increased nonsupervisory, voluntary referrals, the evidence to date—though limited—does not support the view that such voluntary referrals are any less impaired in terms of alcohol involvement than their counterparts referred under mandatory auspices (chapter 8). Again there is some suspicion that the term *voluntary* may be used in a somewhat cavalier manner in some organizations, reaffirming the need for proper definition of terms in evaluations of EAP.

3. It is possible that employers will generally be satisfied with less program impact than unions or interventionists. The real concern of employers may be with control of job-performance standards in terms of quantity and quality of output: their concern is not with the control of alcoholism, drug abuse, or any other condition (chapters 3 and 5). Consequently, they are likely to be concerned about the control of problem behavior only insofar as it can be shown to have practical effects on job performance in the present or in the predictable future. To some extent, employers may be moved to greater efforts at controlling specific problems if the costs of doing so are shown to be outweighed by the benefits. The state of the art with respect to demonstrating the cost-effectiveness of early identification, however, is not at a stage where many employers would be impressed (chapter 2). As a result, EAP tends to bog down at the later intervention stages, except in a few rare cases. This is not an indictment of EAP. Rather, it is an observation about the incompatibility

of what is sometimes expected of EAP and its limits in practice. It might be as well to accept the fact that employers do not on the whole become excited about referral rates, penetration rates, or related statistics as such, but rather they judge the effect of any given policy, procedure, or program by its impact on the overall ability of the organization to get its work done on time while maintaining a satisfactory profit or productivity margin.

Alternative Strategies

So far, EAP emerges overall as a practical, useful device for management of certain types of employees with relatively advanced problems in certain kinds of organizations. While this may be enough to sustain the current level of effort in the United States and in Canada, it may not hold enough promise for a bright future. Given the limitations described, EAP may run out of steam unless its difficulties are resolved. The balance of this chapter explores ways in which EAP can be tied in with other policies, procedures, or programs in order to potentiate its effect and ways in which alternative strategies may effect the same objectives. These observations do not imply that EAP is virtually a dinosaur whose time has run out. Rather, it is argued that in order to survive with credibility and expand on a stable footing, the links between EAP and other forms of intervention must be perceived, confirmed, and exploited. On the other hand, it must be recognized that on occasion EAP is simply not part of a solution to an employer's problems whereas another form of intervention (or no intervention) may be.

Preventive Health Programs

A health-oriented approach to both early recognition and prevention of problems might be more effective than an approach based on problem identification for certain groups: executives and white-collar workers in particular. This approach might be more effective with groups whose work performance was difficult to evaluate on a routine basis, who were not easily amenable to coercion, and who might respond to a form of intervention or prevention which emphasized growth, development, and maximization of potential rather than minimization of damage. We stressed that elements of damage reduction would always be present even in health-oriented approaches but the distinction between these and frank problem identification approaches was one of emphasis. Chapter 6 discussed a type of health-oriented approach in which the employer would introduce a program which educated employees in such basic concepts as stress reduction, weight control, exercise, and diet and also involved them in actual courses of action designed to implement such concepts. The extensiveness of these programs varied a great deal: some applied only to executives, some to all employees; some provided many facilities, others few. In some cases, special staff were hired to run the program while in other cases the whole service was obtained by contracting with an agency in the community. In terms of the earlier identification of problems due to alcohol or drug abuse, these approaches are largely untested. However, they are presented in the context of EAP auxiliary approaches because they deserve to be tested as such. We suggest that they be tested in relation to a wide range of preventive activities and not just to alcohol and drug abuse.

Health and lifestyle programs need not and probably would not be run by medical departments in most organizations, though one might expect a considerable degree of cooperation among responsible parties. The location of any program within the organization is important because of its visibility and credibility. However, the location and management of the program would have to be compatible with the overall structure of the organization, first, for acceptance and then for effectiveness over the long run.

Another approach is multiphasic health screening (MHS) which is an extension of services provided by existing medical departments. Collings, Fitzpatrick, and Stratton (1972) point out that MHS means many things to many people. They stress that it is an approach subject to extensive adaptation to fit various needs, though it grew out of specialized monophasic health surveys for such conditions as tuberculosis in the 1930s and 1940s.

Collings et al. give an example of MHS in the New York Telephone Company, but emphasize that this version is only one among many adaptations. The major program elements in this case are preemployment selection, placement, absence surveillance, treatment of injuries, early care of nonoccupational diseases, health education, selected immunizations, and periodic health assessment. Consequently, prominent activities in such a program are case finding, sampling to establish population norms, screening for high-risk cases, and periodic health examinations. Collings et al. note that the tests which can be used often produce continuous measures rather than pass-fail outcomes, with the result that the term *screening* is becoming increasingly crude. Nonetheless, all tests have a screening potential simply by someone applying a pass-fail criterion to the results. The elements of control in these techniques are obviously quite marked and the potential for abuse should not be overlooked. The stated objectives of MHS at New York Telephone are to improve the work efficiency of employees; to reduce the impact and slow the progression of existing disease; to prolong life and the span of useful functioning; and to prevent development of future disease. In this case, testing is voluntary and confidential. Employees with positive results are referred to their own physicians but they are actively followed up by the company. Both stationary and mobile testing units are used, though the content of the test battery depends on location. The main vehicle of publicity is the supervisory staff armed with brochures.

It is quite clear that both the health and lifestyle approach and the multiphasic health screening approach depend on large organizations for their sustenance or at least on organizations with sufficient resources to purchase these services from community agencies. Since neither approach has been appraised in terms of its value as an auxiliary or substitute for EAP, comparative usefulness of such methods must await procedural investigations.

A possible obstacle to implementation of extensions to industrial health services is the poor reputation reportedly enjoyed by industrial physicians. In reviewing the credibility of occupational medicine Keene (1974) suggests that industrial physicians, through exposure in the mass media, are often seen as management lackeys and as not serving the health needs of employees. He cites the "Brodeur articles" which appeared in the *New Yorker* (October 29 to November 26, 1973) as a particularly good example of attacks on industrial health practices. Much of the animosity has originated in the prevalence of such diseases as asbestosis, angiosarcoma of the liver, and cancers of the stomach, rectum, and colon, all thought or known to result from industrial pollutants. Though these diseases may be preventable, industrial physicians have not exerted much effort in persuading employers to take appropriate action. Even the Conference Board (an independent, nonprofit, business research organization) in its report, "Industry Roles in Health Care" (Lusterman 1974), concluded that industry had never been a positive factor in shaping health care policy in spite of the fact that it ended up paying a significant portion of the nation's health bill. Keene recognizes the truth in some charges against occupational medicine and argues that corrective action has to be taken on several fronts. For our purposes, the most important of Keene's recommendations are (1) that industrial physicians be better trained and selected; the residual problem of incentives to enter industrial practice would need to be overcome, probably by (2) having the industrial physician report directly to a senior executive and ensuring that (3) he contribute to a health-oriented management policy; and (4) better relationships with government health agencies must be formed. Adversary relationships between industrial medical departments and government agencies are simply dysfunctional, particularly with the advent of such sweeping federal legislation as the Occupational Safety and Health Act (OSHA; 1970). If health services include prevention, industrial medicine must reorganize its goals and responsibilities to achieve the necessary credibility to become an effective auxiliary for EAP.

Occupational Safety and Health

The Rationale. In the United States, Canada, and the United Kingdom occupational health is becoming an increasing concern of legislators who have chosen to develop omnibus statutes which deal also with employee safety. Consequently, a whole system of regulation by federal agencies has come into existence which represents another context for the further development, support, and extension of EAPs.

The rationale for integrating safety programs and EAPs has been rarely described in the literature. However, a clear statement of the connection was made by Levens (1976) who urged more recognition of the fact that alcoholics cost industry a lot more in losses due to accidents than normal employees. He cites a number of studies which confirm this fact. The best-known studies are Maxwell's (1959) where the accident rate of alcoholics on and off the job combined was over 3½ times that of a control group and Pell and D'Alonzo's (1970 and 1973). In the 1970 study Pell and D'Alonzo showed an accident rate for alcoholics almost identical to that reported by Maxwell in 1959 in comparison with a control group. In 1973 they showed a mortality rate for alcoholics due to accidents that was twice as high as that for a control group. All these findings are subject to the methodological problems reviewed in chapters 2 and 3. Nonetheless, the weight of the evidence clearly suggests that, whatever is meant by alcoholics in these studies, such people do cost themselves and industry a great deal more than other employees in losses due to accidents. Further, accident losses are a cost line on which considerable improvements have been noted as a result of EAP-like interventions. Examples of such reports are Asma, Eggert, and Hilker (1971) and Alander and Campbell (1973).

However, it has been noted on occasion that not all those who are classified as alcoholics cause or are associated with the same amount of loss from accidents. Characteristically, this was first intimated by Trice (1962) who observed that AA members reported less accident involvement than might have been expected in reconstructing the events which led to their referral for treatment. Pell and D'Alonzo (1970) noted, too, that over half the known and suspected alcoholic groups in their study had reasonably good attendance records (and presumably, therefore, fewer accidents) during the year of study. This suggests that a special subgroup of the alcoholic population is responsible for a disproportionately large amount of the losses ascribed to the group as a whole. In a study of a navy population Borthwick (1977) observed that although the personal injury rate for the majority (80 percent) of referred alcoholics was above average for the navy three and four years before the treatment intervention (27.9 per 1,000 in comparison with 18.2 per 1,000), the rate was 84.4 per 1,000 for a special subgroup (20 percent) of that population. Even more interesting is the observation that as the time of treatment intervention approached—evidenced presumably by increased warnings, discipline, and documentation of poor performance—the majority of alcoholics in the one or two years prior to the crisis had a *lower* accident rate than the navy as a whole (9.3 per 1,000 as opposed to 18.2 per 1,000). In distinction, the special subgroup of alcoholics manifested a rate of 111.1 per 1,000—a substantial increase. In addition, one or two years after treatment the majority had returned to a personal injury rate of 20.8 per 1,000 while the subgroup was still at 74.1 per 1,000. The special subgroup is not an unfamiliar phenomenon to those acquainted with the principles of loss control management (Bird and Loftus 1976) in which they are referred to as the "critical few," a title reflecting a basic management concept first elaborated by Pareto.

It would be idle to claim that the navy study indicates that the majority of alcoholics are good workers because they have less than the average number of accidents once confronted with their behavior. After all, these people were subsequently referred for treatment, suggesting that even though they were being very careful not to have accidents, they were still not doing their jobs very well. From a safety viewpoint the figures simply suggest that alcoholics are more at risk at certain stages of their career than others and that the activation of an EAP or alcoholism control policy promotes widely different behavior in some than in others. While the majority seem to respond to the "lowering of the boom" in a defensive manner (far fewer accidents), a critical few respond in an apparently self-destructive fashion. This cautionary material should not be regarded as a rebuttal of Leven's argument that safety professionals and EAP staff should collaborate as much as possible.

Indeed, there is another line of reasoning which would suggest even more the need for collaboration, namely, that the so-called normal drinker who drinks too much on occasion is a potential safety risk. An example of how this risk develops is provided by Wolkenberg, Gold, and Tichauer (1975) in a study of the delayed effects of acute alcoholic intoxication on job performance. This report is based on an experiment with nine normal males in a simulated industrial work situation. The importance of the experiment is disproportionate to the size of the sample, utilizing as it did a sophisticated battery of performance monitoring tests at three stages of alcohol intoxication—peak intoxication, the morning after, and the afternoon after—as well as at a sober baseline stage before drinking began. Few such studies have been done on the aftereffects of drinking, though several have been conducted on the immediate effects of alcohol ingestion on performance. One study of aftereffects by Ryback and Dowd (1970) reported by Wolkenberg et al. showed that even thirty-four hours after ingestion of alcohol, professional pilots still manifested relevant performance effects, namely, coriolis acceleration on positional nystagmus in several instances. In the Wolkenberg study the eye-hand coordination was significantly affected on some measures up to eighteen hours after the drinking episode. Delayed reaction time and certain motor sensory impairments were found relative to baseline performance. A very interesting finding, however, was that people with low blood alcohol concentrations (BAC) actually performed *better* on both the morning and afternoon following the drinking episode than at baseline. Wolkenberg et al. attributed this phenomenon to an overcompensation effect in the low BAC subjects. At a certain relatively low BAC level, he hypothesized that with great self-control subjects were able to do better than normal with an effort born of pride, competitiveness, and a desire to show that they could hold their liquor. This effect was not seen in high BAC levels. This is further suggestive though not confirmatory evidence of the phenomenon in which heavy drinkers at certain stages of their careers may actually perform better and have fewer accidents than their normal drinker counterparts.

Spinal curvature distortions were clearly evident on the morning after but not on the following afternoon. Again the type of distortion varied, depending on whether the group had a high or low BAC. The distortions were interpreted according to whether, in a real situation, they might contribute to a forward or a backward fall on attempting to lift a given weighted object. The low BAC group exhibited patterns which might contribute to a backward fall. The backward effect is again suggestive of overcompensation among the low BAC group: trying too hard and overdoing it when the body is not responding as usual. Wolkenberg et al. note in conclusion that "the concept of safe perfomance implies that an individual behaves in an expected manner, using motion patterns purposefully designed into the work situation" (p. 117). Where motions become unpredictable and unexpected, potentially hazardous conditions can arise. The study points out the need for further research on the neglected effects of normal but acute episodes of heavy drinking on job performance and safety.

The fact that a rationale exists for developing functional links between safety program management and EAPs does not tell us in what manner this liaison would best be achieved. Levens (1976) suggests that a safety professional might actually run an EAP with the assistance of a part-time or full-time EAP professional. At the very least, he suggests cross-fertilization of personnel from both types of programs.

In a pilot investigation conducted in Ontario, the researchers found that among seven prominent, large organizations with EAPs, four had either formal or informal cross-appointments between the groups set up to manage the EAP and safety-related matters (Shain and MacDougall 1979). In the case of an automobile manufacturer, there was only one committee dealing with both areas. Recent legislation in Ontario provides an impetus to employers to develop closer ties between the functions of alcoholism control and accident control by making them more responsible for worker safety and for violations of safety codes by workers. Such a functional link will be more likely to emerge in environments where there is a willingness or at least an incentive to treat excessive alcohol or drug use (not just the obvious abuse of these substances) as an unsafe practice subject to remedial action by employers and employees.

Legislative Approaches in the United States. If the development of closer working relationships between EAP and safety professionals depends on a greater awareness of how the use of alcohol and other psychoactive substances can be an unsafe practice under certain circumstances, one might expect to find increasing evidence of such an awareness in legislation dealing with safety and health. Both the United States and Canada in the last decade have enacted legislation to bring together a large body of scattered laws under omnibus statutes in order to bring some level of consistency and vision to this complex area. We must look to these statutes for emergent evidence that alcohol and other substance use can be an unsafe practice. Such a legislative link would at least provide room for the development of integration between EAP and safety programs.

In the United States, the principal piece of legislation in our area of concern is the OSHA (1971, P.L. 91-596). Hohn (1972) explains that the act covers 57 million workers in 4 million places of employment. Its objectives are "to assure so far as possible every working man and woman in the nation safe and healthful working conditions." This ambitious legislation is jointly administered by the Department of Labor which sets, promulgates, and enforces OSHA standards and by the Department of Health, Education and Welfare which, through the National Institute for Occupational Safety and Health (NIOSH), conducts research for the development of criteria and technical bases for transmission to the Department of Labor which in turn makes and enforces regulations. In addition, the Department of Labor develops and administers educational and training programs in health and safety for workers and employers.

In practice, the NIOSH places considerable emphasis on the control of such toxic substances as beryllium, carbon monoxide, lead, silica, mercury, asbestos, and cotton dust, and such noxious conditions as heat, noise, and radiation.

However, the NIOSH mandate permits other types of hazards (human in origin) to be explored and reported (Hohn 1972). In particular, this agency can review OSH data to determine unrecognized hazards and may conduct epidemiological research to determine the health risk status of specific occupational groups. Further, NIOSH can study psychological and motivational factors involved in worker health and safety. This includes studies of hazards beyond the purely physical and chemical such as stress related to jobs involving rapid assimilation and processing of large amounts of information; complex, fast decision making affecting personal or group security; and adherence to machine-paced schedules and unnatural work-rest regimens. Some of these work conditions are reminiscent of Roman and Trice's delineation of certain work factors associated with alcoholism (1970). In addition, the NIOSH mandate includes physiologic and ergonomic studies whose thrust is developing standards for acceptable stress levels associated with interactions between worker and environment. In theory, the terms of reference of this agency are broad enough to cover the study of alcohol and drug use as they affect worker health and safety and also the study of how work itself may contribute to the abuse of these substances. It might be expected, therefore, that the agencies created by OSHA would contribute to the development of further theoretical and programmatic links between substance use and abuse and safety. Indeed, there appears to be scope for considering the use of alcohol and other drugs as an unsafe practice for whose elimination employers may in some ways be responsible.

Since the passage of OSHA, commentary on its implementation has not been very favorable. Collier (1973) noted that in the first seven months of 1973 the average penalty under OSHA was \$625 for serious violations and \$45 for nonserious violations, hardly major deterrents. He noted, however, that the act was still new and much more information was needed. In 1978, nonetheless, Pachauri commented that the public affairs journals indicated that OSHA was a failure. In conducting a review of commentaries on OSHA Ellis (1975) concluded much the same thing, reporting that the controversy centers around the apparent unenforceability of legislation so broad and yet so detailed. In practice, the implementation of OSHA appears to have followed the line that safety is largely an engineering problem: people will always take risks and the best we can do is engineer the work environment so as to minimize harm and loss. Certainly, this emphasis is contrary to the hopes that many had for the legislation (Hohn 1972) which was expected, through NIOSH, to pursue human factors and motivations in safety and health control. Ellis, in fact, is quite skeptical about the overall value of safety laws and inspections as a means of accident control. He argues that little empirical evidence of their value exists and that the overall reduction in the rate of serious industrial injuries since the 1920s may be due to other factors; for example, the overall improvement in the health of Americans may have led to an increase in perceptual-motor control which in turn decreases the risk of accidents. Ellis cites studies in which organizations falling outside the sphere of government control appear sometimes to do better than those within it as far as safety records are concerned. He also cites studies in which companies low on safety standards compliance appear to have fewer accidents than those high on compliance doing the same kind of work. On the other hand, Ellis also cites a Wisconsin department of industry study in which it was concluded from a review of workmen's compensation claims that injury could have been prevented in about 25 percent of all cases through proper enforcement of standards.

With these reservations, it would be inadvisable to simply accept as given the view that safety inspections and rules *as such* promote better safety records. The complexity of the variables involved in making a useful study of what contributes to a safe environment is suggested by Simonds and Shafai-Sahrai (1977). They took eleven pairs of companies matched for location, size, and the nature of work but where, within each pair, the occupational injury rate varied considerably. The purpose of the study was to determine what factors apparently affected the frequency of injuries. Since Simonds and Shafai-Sahrai had controlled certain gross variables such as the size and type of organization through matching, they looked for factors related to management, type of work force, physical conditions, and actual safety promotion for explanation of the differences in injury rates. Several such factors were found to differentiate high and low injury rate companies, but the same factors did not always reoccur in the same configurations. An interaction was suspected between the following sets of variables which could not be extricated in the present study: management support for and involvement in the safety program; better injury record-keeping systems; implementation of accident cost analysis; smaller spans of control at the foreman level; recreational programs for workers; higher average age of workers with more experience and a greater proportion married; a roomy, clean shop environment; and more and better safety devices on machines. Rather surprisingly, they found that the quality and quantity of the safety rules themselves were not related to differences in injury rates and that efforts to improve safety through the employee's family were not relevant in that context. These findings tend to place Ellis' (1975) concern about the value of safety rules and inspections in perspective: it is perhaps not the rules themselves which are important, but the manner in which they are implemented and the settings in which they are tried.

The Simonds and Shafai-Sahrai findings about the effect of management involvement are particularly interesting. The most important managerial actions associated with lower injury rates were personal conduct of safety audits and inspections; personal review and analysis sessions to compare the results of carrying out safety plans with projected objectives; and a requirement that safety figures, reports, and achievements be included on the agenda of company board meetings. One might speculate that a factor underlying these managerial actions is the structuring of the safety program control features into the main current of job-performance control. These findings present many interesting parallels with the management of EAPs in terms of what features are essential to the effective implementation and operation of a program.

Legislative Approaches in Ontario. In the United States it appears that a legislative framework exists for the further exploitation of alcohol and drug use or abuse as unsafe practices but the realization of the potential has scarcely begun. In Canada a similar trend may be discerned. As an example, Ontario's legislative approach to safety and health is worth attention. In a review of the history of such legislation in Ontario, Shain and MacDougall (1979) concluded that until the passage of the Occupational Health and Safety Act (OHSA) in 1978 in that province, most statutes and regulations dealing with health and safety in different work environments were based on the premise that the dangers of the workplace are largely external and mechanical rather than human. "Tools malfunction; machines or workplaces are unsafe; products are dangerous: for the most part, people are not." The omnibus OHSA is not an about-face on this subject, but it does include several provisions which conspire toward the possibility that alcohol and drug abuse could be considered as unsafe practices within the meaning of the act and that correspondingly employers would be responsible for the consequences of the behavior of employees who came to work impaired or who actually drank or ingested drugs on the job. There is no hint, however, that the legislators intended to include alcoholism and drug abuse as occupational diseases.

Major provisions of the act are concerned with the mandatory creation of joint health and safety committees and the right to refuse to work in an unsafe environment. Although most organizations of more than a few hundred employees had some form of safety committee or someone in charge of safety before the OHSA, the terms of reference of these committees are extended by the new legislation as follows (Section 7, subsection 5).

"It is the function of a committee and it has power to (a) identify situations that may be a source of danger or hazard to workers; (b) make recommendations to the constructor, employer or group of employers, as the case may be, and the workers for the improvement of the health and safety of workers; (c) recommend to the constructor, employer or group of employers as the case may be, and the workers, the establishment, maintenance and monitoring of programs, measures and procedures respecting the health and safety of workers; and (d) obtain information from the constructor or employer respecting (i) the identification of potential or existing hazards of materials, processes or equipment; and (ii) health and safety experience and work practices and standards in similar or other industries of which the constructor or employer has knowledge."

These are quite broad terms of reference, affording the joint committee considerable scope for inclusion of alcohol and drug use as health and safety related matters should they see fit. The preexistence of a safety committee or "one of like nature" according to Section 7 (1) of the act would preclude the need for the establishment of a new committee. It remains to be seen whether an existing EAP committee would be classified as a safety committee or "one of like nature."

The new act places a burden on employers and supervisors to take "every precaution reasonable in the circumstances" to ensure that persons under their control comply with the act and that workers are protected: a duty more onerous than mere compliance. However, the worker himself is enjoined not "to operate any equipment, machine, device or thing or work in a manner that may endanger himself or any other worker" (Section 17, subsection 2). If employers are to be held responsible for the enforcement of the workers' duties under the act, it seems likely that employees will be under greater surveillance with respect to safety violations. In the case of the drug abuser or alcoholic, a situation could easily arise in which the employer had to use discipline in order to stay within the provisions of OHSA.

An organization which already had an EAP would probably use such a mechanism under some circumstances instead of discipline since the latter approach tends not to be effective for any of the parties involved. This would be a prime example of circumstances bringing EAP and safety control closer together. It is possible that the recognition of employees whose behavior may represent a safety hazard under the strict regulations of the new Ontario statute would be a form of earlier identification than is now possible under the auspices of EAP. It is worth noting in particular that supervisors are specifically identified along with employers under the provision requiring every reasonable precaution to be taken to protect the worker. This may well act as an incentive to supervisors to activate the EAP under the auspices of safety violations which can now be interpreted, in theory, as indicators of deteriorating job performance. Only experience will tell whether this provision does in fact lead to earlier identification of alcohol and drug abuse, but it is a highly researchable topic. Further, consultants and other interventionists involved with employers might pay particular attention to the links noted so far between safety control and EAP in addressing the needs of their clients.

Loss-Reducing and Gain-Maximizing Management Strategies. Health and safety are not concerns which are limited to the legislative arena. Although legislation has often provided a much needed spur to the development of healthy (or nonharmful) and safe working environments through statutes and regulations and such economic incentives and deterrents as the workmen's compensation laws, employers have not been blind to the relationship between such environments and efficient, effective production. So much is this the case that it is possible to identify more than one school of thought in management where safety and the control of losses associated with its violation are considered key factors. One example of this approach is loss control management (Bird and Loftus 1976). Essentially, this is a systematic attempt to identify and control conditions and events which tend to downgrade the effectiveness and efficiency of a business or other task-related set of activities. This is achieved primarily through the identification and remediation of aspects of management control that are deficient in some essential respect, such as planning, organizing, leading, and monitoring. Weaknesses in these areas are considered to lead in a dominolike chain of consequences to poor enforcement or even nonexistence of standards which in turn leads to loss, causing unsafe acts or conditions (Heinrich 1959). Within this context, safety is considered to be a product of particular interactions between people, equipment, material, and environment. Stated in this manner, loss control management begins to take on aspects of ergonomic approaches to management, which emphasize the maximization of human resources through their proper matching with appropriate jobs.

Bird and Loftus (1976) consider that the rate of serious and disabling accidents in a given workplace bears an ascertainable and more or less constant relationship to other classes of loss causing accidents and incidents. For example, for every one serious or disabling accident [as defined by the American National Standards Institute (ANSI) code], Bird (1974) found that there were approximately 10 minor but reportable injuries, 30 property damage accidents of all types, and 600 incidents with no visible injury or damage: the so-called near-miss accidents. These ratios were based on an analysis of 1,753,498 accidents reported by 297 cooperating companies representing 21 industrial groups employing 1,750,000 people who worked over 3 billion man-hours in the exposure period under study. The implication of this ratio of serious to other types of accidents appears to be that if attention is paid to the circumstances leading to the less serious losses, there will be a corresponding reduction in the rate of the more serious losses. In some ways this argument is similar to the one advocated for the control of the adverse consequences of drinking: namely, if the overall per capita consumption of alcohol is reduced, the incidence of problem drinking will also be reduced (Schmidt and Popham 1978). In fact, the reduction of per capita consumption of alcohol may well be relevant to the control of accidents in the workplace: Wolkenberg et al. argued that even acute, normal episodes of drinking out of work can affect work performance and behavior in safety-related ways up to eighteen hours after ingestion. The ANSI has classified drinking and drug use as potentially unsafe practices along with acts such as operating without authority, failure to warn or secure, using defective equipment, and horseplay (ANSI Z.16.2-1962, R1969). Correspondingly, drug abuse and alcoholism are activities and states that should be eliminated in the context of loss control management, which is concerned with loss-inducing events of all kinds from job injuries, absenteeism, and general property damage to vandalism, pollution, and waste. It is not without significance that a chapter by Von Wiegand, a respected student of alcoholism and its control in industry, was included in the Bird and Loftus account of loss control management.

It is likely that loss control management is a stage in an evolutionary process which according to Bird and Loftus is leading already from safety programs and injury prevention as such to total accident control and then to total environmental control. It is not clear, however, to what extent this movement is led by or responded to by senior managers and executives. The history of loss control management has been one of middle managers attempting to diffuse a method which one might have expected to emanate from the executive suites. This, too, is a process in flux, so situations can be identified in which executives are in fact managers of loss control teams. This parallels the type of managerial involvement that can be found in EAPs: often middle managers are in the position of constantly legitimizing "their" programs to their superiors in ways that imply the marginality of the activity. As Simonds and Shafai-Sahrai showed in the case of safety programs, the "ownership" of such programs by managers probably has a lot to do with their success in the sense that such support is a prerequisite for the effective "system" functioning of any such activity.

Loss control management, in its emphasis on safety as the product of specific interactions between people, places, and things, contains elements of ergonomic approaches to management. The main philosophical difference appears to be that, in spite of its evolutionary nature, loss control management is still concerned with minimizing losses, while ergonomic approaches emphasize the maximization of human potential by relating people to the jobs for which they are best fitted. An example of the latter is human resources management and accounting (Flamholtz 1974, Woodruff 1970). In this approach, an inventory of human resources is undertaken and related to a corresponding inventory of job requirements. On this basis, an approximation of the best "job-person" match is made. These systems require elaborate record-keeping methods, where the collection and analysis of relevant data are highly visible, valued functions required and monitored by senior management.

The relevance of this approach as an auxiliary for EAP is that it deals with some of the issues raised by Roman and Trice (1970) concerning those aspects of work which are or may be associated with higher rates of problem drinking. The factors identified by Roman and Trice are (1) absence of definition in job role; (2) discretionary hours; (3) isolation from supervisors and associates; (4) work addiction; (5) occupational obsolescence; (6) occupying a novel role; (7) having a job where drinking is part of it; (8) having a job where pathological drinking serves the power needs of others; and (9) moving from a job involving heavy drinking but with social controls to another job without controls. It can be seen quite readily that a more effective job-person fit could avoid some of the problems associated with the factors just listed: for example, people with low tolerance for isolation should not be put in jobs where such a condition occurs often. Similarly, those who need supervision, structure, and direction should not be expected to perform as autonomous self-starters. Some work situations are negative and stress-inducing for some people while positive and growth-inducing for others.

The principle of ergonomics is to make sure that every effort is made to fit the right person to the right job. In so doing, it is possible that excessive alcohol or drug use as available responses to the stress of being in the wrong job may be reduced. Ergonomics, however, is broader in scope than the example of human resources management and accounting implies. At its broadest, ergonomics is an attempt to bring sciences such as medicine and its subdisciplines, psychology and sociology, to bear on the challenge of improving people's relationship with work. Even where the right person is doing basically the right job, often there are many dissatisfactions that could be eliminated or reduced through the application of rational principles. Note that the OSHA in the United States created an agency (the NIOSH) whose mandate includes ergonomic studies.

Structural Modifications in the Workplace. The ergonomic approach to management is on the border between programmatic and structural responses to organizational challenges or problems. That is, ergonomics begins to go beyond the introduction of ameliorative measures and programs to consider the organization of work itself as the proper focus for effective change. As such, the structure of organizations in its most fundamental terms becomes the subject of inquiry. It is at this point that we begin to deal more in alternative than in auxiliary approaches to the management of alcoholism and drug abuse by programmatic means such as EAPs. The structural approach is predicated on the view that major problems will respond only to basic changes in the way an organization is run. That is, assuming the goals of the organization are appropriate and clear, it will be necessary to consider the genesis of management problems in terms of how control is brought to bear on the key tasks of the particular workplace. This involves a review of basic control-related systems such as the division of labor, communication methods, and power channels, and their relationship to one another and to the overall task of the organization.

An example of such an approach to the organization of coal-getting was discussed in chapter 3. In this case benign effects were achieved on productivity and absenteeism when the traditional division of labor involving highly specific work roles was modified so that more interdependent work groups were created (Trist and Murray 1948). The results were interpreted as indicating the superiority of the more flexible division of labor for the kinds of task that were most common in coal mines. It is essential to note that such a division of labor is not advocated as a panacea for all ills. Indeed, the principle of the thing is that certain organizations better serve some goals than others: the challenge is to find the appropriate match of goals and implementing systems.

Although the technology of a given organization tends to constrain the variety of methods that can be used to carry it out, there is often room for creating more adaptive systems which can achieve organizational goals with less fallout from human stress and resulting problems. Although his study was not designed to measure the human consequences of different management structures, Melman (1976) reported provocative findings on the relative efficiency of managerial versus cooperative decision making among six matched pairs of manufacturing enterprises in Israel. The results indicated that both forms of management could be efficient and that modern manufacturing plants are not dependent on the use of managerial-hierarchical control. These findings need replication in various social, cultural, and economic conditions, but they suggest with some vigor that where two forms of management are equally efficient in terms of productivity, it makes sense to opt for the method which produces the least ill effects in terms of human distress. It cannot be stated at present that a reduction of such distress will result in less incidence of problems due to alcoholism. Nonetheless, an apparently logical chain exists which does lead to such a conclusion, and it is therefore important that such structural measures as have been touched on here be subjected to empirical scrutiny to test the mettle of this chain.

Some similar observations were made by the special task force to the secretary of Health, Education and Welfare (O'Toole, chairman) in their report entitled *Work in America* (1973). In their lengthy discussion of how work affects the mental health of American men and women, the task force touches on alcoholism and drug abuse as possible functions of "job insecurity, unpleasant working conditions, or hazardous work" (p. 85). Drawing for support on McLean (1970), they admit that any evidence they reviewed linking job stress and alcoholism was of a suggestive nature. It was neither causal nor conclusive. It need hardly be stressed that such connections, if they exist, are extremely hard to document. A principal difficulty in this regard is the probable effect of interactions between the kinds of work people do and the kinds of people who do it. People select themselves into certain jobs to some extent, but by the time they are ready to accept employment, several determinants have had and continue to have influence, reducing the actual range of choices. For example, a person's sex, education, cultural and economic background, language, parentage, and various combinations of these factors all act in such a way as to produce constraints on freedom of choice in relation to employment in practice.

It is unlikely that, as interventions, structural solutions carry as much credibility as programmatic responses to identified problems. First, structural approaches are by definition more basic, require more thorough working through, and certainly require a high level of organizational commitment in order to succeed. It is difficult to be halfhearted about such changes since they resemble the overhaul of a motor vehicle: while disassembled they will not run. Programmatic interventions (EAP among them) can be more or less integrated into the major control systems of the organization and can offer more or less benefit depending on this degree of integration. However, to succeed, they must be compatible with the existing structure of the host organization and will simply atrophy if they are not. That is, the introduction of a new program, such as EAP, will not affect the overall structure of the organization even though it may suggest the need for such change. Second, structural approaches tend to carry with them the implication that something about the work environment itself is causing or contributing to the problems for which the structural change is the proposed solution. Programmatic solutions tend to imply that the work situation is alright and that the problem lies in the employee. Obviously, some basic differences in world view underlie such variations. Similarly, programmatic approaches tend to emphasize the gradual identification of populations at risk (alcoholics, for example) while structural approaches emphasize reducing the incidence or precipitation of problems due to being at risk and to some extent also seek to reduce the prevalence of the predisposing conditions leading to the incidence of these problems. By implicating the workplace itself in the genesis and manifestation of problems such as alcoholism, structural solutions set themselves distinctly apart from programmatic approaches.

Whether structural approaches are really a viable alternative to EAPs in the control of alcoholism and drug abuse in the workplace is a question which must stand the test of future empirical trial. Although many suspect that these problems are correlated with the nature and organization of work itself in various forms, a definitive test of this connection has not been made. Until such time as these important tests are made, it will probably be most practical to emphasize those methods and approaches which can serve in an auxiliary capacity with EAP and which have been reviewed here.

Appendix A Employee-Assistance Programs as Conflict-Avoiding Devices and the Influence of Arbitral Decisions on Their Development

Martin Shain and
Peggie Walden

Arbitral Decisions

Chapter 1 raised the possibility that the origins of employee-assistance programs (EAPs) might lie in some not altogether obvious places. Although such programs are often presented as though their rationale pertained largely to the economics of production, evidence can be adduced to broaden this perspective and suggest that the economic rationale may be a rationalization. It was put forward, for example, that the human-relations movement in industry in and of itself may have been instrumental in setting a climate of which EAP was a natural manifestation. That is, EAPs may have developed not because they could have been shown to save money but because they reflect increasing pressure on industry to do business in a certain way, namely, conserve human resources. Similarly, other external pressures to protect their human investments have been exerted on industry. One of the more significant is the increasingly consistent message of labor arbitrators in industrial disputes that dismissal and heavy discipline are inappropriate for coping with employee disabilities related to such things as excessive drinking, drug use, and mental health problems. This trend is observable both in Canada and the United States. If the participants in labor disputes realize that arbitrators will reject certain kinds of disciplinary decisions by employers, it is possible and even likely that they will turn increasingly to a form of handling problem employees in ways that will avoid arbitration altogether. EAPs, then, have a role as conflict-avoiding devices. Their development as conflict-avoiding devices in response to arbitral decisions is the subject of this exploratory inquiry, which is based on a study of such decisions in Ontario and draws for comparative purposes on cases from the United States and from elsewhere in Canada.

Arbitration law is that body of jurisprudence developed by arbitrators whose activities in Ontario are governed by statute and whose offices are invoked for grievances under collective agreements. In the United States, arbitrators are appointed solely as a function of contracts between employers and employees. It is a body of law which is distinct from though related to curial law (created and implemented by the courts). Arbitral law is a unique institution for the government of industrial disputes. However, we are concerned with the social and economic role of arbitration as it bears upon the management of alcoholism and substance abuse in industry.

EAP itself is a term applied to a variety of procedures adopted by employers to identify and treat mental and social problems which affect job performance. One of the most commonly presenting problems is alcohol abuse. These procedures are invoked as an alternative to regular disciplinary practices, though the latter are reactivated if attempts to involve the problem employee fail. These procedures are sometimes incorporated into a written policy, ideally involving the union and management as joint partners. Although self-generated referrals for treatment are increasingly common, the procedures typically involve some variant of corrective discipline in which successive warnings and documentation of deteriorating job performance, if unheeded, yield to a confrontation in which the employee is given a choice between seeking help through the program or being subject to regular discipline. This help varies tremendously, ranging from attention by the plant physician to residence in a specialized facility which may be a long way from home. Apart from humanitarian value, these programs have been considered as money savers. Indeed, once the problem employee is identified, his chances of recovery, at least in terms of job performance, are quite favorable. Relative to the alternative, disciplinary method of handling alcoholic employees, the record of EAPs for identified cases is encouraging. In a study of disciplinary management of alcoholic and other problem employees in Ontario, Adams (1978) concluded that although arbitral reinstatements of such employees were very common, the prognosis for subsequent satisfactory job performance and job retention was very poor. These findings reflect those of Trice and Belasco (1966) in the United States. Both studies concluded that arbitration was a weak method for employers and unions for controlling alcohol abuse in the workplace. Also the employee gained very little even when reinstated because decisions took too long to come down, back pay was often not awarded, and the chances of relapse were high.

In documenting the nature and development of the arbitral decisions in Ontario and elsewhere in Canada which have led to this state of affairs, we suggest a possible relationship between the substantive and procedural requirements made by arbitrators with respect to achievement of just discharges involving the abuse of alcohol and the content of various ultradisciplinary methods now used by industry with increasing frequency to avoid the conflict, nuisance, and ineffectiveness in grievances about such cases. EAP of course is a prime example of such ultradisciplinary practices. To a great extent the reader will be aware that a connection between arbitral decisions about discharges for alcoholism and the content of EAPs is largely a matter of deduction. Nonetheless, we hope to show that the arbitral process, by not serving the interests of management, union, or employees, acted and still acts as a pressure on industry (and on the unionized public sector) to develop methods which serve their needs better. Arbitrators in the United States and Canada have argued that this is the case and that alternative means for management of alcohol-abusing employees should be sought (Somers 1975, Weiler 1976, Adams 1978).

The implications of the refusal of arbitrators to uphold discharges in cases involving alcohol abuse (55 percent according to Adams) are quite far-reaching. If discharge is not a reliable method of controlling alcoholism in the workplace, it means that responsibility for an impaired subgroup of the population cannot be shifted onto social institutions and agencies save as a last resort. By creating a situation in which the employer has to come up with ultradisciplinary means for controlling alcoholism (at least where the employing organization is unionized), a substantial reallocation of fiscal liability is shifted from the state to the private sector, though the trend is also manifest in the public sector. A similar point was first made by Trice and Belasco (1966). We turn now to the process whereby this state of affairs appears to have come about.

Alcoholism and Labor Arbitration

The general problem of alcoholism in industry has rarely been discussed in reported Canadian arbitration decisions. No doubt, this is partly a result of the arbitration process itself. Cases involving employee drinking come before an arbitrator as an issue of discipline for misconduct imposed by the employer under the management's rights clause found in the majority of collective agreements.

Thus the usual case involving alcohol in industry arises out of a specific incident or act of misconduct such as drinking on the job or reporting for work in an intoxicated condition. Less obvious cases which may involve an employee with a drinking problem are those in which the worker has been discharged or otherwise disciplined for excessive absenteeism, negligent work, or unsatisfactory service. However, whatever the background or incident which provoked the disciplinary action of the employer, the issue comes before the arbitrator as the narrow question: Has the grievor been disciplined for just cause?

The Meaning of Just Cause in Discipline Cases

When contractual doctrines became infused into the master-servant relationship, it was generally held that an employer could discharge an employee summarily only for just cause, or without cause only on proper notice. In practice, of course, for most wage earners the employment contract could be terminated by the employer virtually at will, lack of job security being one of the factors which led to unionization. At common law, however, summary dismissal was allowed only for just cause. This meant that the question in each case would be whether the particular act or breach of the employment contract by the employee was one which went to the root of the agreement and so justified the other party in treating the contract as terminated. At common law, certain acts, such as willful disobedience or theft of the employer's property, were automatic grounds for dismissal.

From the beginning, most collective agreements between employers and unionized workers contained the "discharge only for just cause" provision. Since few agreements specifically spelled out what circumstances would amount to just cause, it became the province of grievance arbitrators to give meaning to this language in the industrial relations context. In effect, the resolution of disputes in the collective bargaining regime called for a new jurisprudence which, as Carrothers (1961) observed, was a slow and laborious process simply because principles, rules, and standards take time to develop particularly when the status of arbitration tribunals is unclear and they are not bound by precedent.

This uncertainty about the scope of arbitration is reflected in the early cases. In the 1940s and 1950s there was a lack of agreement among arbitrators about the extent to which they could interfere with the exercise of management's disciplinary powers. Once a finding of just cause was made, some arbitrators felt it was beyond their authority to overrule management, though they occasionally expressed the opinion that the penalty imposed was too severe under the circumstances.

Gradually, some general principles evolved, chiefly in the area of procedural doctrines, as a means of protecting employees from arbitrary or unreasonable disciplinary acts by employers, while still upholding management's right to discipline as expressed in the contract. In developing these doctrines, arbitrators drew on a variety of sources—not only contract law but also criminal law and notions of due process.

The following arbitral statements from *Re Lumber and Sawmill Workers Union and K.V.P. Co. Ltd.* (1956) 16 L.A.C. 73 (Robinson) summarize some of these principles:

> The burden of proof rests on the company to establish that a "just cause" is present. *Re United Brewery Workers and Dow Kingsbeer Brewery Ltd.* (1958) 8 L.A.C. 198 (Laskin).
>
> And it is for the arbitrator to develop the meaning of that phrase in the specific circumstances. Consequently, rules of conduct unilaterally promulgated by the employer "are merely an advance indication by the Company of how it proposes to exercise its disciplinary powers. In any particular instance of discharge the Company's action must find acceptance in the arbitration board's view of reasonable cause. . . ."

> *Re UEW and Canadian General Electric Co. Ltd. (1951) 2 L.A.C. 688 (Laskin).*
>
> But if such rules are to lay the foundation to a Company's claim that just cause exists, these rules must be brought to the attention of the employee before this conduct occurred. They must be clear and unequivocal. And they must be enforced by the Company from the time introduced.

The effect of these procedural protections and due process requirements was to incorporate notions of the "rule of law" into the exercise of management's contractual right to discipline employees.

The early cases involving employee drinking, since they arose under the just-cause provision, illustrate the development of these doctrines. For example, in the *Dow Kingsbeer* case the grievor had been discharged for being intoxicated on the job. At the arbitration hearing, the supervisor testified to the grievor's mien and behavior as he observed him during the shift, and to the grievor's inadequate job performance on that day. Further, the company introduced evidence as to the grievor's recurring problems with alcohol over a period of time, evidence which was not denied by the grievor. However, the arbitrator ordered that the grievor be reinstated with full compensation because the company had failed to satisfy the burden of proof that the grievor had actually been drinking on the job on that day. This case could be read as holding that an employee's confirmed status as an alcoholic was not sufficient cause as such for discharge, without proof of some specific culpable act or course of conduct.

Other cases involving employee drinking on the job, usually in breach of company rules, illustrate the elaboration of the due process protections which were built into the just-cause concept by arbitrators. For example, in *Re Brewers' Warehousing Provincial Board and Brewers' Warehouse Co. Ltd.* (1958) 8 L.A.C. 302 (Curtis), though the grievor was found by the arbitrator to have been drinking on the job in breach of company rules, his discharge was overturned and the grievor was ordered reinstated because of the company's failure in the past to consistently enforce the rule. To single out the grievor for discharge was held to be an unfair exercise of management's disciplinary powers. Similarly, in *Re Council of Brewers' Warehousing Workers and Brewers' Warehouse Co. Ltd.* (1955) 7 L.A.C. 216 (Bigelow) a grievor discharged for drinking in his lunch hour was ordered reinstated because the language of the rule (no drinking during working hours) was found to be ambiguous and therefore to be construed in favor of the grievor. Thus while never questioning management's right to discipline for misconduct, arbitrators developed doctrines designed to ensure that these powers were not exercised in an unreasonable, unfair, or arbitrary fashion.

As well as these restraints on the manner in which management used its powers, arbitrators also expanded the question of just cause to include not only a consideration of the offense but also of the offender. They began to look not only at the specific act or incident which had prompted the disciplinary action and the manner in which management exercised its disciplinary powers, but also they took into consideration the previous work record and seniority of the employee in deciding whether or not the employer had established just cause. This was a recognition of the important rights and interests of the employee which were at stake in a discipline case, and as such went beyond common law contractual principles: in ordinary breach of contract cases, in deciding whether or not there had in fact been a breach of contract, the court would not be concerned with the personal factors of the contract breaker. In developing this aspect of just cause, the arbitrator's closest analogy would be to the sentencing process in criminal law, where such factors as the status of the offender and his prospects for rehabilitation are considered as well as the seriousness of the offense and the need for deterrence.

The development of the meaning of just cause in this way gave arbitrators a degree of flexibility in deciding discipline cases by allowing them to modify penalties imposed by management in cases where they felt the grievor's conduct merited some form of punishment but not necessarily the extreme measure of discharge. In doing so, they imposed a heavier onus on employers than before to justify their actions. This approach was neatly summed up by the arbitrator in the *KVP* case in 1965: "The prevailing rule now appears to be established that when the question arises whether or not the penalty was for just cause, the company must establish just cause not only for the imposition of a penalty but also for the particular penalty imposed."

Such flexibility was felt to be essential if the legislated compulsory arbitration of these disputes was to achieve its goal of ensuring harmonious labor relations; after all, organized labor had, through legislation, losts its right to strike during the life of the collective agreement to protect the interests of its members.

In *Re USW and the Steel Equipment Co. Ltd.* (1964) 14 L.A.C. 356 (Reville), the arbitrator set out a lengthy list of criteria developed by arbitrators in considering whether to assess a lesser penalty in discipline cases (citations omitted):

1. The previous good record of the grievor.
2. The long service of the grievor.
3. Whether or not the offense was an isolated incident in the employment history of the grievor.
4. Provocation.
5. Whether the offense was committed on the spur of the moment as a result of a momentary aberration, due to strong emotional impulses, or whether the offense was premeditated.
6. Whether the penalty imposed has created a special economic hardship for the grievor in the light of his particular circumstances.

7. Evidence that the company rules of conduct, either unwritten or posted, have not been uniformly enforced, thus constituting a form of discrimination.
8. Circumstances negating intent, for example, likelihood that the grievor misunderstood the nature or intent of an order given to him, and as a result disobeyed it.
9. The seriousness of the offense in terms of company policy and company obligations.
10. Any other circumstances which the board should properly take into consideration. Every case must be determined on its own merits and every case is different, bringing to light in its evidence differing considerations which a board of arbitration must consider.

Such a list of factors gave arbitrators, who wished to exercise their remedial powers, plenty of scope. However, in the employee-drinking cases arbitrators seem to have given greatest weight to the employee's previous record. With the adoption by many employers of progressive discipline procedures at the plant level, in many cases of employee drinking, by the time management imposed the ultimate penalty of discharge and the case was taken to arbitration, few employees with a drinking problem would be able to present the arbitrator with an unblemished disciplinary record. In such a case, there would be little basis on which an arbitrator could mitigate the penalty, even if he wished to do so, unless he was prepared to break new ground in these cases. Few arbitrators were disposed to do so. Thus the grievor in *Re OCAW and Regent Refining (Canada) Ltd.* (1964) 15 L.A.C. 215 had his discharge sustained for reporting for work in an impaired condition. Since he had had two previous warnings about such conduct, the arbitrator held the discharge was for just cause.

Nevertheless, by the mid-1960s it was generally accepted that arbitrators had the authority to modify penalties imposed by management, in appropriate circumstances, under the rubric of determining just cause. "To find just cause we must have regard both to the offence and to the penalty" [*Re Port Arthur Shipbuilding Company* (1966) 17 L.A.C. 109 at 113, Arthurs]. In the industrial context, cases were no longer to be confined by the common law straitjacket with its all-or-nothing result. Where an arbitrator found the conduct of the grievor to merit some form of discipline (and that drinking on the job or reporting for work impaired merited some form of punishment was universally accepted), he had the authority to consider whether the specific form of discipline used by the employer was just and reasonable in the circumstances.

The benefits of this approach to discipline in the industrial context, whereby there were no fixed consequences for specified types of conduct, and the philosophy behind it were expressed by Justice Laskin (once a labor arbitrator himself):

> . . . experience has shown that there must be a pragmatic and not a cut and dried, Medes and Persians approach to discipline. Employers and unions are wise to leave room in collective agreement administration. . .

> for consideration of the worker as an individual, and not as simply part of an indistinguishable mass. The formulae of "just cause" or "proper cause" . . . join to the pragmatic case by case approach a sensible individualization in the assessment of punishment for misconduct.

While there is no doubt that in many cases this personalized approach to discipline—a major departure from the common law of master and servant—benefited many individual employees, it also enabled arbitrators to avoid the necessity of developing new principles to resolve the inherent conflict of interest between employers and employees. Or perhaps one should say, it allowed arbitrators to continue to operate from the basic premise expressed in the management rights clause: management's interest in operating an efficient business operation was the ultimate principle which in the end must override employee interests.

A disadvantage of the personalized approach in discipline cases is its uncertainty and unpredictability, elements for which most business operations, especially large ones, have a low tolerance. Possibly this uncertainty influenced both employers and unions to seek remedies of the EAP type for dealing with problem employees outside the grievance-arbitration system.

In summary, by the mid-1960s arbitrators in Ontario had elaborated the meaning of just cause along two lines: (1) they developed due process limitations on the exercise of management's disciplinary powers; and (2) they personalized the disciplinary process: to make the punishment fit the criminal as well as the crime. Both these devices were used in the employee-drinking cases which arose, with various results. However, at no time was the appropriateness of disciplinary procedures as such questioned in the cases: given that discipline in some form was warranted, the main question was under what circumstances should a particular penalty be modified. In general, since employees in the drinking cases often had a poor previous record, a discharge would be sustained.

In this same period, two cases arose which suggested that the personalized approach to discipline could be further expanded in cases of employees involved with alcohol. In *Re UAW Local 222 and Houdaille Industries* (1966) 17 L.A.C. 420 (Adell), for example, the grievor had been discharged for drinking on the job. The arbitrator, in the course of deciding just cause referred to American cases of a similar nature, in which arbitrators had overturned the discharge of an employee with an admitted drinking problem where the employee offered evidence of his attempts to remedy it. In *Houdaille*, however, the discharge was sustained because the grievor had "little seniority and little such evidence was presented." This case suggested that evidence that a grievor was seeking treatment for his problem might be grounds for an arbitrator to order reinstatement in spite of a prior bad record. In such a case, then, it would be important for a union to become involved in exploring such possibilities to assist its membership.

The issue was canvassed more fully in *Re UAW, Local 112 and Douglas Aircraft Co. Ltd.* (1967) 18 L.A.C. 38 (Arthurs). In this case the grievor had been discharged for unsatisfactory service. His record showed a history of excessive lateness and absenteeism, as well as financial problems including wage garnishments and assignments and difficulties with the income tax department—what the arbitrator referred to as a "seriously disorganized existence." Corrective discipline as well as personal financial counseling had been given by the employer over a period of time but with little success. Finally, discharge had been imposed. Although admitting the bad record of the grievor, the union suggested that the root of the grievor's problems lay in his drinking habits and asked the arbitrator to use his just and equitable power under the contract to reinstate the grievor and afford him the opportunity to rehabilitate himself. In other words, the arbitrator was asked to consider, in deciding the question of just cause, not only the past record of the grievor but also the future chances of rehabilitation.

In response the arbitrator did affirm in principle that the just and equitable language of the contract was broad enough to sustain such an order. However, he went on to uphold the discharge because there was insufficient evidence offered by the union to support their contention that the grievor could henceforth be a satisfactory employee:

> There is no evidence that the grievor has placed himself in the hands of a competent social agency, that he has resolved his monetary and domestic difficulties, or that he has taken any steps beyond admitting that he must work at solving his problems. However commendable, however fundamental such an admission may be, it is not enough to demonstrate the prospects to the full extent of proof required, keeping in mind the black record of the past. As a matter of evidence, then, I cannot make the finding that the grievor was discharged other than for just cause.

The concluding statement by the arbitrator is one of the few general statements on the issue and, as an expression of the prevailing view of the arbitrator's role, it is worth quoting in full (p. 42):

> I would be less than frank if I did not conclude by stating that this case presents in a tangible way a problem of great social dimensions. The individual whose life is ravaged by personal weakness, financial pressures, or family difficulties, represents a burden, not merely to the company, but to society as a whole. His bad credit, his family's basic needs, and his inefficiencies as a worker, all are cost items which are ultimately borne by society. It is therefore particularly tragic when such a person's primary productive activity is terminated. Not only is his job the means by which he bears some of these costs, but as well it may be a vehicle for reintegrating him into the community as a useful citizen. Absent a job, prospects for rehabilitation are obviously much

> lower. Yet it is not fair to ask his company to take the risks, to bear the costs, of helping such an individual in this predicament. Surely such costs ought to be borne by society. Of course, if good corporate citizenship leads the company to undertake responsibility (as it did here in a limited way) it is to be commended. For example, the company might properly have agreed to reinstate the grievor on probation, upon proof that he was in regular attendance at some social agency that certified his reasonable prospects of recovery. Perhaps, in fact, in appropriate cases an arbitrator might so order. Certainly nothing in my award is intended to preclude any act of generosity by the company in "salvaging" this employee. Fortunately, the union has expressed its willingness to assist in such a project. However, if the parties cannot agree to the institution of such a scheme for helping employees in similar circumstances . . . I am afraid that I am unable to compel them to do so. As an arbitrator, my function is to adjudicate the differences between the parties, rather than to fashion for them, out of whole cloth, solutions which they are always free to construct, but have chosen not to.

This was plainly put. While the language of the arbitrator suggested the possibility of a probationary reinstatement under certain circumstances, the onus would be on the grievor to establish by concrete evidence his good prospects for rehabilitation. Once the company had made out a case for discharge on the basis of the grievor's past record, the burden of proof on the union required by the adjudicator would be onerous indeed. Resort to this approach would be risky; far better perhaps to rely on other defenses where available or on other methods, as the arbitrator himself suggested.

Nevertheless, consideration of the likelihood of future improvement as a further ground for a no just cause finding was at least raised in these two cases. The *Douglas Aircraft* decision further spelled out what kind of evidence would be required to convince an arbitrator to order reinstatement in such cases. In this case, the arbitrator strongly suggested that the major responsibility for fashioning remedies to deal with the problem lay with the parties themselves: they should not look to the arbitrator to assist them. Clearly, this arbitrator did not believe that the company could be compelled to bear the cost of helping to salvage such employees.

The Port Arthur Shipbuilding Case

What, if any, further developments along the lines suggested so far might have taken place in the arbitrators' cautious but steady expansion of the meaning of just cause, we do not know. The decision by the Supreme Court of Canada in *Port Arthur* (1968) 70 D.L.R. (2d) 693 seemed to cut the ground from under the developing arbitral jurisprudence.

The *Port Arthur* case concerned the discharge of three employees who had taken unauthorized leaves of absence to work elsewhere in anticipation of the usual seasonal layoff. At arbitration, the discharges were overturned and a suspension was substituted. In accordance with generally accepted arbitral practice, the arbitrator took into account the lengthy seniority, the previous good records, and the unlikelihood of a repetition of the offense in holding that there was not just cause for discharge.

The decision was ultimately appealed to the Supreme Court of Canada, where the company's position was upheld and the arbitrator's award quashed. The Court took the position that under the collective agreement the employer had the unilateral right to discharge for proper cause, and that meant cause as seen in the common law. The Court's view of the arbitrator's jurisdiction in discipline cases was stated succinctly (p. 696):

> The task of the board of arbitrators in this case was to determine whether there was proper cause. The findings of fact actually made and the only findings of fact that the board could possibly make establish that there was proper cause. Then there was only one proper legal conclusion, namely that the employees had given the management proper cause for dismissal. . . . Once the board had found that there were facts justifying discipline, the particular form chosen was not subject to review on arbitration.

Thus in one blow the Court seemed to destroy the entire body of arbitral law in discipline cases, so slowly and painfully built up. The arbitrator's remedial authority to modify penalties—to make the punishment fit the offender—was rejected as unsound. It was a reaffirmation of common law principles.

The significance of the decision for all discipline cases is apparent: an arbitrator would be confined either to upholding the penalty imposed by the employer, however severe, or to completely exonerating the grievor and ordering reinstatement with full compensation. The fine-tuning and personalized approach necessary to foster harmonious labor relations would be impossible. Given the great variety of behaviors that could be characterized as offenses in the industrial setting, and therefore deserving some form of discipline, a union would have to make a very strong case to persuade an arbitrator to find in the grievor's favor.

This state of affairs would have particular consequences for employee-drinking cases. Acts of misconduct involving drinking, once proved, had always been considered by arbitrators to be grounds for some form of discipline; the remedial authority had at the most been exercised to reduce a penalty, not remove it. The rule of the *Port Arthur* case, if followed, would mean that, unless the contract itself specifically gave the arbitrator the power to modify a penalty imposed by management, he would be compelled to uphold management's decision, regardless of the grievor's previous good record or his chances for rehabilitation.

Two cases decided after *Port Arthur* illustrate the harshness of the rule. Since both cases are only briefly reported, it cannot be certain that the decision was influenced directly by the Court's pronouncements. However, the results would seem to be unduly severe in the light of earlier authorities. Thus in *Re USWA and Northern & Central Gas Co. Ltd.* (1969) 20 L.A.C. 361 (Hanrahan) the arbitrator upheld the discharge of a grievor who was intoxicated while performing dangerous emergency work, despite his ten years' seniority. Again in *Re UAW Local 252 and Fruehauf Trailer* (1970) 21 L.A.C. 430 the same arbitrator upheld the discharge of a grievor with seventeen years' seniority and one previous warning, for being intoxicated and involved in an accident on the company parking lot while leaving work. However, we cannot be sure that, absent the *Port Arthur* rule, the result would have been different. Some arbitrators had always taken a hard line in drinking cases where safety risks were alleged. Nevertheless, the *Port Arthur* case was perceived by many arbitrators as overruling their previous practice.

One likely result of the *Port Arthur* decision was the inclusion in some collective agreements of a provision specifically authorizing the arbitrator to modify a penalty on just and equitable grounds. Where this was done, arbitrators were able to use the contractual provision as authority to exercise remedial powers as before and so avoid the harshness of *Port Arthur.* Without such a provision, however, arbitrators had to fall back on earlier doctrines to take the sting out of the rule.

Reasonableness of the Rule

In cases involving discharge for breach of a company rule, for example, arbitrators continued to make use of the principles outlined in the *KVP Co.* case: before a breach of a rule could be considered just cause for discipline, the rule must be shown to be "consistent with the collective agreement, clear and unequivocal, known to the employees, consistently enforced and reasonable" [*Re General Spring Products* (1968) 19 L.A.C. 392 (Weatherill) at 393]. The test of "reasonableness" was whether or not the rule related directly to the employment relationship itself. Thus in *Re National Steel Driving Co. Ltd.* (1969) 20 L.A.C. 402 (Palmer) a company rule imposing dismissal in the event of a wage assignment or garnishee order was considered an inappropriate way of protecting the company's interest; the grievor was ordered reinstated on condition that he obtain a consolidation order.

Culminating Incident

Similarly, the doctrine of a culminating incident could be used to overturn a discharge. This doctrine held that the company could rely on evidence of the grievor's past record to meet the just-cause standard *only if* the specific incident which had invoked the penalty was by itself sufficiently serious to merit some form of discipline.

The Innocent Employee

In other cases arbitrators developed the doctrine of "innocent or blameless" conduct, that is, conduct which could not be the subject of discipline because the conduct involved was beyond the control of the employee. This was most often used in cases where a grievor had been discharged for excessive absenteeism because of medical problems or disabilities. By removing the issue entirely from the realm of discipline, arbitrators, in ordering a grievor reinstated on conditions, could avoid the appearance of modifying a penalty imposed by management.

The leading case in this area is *Re UAW and Massey-Ferguson Ltd.* (1969) 20 L.A.C. 370 (Weiler) in which a grievor with chronic, recurring medical problems had been discharged for excessive absenteeism. In explaining why the penalty of discharge was inappropriate in such cases, the arbitrator stated the reasons for rejecting disciplinary procedures (p. 371):

> If a person is absent without excuse, especially if he falsifies his reasons, he can be disciplined. On the other hand, if he is sick or hurt and disabled even for a very lengthy period of time, it is hard to see why he should ever be discharged. He can be laid off and replaced without loss to the employer, and retain his seniority rights to return if he becomes able. This conclusion appears particularly true here where there are very lengthy disability benefits payable to employees. A person should not be able to be deprived of the latter because the company discharges for excessive failure to come to work.

The first two doctrines probably would have done little to help the employee found drinking on the job or reporting unfit for work if the issue went to arbitration: such acts of misconduct had always been considered to merit some form of discipline. However, they may have "saved" a grievor with an alcohol problem whose case came before the arbitrator in some other form, so that drinking never came into it.

As for the innocent absenteeism doctrine, while the nonpunitive approach to dealing with medically unfit or disabled employees might have been used by analogy in alcohol cases, this seemingly was rejected in *Re Retail Wholesale & Department Stores Union and Dominion Stores* (1971) 23 L.A.C. 226. In that case, the grievor, who had been employed by the company for five years, had a poor attendance record which he admitted was caused by his drinking habits. In the course of its argument on behalf of the grievor, the union suggested that the case fell within the ambit of innocent absenteeism as defined in the *Massey Ferguson* case and that discharge was an inappropriate remedy. However the arbitrator rejected the analogy (p. 288): "We have carefully considered these cases but we are of the opinion that their reasoning is inapplicable to the present case because the nature of the absenteeism dealt with in those cases is not in the same category as that which we have to deal with here where the element of self control enters into the matter." [Principle reaffirmed in pronouncements in *Re National Auto Radiator Co. Ltd. and U.A.W. Local 145* (1946) 11 L.A.C. (2d) 48–absence due to drunkeness is not innocent absenteeism.]

Legislative Amendment

Other techniques were used in various situations effectively to get around the *Port Arthur* rule. However, the best solution to remove the uncertainty left by *Port Arthur* was deemed to be a legislative amendment to forestall future judicial review of the arbitrator's authority to modify penalties. In November 1970 the Ontario legislature enacted s.37 (8) of the Labour Relations Act, R.S.O. 1970, C.232, to take effect January 1, 1971, specifically empowering arbitrators to modify penalties in discipline cases: "Where an arbitrator or arbitration board determines that an employee has been discharged or otherwise disciplined by an employer for cause and the collective agreement does not contain a specific penalty for the infraction that is the subject matter of the arbitration, the arbitrator or arbitration board may substitute such other penalty for the discharge or discipline as to the arbitrator or arbitration board seems just and reasonable in all the circumstances."

For the most part, the amendment is now treated by arbitrators as restoring their remedial authority to fashion appropriate penalties in discipline cases and most of the pre-*Port Arthur* doctrines continue in use.

The more recent cases involving employee drinking indicate a more lenient approach on the part of some arbitrators, though they are still dealt with in the context of disciplinary proceedings. For example, in *CUPE and Ottawa Civic Hospital* (1972) 24 L.A.C. 145 (Roberts) the grievor, a hospital dishwasher, had been discharged for being intoxicated on the job. The arbitrator overturned the discharge and substituted a suspension, in spite of the fact that the collective agreement specifically called for immediate dismissal as the penalty for being intoxicated on the job and the grievor had received prior warnings. The arbitrator's reason for not upholding the discharge was that the employer's interests had not been damaged in any way by the grievor's condition on that evening. Although it is not spelled out in the case, clearly the arbitrator felt some compassion for the grievor's position and the difficulty he might have in finding another job should he lose this one: in reaching his result, he had to ignore both the terms of the collective agreement and the wording of 3.37 (8) of the OLRA.

Again in *Brewers Warehousing Co. Ltd. and United Brewers' Warehousing Workers Provincial Board* (1973) 4 L.A.C. (2d) 40 the discharge of the grievor, a brewery truck driver, for being impaired on the job through drinking was overturned and a lengthy suspension substituted by the arbitration board. The grievor had only fifteen months' seniority and had had several prior warnings about drinking on the job. However, because of the company's past record of laxness in imposing discipline, it was held to be unfair to allow them to discharge the grievor. Instead, the arbitrator reinstated the grievor, but on probation: any future drinking on the job would be grounds for instant dismissal.

This more lenient approach may be a reflection of changed attitudes about drinking on the job. It is also part of a trend to consider the consequences of discharge to employees as deserving of greater consideration than in the past. In a free enterprise economy, where the state provides only a minimum level of welfare benefits, the loss of a job can have disastrous consequences for an employee and his family. Employment, especially in a unionized work force, carries with it many valuable rights such as sickness and accident benefits, dental plans, and pensions rights, all of which can be lost when employment is terminated. No doubt for this reason there is an increasing trend in arbitration cases to impose a heavy burden on employers to justify a discharge. For example, in recent cases involving excessive absenteeism for medical reasons, the onus is on the employer to establish (1) undue absenteeism in the grievor's past record, and (2) that the grievor is incapable of regular attendance in the future. In *Re UAW Local 458 and Massey Ferguson Industries Ltd.* (1972) 24 L.A.C. 344 (Shime) the grievor had been absent for two lengthy and many short periods because of medical problems requiring surgery; he was ordered reinstated on probation.

The issue of how to deal with the alcoholic worker was discussed in a recent decision of the British Columbia Labour Relations Board, which is empowered under the BC Labour Code to hear grievance arbitrations. In *Hiram Walker and Sons Ltd. and Canadian Union of Distillery Workers*, June 18, 1976, no. 38, the grievor had been discharged for reporting to work under the influence of alcohol. The grievor was an admitted alcoholic but his work record, apart from the incident which had provoked his dismissal, was good and he had received no previous discipline relating to drinking. The arbitrator held that discharge was an excessive penalty and, considering the good record of the grievor and the company's failure to use progressive discipline, ordered the grievor reinstated with a three-day suspension. Within a week of his discharge the grievor had apparently joined Alcoholics Anonymous and as of the date of the hearing (five months after the discharge) had consumed no more alcohol. In rejecting the employer's argument that the discharge was justified on the grounds that at common law reporting for work in an unfit condition was grounds for summary dismissal, the arbitrator reaffirmed that common law principles no longer applied in a collective bargaining regime—there could be no fixed penalties for specific acts of misconduct. Furthermore, in the course of her lengthy discussion of the issue, the arbitrator specifically referred to alcoholism as an "illness" and therefore by its very nature a different type of offense than insubordination or willful disobedience. Nevertheless, while discharge was held to be inappropriate in the circumstances, a suspension was ordered:

> Suspension may sound inconsistent, after we have stated that alcoholism is basically an illness. We would not suspend someone . . . who sustained a broken leg. Why treat this "illness" differently? Because the realities of the situation in the workplace demand it. Drinking is a universal problem. Broken legs are not. . . . There is the already stated need for deterrance, and the probable value of some shock needed to the alcoholic employee. He or she must realize the necessity to seek treatment, and the very real threat of loss of a job may assist in bringing the employee to this realization.

While the arbitrator was careful to stress that "every case must be judged on its own facts, keeping in mind the differences in individuals, the working environment, and conditions generally," the case suggests a new response to dealing with the alcoholic worker at arbitration. By refusing to uphold a discharge in a situation which at least at common law would clearly have been grounds for instant dismissal, the arbitrator could indirectly put pressure on management in this case to adopt a more enlightened policy in dealing with the alcoholic worker. In the concluding paragraphs of the decision, the arbitrator took notice of the policies of other employers (EAPs), while affirming that it was up to the parties to develop such a scheme through negotiation: "Dealing with an alcoholic in the workplace by means of the adversary system is no answer. The parties must be aware of the desirability and need to deal with the problem through other means, by way of education and development of programs, rather than merely relying on discipline" (p. 28).

Thus the decision in *Hiram Walker* may be significant for the future development of arbitral jurisprudence in employee-drinking cases. It reaffirms that common law principles no longer apply in a collective bargaining regime, that conduct which at common law would have been grounds for instant dismissal will be treated differently in the arbitration system. However, given the nature of arbitration as it has developed, with its emphasis on individualized justice, we can only search in vain for a definitive statement that as a matter of substantive arbitral law, opportunity for treatment for alcoholic employees without loss of income, not discharge or discipline, is the appropriate remedy. Even in *Hiram Walker* where a suspension was substituted for the discharge, the arbitrator was careful to stress that each case would turn on its own particular facts.

A suspension, in lieu of discharge, is important because it maintains the employment relationship. However, a suspension without more in such cases may be only a temporary solution, merely delaying the inevitable discharge. The dilemma posed by such an order may act as an incentive on both the union and management to cooperate in seeking other remedies. At the same time, it should be noted that the cost of a suspension (loss of income) falls most heavily, not on the employer or the union, but on the individual grievor and his family. Presumably, this is the intended "shock value" of the suspension order.

In *Hiram Walker*, the arbitrator cited with approval an American case, *Giant Eagle Markets Inc. and General Teamsters, Chauffeurs & Helpers Local 249* (1975) ARB 8145 (Emerson), in which a grievor with a truly horrendous employment record involving drinking over a period of years was finally discharged when found drinking on the job despite repeated warnings. The arbitrator dealt with the grievor as a man suffering from an illness and ordered that he seek medical treatment. He overturned the discharge and ordered that the employer reinstate the grievor with full seniority from the date of discharge when and if the employee was rehabilitated to the point where he could be certified as fit to resume work. The policy reasons behind this order were clearly enunciated by the arbitrator:

> . . . where the company discharge of the employee is affirmed by the arbitrator, particularly where alcoholism is involved, the "drunken" former employee for his own fault is cast out into society with sometimes little consideration for his case and treatment either by Alcoholics Anonymous or by private or public psychiatrists. He won't ask for help. The result often is that he is, or becomes a derelict, and his family destitute and fraught with all sorts of social problems.

Moreover, the difficulty which even a "reformed" alcoholic might experience in finding another job and the fact that he was already skilled in this job, were sound reasons for imposing an obligation on his present employer to reinstate him when he was rehabilitated.

Since this reasoning was cited with approval by the arbitrator in *Hiram Walker*, perhaps in future cases such an order would be made by a Canadian arbitrator. Indeed, the possibility of such an order was first raised in *Douglas Aircraft* (1967). Again, while an indefinite suspension in lieu of discharge is certainly an advance in that it preserves the employment relationship and protects the employee's accumulated rights while he seeks treatment, at the same time the cost of the suspension falls most heavily on the grievor and his dependents. The employer can always replace an employee while he is away from the job.

Other American cases have gone even further than *Giant Eagle* by ordering that an alcoholic employee be returned to work while undergoing treatment, thus ensuring that he is still able to earn a living. In *Acme Block & Supply Co. and International Brotherhood of Teamsters, Local 486* (1970-72) ARB 8489 (Keefe) a grievor who had been subject to "alcoholic seizures" for several years was finally discharged when he was involved in an accident while operating a forklift truck. The employer's insurer had informed the company that they would not assume the risk of accidents involving such an employee. Nevertheless, the arbitrator refused to uphold the discharge and ordered that the grievor be given an opportunity to seek treatment. He was reinstated on condition that he attend Alcoholics Anonymous and follow a strict regimen of medical treatment; failure to comply with the order would be grounds for dismissal: "This then is the avenue which must be explored. It would be wrong to deny the Grievant opportunity to earn a livelihood if he is physically capable of performing constructive services."

Similary, in *Charleston Naval Shipyard and Charleston Metal Trades Council* (1970-71) ARB 8301 (Kesselman) the grievor had been suspended three times in the previous nine months for being on duty while under the influence of alcohol, and when he again reported for work in an intoxicated condition he was discharged. The arbitrator overturned the discharge and ordered the grievor be returned to work. The grievor had had nineteen years of good service, his drinking had only begun in the two years prior to his discharge, and the arbitrator declared that the company should have taken more steps to correct the grievor's problem: counseling not discharge was the proper remedy. Again the arbitrator stressed the policy considerations behind such an order: the grievor was 47 years old at the time of discharge and if he lost this job he might never find another one. "We all share a moral obligation toward those less blessed than ourselves to make a maximum effort to help them enter and stay in the mainstream of American life."

Whether a Canadian arbitrator would be prepared to go so far as to order that an employee who is an alcoholic be returned to work while seeking treatment is debatable. In certain cases, such an order might be undesirable, but underlying the American cases cited so far is the desire to ensure that the alcoholic employee not be deprived of an income during treatment. In the last two cases, the arbitrators were prepared to let the employer bear the cost of these problem employees, by returning them to work, in the absence of any other provision for income maintenance.

In fact, in the future where the parties have negotiated a group accident and sickness insurance policy, the possibility of the employee claiming benefits may ultimately be a crucial factor in finding that there has been no just cause for dismissal. We have seen this pragmatic aspect taken into account in the so-called innocent absenteeism cases (*Massey Ferguson*) and again in the *International Woodworkers' of America, Local 217 and Weldwood of Canada Ltd.* (1976) 67 D.L.R. (3d) 544 S.C.C.). In *Weldwood* the grievor had been discharged for being impaired on the job. Her health and work had been on a decline for several years, partly due to alcoholism, and she had the highest incidence of absenteeism in the company. The arbitrator discarded absenteeism as a possible ground for discharge, but found that in fact she had been impaired on the job, not through alcohol as the employer alleged, but through the medication she was taking for her asthmatic condition. He rejected the employer's contention that impairment, for whatever reason, was just cause for discharge, and held that she had not been discharged for just cause because under the collective agreement the grievor would be entitled to claim a leave of absence for illness. The award was upheld as valid by the Supreme Court, in line with its more recent policy of restraint in arbitration cases.

If *Weldwood* says impairment on the job is not just cause for discharge where the collective agreement provides for other remedies (in *Weldwood*, a leave of absence), and *Hiram Walker* says that impairment on the job through alcohol is not in itself just cause for discharge, then together the cases suggest the importance of having a group insurance policy which includes coverage for alcoholism as an illness for which employees are entitled to claim benefits while undergoing treatment. Of course, such coverage would presumably have to be left to the collective bargaining table: it is unlikely that a Canadian arbitrator would impose such an arrangement on management without some provision in the agreement, given their refusal to deal with alcoholism as an illness. Today, some unions have already negotiated such coverage, and where this is the case, presumably the question of discharge would be less likely to arise.

In the final analysis, though the decision in *Hiram Walker* may suggest a new response in employee-drinking cases at arbitration, it is valuable only as a last resort. The delay involved in taking a grievance all the way to arbitration, and the frequent practice among arbitrators in discipline cases of not awarding compensation for lost time between the discharge and the date of the award, are powerful arguments for seeking other remedies outside the system to deal with the problem of the alcoholic worker, both on financial and rehabilitative grounds, on a more immediate basis.

Conclusion

The history of arbitration law has been one of successive modification to the common law pertaining to master-servant relationships. From imposing the conditions of the rule of law to introducing concepts of individualized justice, arbitrators have, haltingly at times, created a backpressure on industry to cope creatively and constructively with problems due to alcoholism and certain other mental health problems. The language of arbitral pronouncements on the subject of just cause bears a striking resemblance to the language of EAPs with their emphasis on progressive, corrective discipline, consistency, and fair play. Perhaps it is the uncertainty of outcome in cases involving alcoholism that has caused some employers to avoid the need for recourse to arbitration. Increasingly, however, there are signs that arbitrators rightly or wrongly will consider alcoholism as a treatable disease, compelling employers to deal with the problem in a more constructive way to begin with. Consciously or unconsciously, arbitrators act as social policymakers in the area of alcoholism in the workplace. In Canada, the process has been more one of default than in the United States where more radical proactive measures have been taken by arbitrators to impose social responsibility for alcoholics and problem drinkers on industry. Yet in both countries, arbitrators have argued that the grievance process is unable of itself to provide answers for the major problems raised by alcoholism in industry. There are both institutional and ideological reasons for this.

As an institution designed to resolve disputes between employers and employees, arising ostensibly out of the administration, application, and interpretation of collective agreements, the grievance arbitration system has closely followed the traditional adjudicative model with its emphasis on the resolution of a particular dispute between two parties. This institutional framework, by its very nature, imposes certain limitations on the way in which social problems can be dealt with. It has been one influence in the growth and proliferation of social legislation in modern society. This is even truer in the case of labor arbitration, as it has developed, where precedent is eschewed and the pragmatic, individualized case-by-case approach to dispute resolution is considered to be its chief virtue.

More important than the institutional limitations of grievance arbitration is the ideological bias of the system. It operates within the narrow social context of the industrial setting, where the overriding "social" purpose is the maintenance and promotion of an efficient and profitable commercial enterprise. The acceptance, by most arbitrators, of this goal as the standard against which all other considerations must ultimately be measured, necessarily narrows the boundaries within which they can resolve the basic conflict of interest between this goal and the interests of employees as human beings, not merely sellers of labor power. This ideological premise on which the system rests limits the degree to which most arbitrators have been prepared to fashion new principles and remedies. An examination of the cases involving alcoholic employees, where the emphasis has been on punishment rather than rehabilitation, illustrates these weaknesses of the system and underscores the necessity for the parties to develop remedies of their own.

Finally, even apart from the institutional and ideological drawbacks to grievance arbitration as an agency for developing enlightened social policy, such practical problems as the delay, uncertainty, and expense involved in taking a case to arbitration, especially in recent years, must surely have influenced both labor and management to find other methods for coping with the problem of alcoholism in the workplace.

Appendix B
The Key-Elements Interview Questionnaire

A. *Company/Agency Characteristics*

1. Name of company/agency.
2. Head office, branch office.
3. Public, private, other.
4. Will the information recorded here pertain to:
   a. the company/agency as a whole?
   b. a branch, division, or affiliate of the whole?
5. If 4b, please specify.
6. How many employees in the organization which is the subject of this interview?
   a. Number of permanent employees.
   b. Number of seasonal employees.
7. Informant for present interview: name, position.
8. What percentage of employees are unionized?
   Specify unions by name.
9. What is the business of this organization?
10. Is there a medical department?
    a. None.
    b. Physician on Staff.
    c. Physician on Call.
    d. Nursing Station.
    e. Other.
11. Are medicals performed on all employees routinely?
    a. Wage earners, every year.
    b. Wage earners, on a rota basis.
    c. Salaried employees, every year.
    d. Salaried employees on a rota basis.
    e. No routine medicals.
    f. Other arrangements.
12. How serious do you judge the problem of alcohol and drug abuse to be in your workforce?
13. What percentage of your workforce do you estimate to be consuming alcohol and drugs at "problem" levels?
14. What kind of reporting system do you have in this organization? (Line, functional, mixed)

15. How does your EAP (practice or procedure re substance abuse) fit into this reporting system?

B. *General Policy, Practice, Procedure*

16. What practice, policy, or procedure governs the management of the following problems? (Check)

Problem	Nothing	Written Policy	Unwritten Policy	Time-Honored Procedures
Alcohol Abuse				
Drug Abuse				
Mental Health Disorder				
Employee's Family				
Other Problems (Specify)				

17. What is the date of origin of these policies, practices, or procedures? (If there have been extensions of coverage, note when. Obtain copy of anything in writing describing the above.)
18. Describe the policy, practice, procedure.
19. Which department is responsible for administering the EAP?
20. What pressures or influences governed the development of the policy, practice, procedure?
21. Is the policy, practice, procedure still in effect?
22. If "Partly" or "Not at All", please outline what happened that resulted in disuse.

C. *Procedural Specifics*

23. Is there a management/union committee to govern the policy, practice, procedure?
    Is the committee active?
    Was the policy, practice, or procedure jointly developed?
    Was the policy, practice, or procedure jointly issued?
24. Who is responsible for the identification of problem employees? (*Responsibility*)
25. Do these identifiers have any special skills or training to help them? (*Skills*)

26a. Who is responsible for confrontation and referral? (*Responsibility*)

26b. Is anyone designated to hear complaints about the operation of the assistance program, policy, practice? (*Appeals*)

27. What signals a "problem employee"? (*Job Performance*)
28. Do you consider that this organization effectively controls job performance?
29. What is your overall rate of absenteeism?
30. How often is absenteeism monitored?
31. How is absenteeism measured?
32. What procedure is usually followed by the identifier? (Document, Warn, Confront, Refer, Followup: "progressive discipline")
33. Are there guidelines to govern those cases which will be dealt with on a *disciplinary* basis (fines, suspensions, discharge, and so on) as opposed to a *rehabilitative* basis? (Discipline/Rehabilitation)
34. How are employees made aware of the choices available to them if they have problems which affect their performance or behavior at work? (Self-Recognition, Program Visibility, Publicity, Employee Education)
35. Does the job-performance review of supervisors include accountability for management of problem employees? (Support)
36. What is the ratio of supervisors to line personnel? (Span of Control)
    a) Wage earners
    b) Salaried
37. Is record-keeping by personnel department or by individual departments such that job deterioration would be noticed within a reasonable period? (*Support and Control*)
38. Does the organization–from your perspective–consider it worthwhile economically to attract employees into a "helping program" before problems on the job have become apparent? (*Early Identification*)
39. Has the organization ever been involved in grievance and/or arbitration proceedings as a result of an employee's drinking, drug, or mental-health problem? (*Legal Pressures*)
40. What is the coverage of the Company/Agency insurance policy with respect to: (*Benefits*)

	Coverage Cost	Payments Disbursed
Alcoholism		
Drug Abuse		
Mental-Health Disorder		

41. Are some employees excluded from coverage by the policy, practice, procedures for problems in work performance? (*Nondiscrimination*)
42. What facilities for the treatment of alcoholism exist in the community? (*Availability of Treatment*)

43. What measures exist to protect the confidentiality of employee records? (*Protection of Reputation*)
44. What effect does a successful treatment referral have on the career of an employee whose work performance deteriorated as a result of drinking, drug abuse, mental-health disorders? (*Clean Slate*)
45. When an employee returns from a treatment program, how, if at all, is his/her progress monitored (*Followup*)

D. *Program Outcome*

46. Do you have any record of the numbers of employees seen under the auspices of the policy, procedure, practice for the following reasons:

	1974	1975	1976	1977
Alcoholism				
Drug Abuse				
Mental-Health Disorders				
Family Problems				
Others: Specify				

47. What are your perceptions about the success or failure of these cases?
48. How could your policy, practice, procedure be improved?
49. What do you consider to be the key elements in a successful policy, practice, procedure?
50. To what extent do you feel that an industry/agency such as yours has a responsibility to help problem employees?

E. *Interviewer's Comments*

1. General tone of interview.
2. Observations about expressed or implied attitudes of the respondent concerning alcoholism, drug abuse, mental disorders—their genesis, prevention, treatment.
3. Other remarks.

The interview questionnaire is keyed to table 1-1 by means of italicized words in parentheses following specific questions. For example, question 25 is followed by (*Skills*). This refers the reader to the corresponding heading in table 1-1 which deals with the constructs of the ideal model of EAP described in chapter 1.

References

Adams, G.W. 1978. "Concepts of Industrial Discipline and Their Results." Part 2. Presentation to the Annual Meeting of the Ontario Labor-Management Arbitration Commission.

Aharan, C.H. 1966. "The Interdependence of Personal and Cultural Variables in Alcoholism." Ph.D. thesis, University of Western Ontario.

Alander, R., and Campbell, T. 1973. "One Organization's Approach: An Evaluative Study of an Alcohol and Drug Recovery Program." Oldsmobile Division, General Motors Corporation, Michigan State University, School of Labor and Industrial Relations.

Archer, J. 1977. "Occupational Alcoholism: A Review of Issues and a Guide to the Literature." In *Alcoholism and Its Treatment in Industry,* edited by C.J. Schramm. Baltimore: Johns Hopkins University Press.

Argyris, C. 1970. *Intervention Theory and Method: A Behavioral Science View.* Reading, Mass.: Addison-Wesley Publishing Co.

Asma, F.E., Eggert, R.L., and Hilker R.R.J. 1971. "Long-term Experience with Rehabilitation of Alcoholic Employees." *Journal of Occupational Medicine* 13:581-585.

Bartell, T. 1976. "The Human Relations Ideology: An Analysis of the Social Origins of a Belief System." *Human Relations*, no. 8, 29:737-749.

Berry, R.E., and Boland, J.P. 1977. "The Work-Related Costs of Alcohol Abuse." In *Alcoholism and Its Treatment in Industry*, edited by C.J. Schramm. Baltimore: Johns Hopkins University Press.

Bergin, A.E. 1971. "The Evaluation of Therapeutic Outcomes." In *Handbook of Psychotherapy and Behavior Change: An Empirical Analysis*, edited by A.E. Bergin and S.L. Garfield. New York: Wiley.

Bird, F.E. 1974. *Management Guide to Loss Control.* Mordialloc, Victoria, Australia. Imageprint.

Bird, F.E., and Loftus, R.G. 1976. *Loss Control Management.* Loganville, Ga.: Institute Press.

Borthwick, R.B. 1977. "Summary of Cost Benefit Study Results for Navy Alcoholism Rehabilitation Programs." Technical Report #346 Presearch Inc.

Cahalan, D., and Room, R. 1972. "Problem Drinking among American Men Aged 21-59." *American Journal of Public Health* 62: 1473-1482.

_____. 1974. "Problem Drinking among American Men." New Brunswick, N.J.: Rutgers Center of Alcohol Studies.

Capitman, W.G. 1973. *Panic in the Boardroom.* Garden City, N.Y.: Anchor Press.

Carrothers, A.W.R. 1961. *Labor Arbitration in Canada.* Toronto: Butterworths.

Cohn. J. 1971. *The Conscience of Corporations.* Baltimore: Johns Hopkins University Press.

Cole, J.J., and Shupe, D.R. 1970. "A Four Year Followup of Former Psychiatric Patients in Industry." *Archives of General Psychiatry* 22:222-229.

Collier, J. 1973. "Inspection and Enforcement at the Workplace." *Monthly Labor Review*, no. 8, vol. 96.

Collings, G.H., Fitzpatrick, M.M., and Stratton, K.L. 1972. "Multiphasic Health Screening in Industry: Concepts, Philosophy and General Descriptions." *Journal of Occupational Medicine*, no. 6, 14:435-445.

Comptroller General of the United States. 1970. *Substantial Cost Savings from Establishment of Alcoholism Programs for Federal Civilian Employees.* Report to the Special Subcommittee on Alcoholism and Narcotics of the Committee on Labor and Public Welfare. U.S. Senate. Washington: U.S. Government Printing Office.

Davis, K. 1967. *Human Relations at Work: The Dynamics of Organizational Behavior.* New York: McGraw Hill Book Co. Inc.

Deniston, O.L., Rosenstock, I.M., and Getting, V.A. 1968. "Evaluation of Program Effectiveness." *Public Health Reporter* 83:323-335.

Dentler, R., and Erickson, K. 1959. "The Function of Deviance in Groups." *Social Problems* 7 (Fall):98-107.

Dunbar, B. 1978. "Report on the Canadian Labor Congress Conference, Quebec City, April 3-7, 1978" Companion Paper #10 to the Report of the Task Force on Employee Assistance Programs. Addiction Research Foundation, 33 Russell Street, Toronto, Ontario.

Edwards, D.W. 1975. "The Evaluation of Troubled Employee and Occupational Alcoholism Programs." In *Occupational Alcoholism Programs*, edited by R.L. Williams and G.H. Moffat, Springfield, Ill.: Charles C. Thomas.

Ellis, L. 1975. "A Review of Research on Efforts to Promote Occupational Safety." *Journal of Safety Research*, no. 7, 4:180-189.

Emery, F.E. 1969. *System Thinking.* Harmondsworth, England: Penguin.

Emery, F.E., and Trist, E.L. 1960. "Socio-technical Systems." In *Management Science, Models and Techniques*, edited by C.W. Churchman and M. Verhulst vol. 2. New York: Pergamon.

_____. 1965. "The Causal Texture of the Organizational Environment. *Human Relations* 18:21-32.

Ennis, P. 1977. "A Review of the Mortimer-Filkins Test for Identifying Problem Drinkers." Substudy #854. Addiction Research Foundation of Ontario, 33 Russell Street, Toronto.

Erfurt, J.C., and Foote, A. 1977. "Occupational Employee Assistance Programs for Substance Abuse and Mental Health Problems." Institute of Labor and Industrial Relations, Worker Health Program, University of Michigan, Wayne State University, Ann Arbor.

Flamholtz, E. 1974. *Human Resources Accounting.* Belmont, Calif.: Dickerson Publishing Co.

Follman, J.F., Jr. 1976. *Alcoholics and Business: Problems, Costs, Solutions.* New York: Amacom.

Freedberg, E.J., and McLatchie, B. 1976. "A Behaviorally Oriented Test Battery for Assessment of Clinical and Normal Populations." Addiction Research Foundation, Substudy #807, Toronto.

Gavin, M. 1978. "Consortium." Companion Paper #9 to the Report of the Task Force on Employee Assistance Programs. Addiction Research Foundation, 33 Russell Street, Toronto, Ontario.

Gillies, M., Aharan, C.H., Smart, R.G., and Shain, M. 1974. "The Alcoholic Involvement Scale: A Method of Measuring Change in Alcoholics." *Journal of Alcoholism*, no. 10, 4:142-147.

Glen, F. 1975. *The Social Psychology of Organizations*. London: Methuen and Co., Ltd.

Groeneveld, J., Simon, J., and Shain, M. 1978. "The Problem Employee's Program of Lifeline Foundation." Substudy #971. Addiction Research Foundation of Ontario, 33 Russell Street, Toronto, Ontario.

Habbe, S. 1969. "Company Controls for Drinking Problems." Studies in Personnel Policy #218, New York, National Industrial Conference Board.

Hayward, B.J., Schlenger, W.E., and Hallan, J.B. 1975. "Occupational Programming: A Review of Literature." Human Ecology Institute, 7334 Chapel Hill Rd., Raleigh, N.C.

Heald, M. 1970. *The Social Responsibilities of Business*. Cleveland, Ohio: Case Western Reserve University Press.

Heinrich, H.W. 1959. *Industrial Accident Prevention*. 4th ed. New York: McGraw-Hill Book Co.

Henderson, R.M., and Bacon, S.D. 1953. "Problem Drinking: The Yale Plan for Business and Industry." *Quarterly Journal of Studies on Alcohol* 14:247-262.

Hitchcock, L.C., and Sanders, M. 1976. "A Survey of Alcohol and Drug Abuse Programs in the Railroad Industry." National Technical Information Service, U.S. Department of Commerce, Springfield, Va. 22161.

Hohn, H.M. 1972. "Occupational Safety and Health Research: New Challenges." *Journal of Safety Research*, no. 2, 4:53-59.

Jacobsen, G. 1975. "Diagnosis and Assessment of Alcohol Abuse and Alcoholism." National Institute of Alcohol Abuse and Alcoholism, Rockville, Md.

Keene, C.H. 1974. "The Credibility of Occupational Medicine." *Journal of Occupational Medicine*, no. 5, 16:309-312.

Kelly, J. 1969. *Organizational Behavior*. Homewood, Ill. R.D. Irwin. Irwin Dorsey Series in Behavioral Science.

Kerlans, M., Mortimer, R., Mudge, B., and Filkins, L. 1971. *Court Procedures for Identifying Problem Drinkers.* Vol. 1: *Manual*. N.H.T.S.A. Report #DOT-HS-800-632. Highway Safety Research Institute, University of Michigan.

Kirkham, P.G. 1977. *Perspective Canada II: A Compendium of Social Statistics.* Report, Statistics Canada, Government of Canada, Ottawa.

Levens, E. 1976. "The Cost Benefit and Cost Effectiveness of Occupational Alcoholism Programs." *Professional Safety* (November):36-41.

Luft, H.S. 1975. "The Impact of Poor Health on Earnings." *Review of Economics and Statistics* 57:43-57.

Lusterman, S. 1974. "Industry Roles in Health Care." A research report from the Conference Board. Report #610, New York, the Conference Board.

Maxwell, M.A. 1959. "A Study of Absenteeism, Accidents and Sickness Payments in Problem Drinkers in One Industry." *Quarterly Journal of Studies on Alcohol* 20:302-312.

McLean, A. 1970. *Mental Health and Work Organizations*. Chicago: Rand McNally.

Melman, S. 1976. "Industrial Efficiency under Managerial versus Cooperative Decision Making: A Comparative Study of Manufacturing Enterprises in Israel." *Review of Radical Politics and Economics*, no. 1, 2:9-34.

Mortimer, R.G. 1977. Personal communication.

Munsterberg, H. 1913. *Psychology and Industrial Efficiency*. Boston: Houghton Mifflin.

National Institute on Alcohol Abuse and Alcoholism. 1977 *Forward Plan: A Preliminary Version of a Five Year Set of Goals and Objectives*. Washington: U.S. Government Printing Office.

Neubeck, K.J. 1974. *Corporate Response to Urban Crisis*. Lexington, Mass.: LexingtonBooks.

Pachauri, R.K. 1978. "The Economics of Occupational Health and Safety." *Journal of Safety Research*, no. 2, 10:78-86.

Payne, W.D., Monti, J.M., and Winer, M.B. 1976. "Industry as a Setting for Drug Abuse Education: A Preliminary Study." *Journal of Drug Education*, no. 3, 6:201-208.

Pell, S., and D'Alonzo, C.A. 1970. "Sickness Absenteeism of Alcoholics." *Journal of Occupational Medicine* 12:198-210.

———. 1973. "A Five Year Mortality Study of Alcoholics." *Journal of Occupational Medicine* 15:120-125.

Perlis, L. 1977. "Unionism and Alcoholism: The Issues." In *Alcoholism and Its Treatment in Industry*, edited by C.J. Schramm. Baltimore: Johns Hopkins University Press.

Perrow, C. 1967. "A Framework for the Comparative Analysis of Organizations." *American Sociological Review*, no. 2, vol. 32.

Roethlisberger, F.J., and Dickson, W.J. 1939. *Management and the Worker.* Cambridge, Mass.: Harvard University Press.

Roizen, R., Cahalan, D., and Shanks, P. 1978. "Spontaneous Remission among Untreated Problem Drinkers." In *Longitudinal Research on Drug Use*, edited by D. Kandel. Washington: Hemisphere Publishing Corporation, John Wiley and Sons.

Roman, P.M. 1977. "Occupational Programming in Major American Corporations: The 1976 Executive Caravan Survey." New Orleans, Tulane Center for Monitoring of Occupational Alcoholism Programming, Tulane University.

———. 1978. "The current status of Occupational Alcoholism: Review and Documentation." In *Third Alcohol and Health Report to Congress, Part II: Scientific Documentation*. Washington: U.S. Government Printing Office.

Roman, P.M., and Trice, H.M. 1970. "The Development of Deviant Drinking: Occupational Risk Factors." *Archives of Environmental Health* 20:424-435.

_____. 1976. "Alcohol Abuse and Work Organizations." In *The Biology of Alcoholism*, edited by B. Kissin and H. Begleiter Vol. 4, pp. 445-517. New York: Plenum Press.

Rosenthal, R., and Jacobsen, L. 1968. *Pygmalion in the Classroom: Teacher Expectation and Pupils' Intellectual Development*. New York: Holt, Rinehart, Winston.

Ryback, R.S., and Dowd, P.J. 1970. "Aftereffects of Various Alcoholic Beverages on Positional Nystagmus and Coriolis Acceleration." *Aerospace Medicine* 41:429-435.

Schlenger, W.E., and Hayward, B.J. 1976. "Occupational Programming: Problems in Research and Evaluation." *Alcohol Health and Research World* (Spring):18-22.

Schlenger, W.E., Hallan, J., and Hayward, B. 1976. "Characteristics of Selected Occupational Programs." Raleigh, N.C.: the Human Ecology Institute.

Schmidt, W., and Popham, R.E. 1978. "Alcohol Problems and Their Prevention: A Public Health Perspective." Addiction Research Foundation of Ontario, 33 Russell Street, Toronto.

Schramm, C.J. 1977a. "The Development of a Successful Alcoholism Treatment Facility." In *Alcoholism and Its Treatment in Industry*, edited by C.J. Schramm. Baltimore: Johns Hopkins University Press.

_____. 1977b. "Development of Comprehensive Language on Alcoholism in Collective Bargaining Agreements." *Journal of Studies on Alcohol*, no. 7, 38:1405-1427.

Schramm, C.J., ed. 1977c. *Alcoholism and Its Treatment in Industry*. Baltimore: Johns Hopkins University Press.

Schramm, C.J., Mandell, W., and Archer, J. 1978. *Workers Who Drink: Their Treatment in an Industrial Setting*. Lexington, Mass.: LexingtonBooks.

Shain, M., and Groeneveld, J. 1976. "The Effect, Effectiveness and Efficiency of the Employee-Assistance Program." Addiction Research Foundation Report, 33 Russell Street, Toronto.

_____. 1977. "An Analysis of Responses to the Report Entitled, 'The Effect, Effectiveness and Efficiency of the Employee-Assistance Program.'" Addiction Research Foundation Report, 33 Russell Street, Toronto.

Shain, M., and MacDougall, J. 1979. "A Study of Occupational Health and Safety Legislation as a Context for Employee Assistance Programs." Report, Employee-Assistance Program Research Unit, Addiction Research Foundation, 33 Russell Street, Toronto.

Shain, M., and Suurvali, H. 1976. "The Alcoholic Involvement Scale in Program Evaluation: Theoretical and Practical Considerations." Substudy #810. Addiction Research Foundation, Toronto.

Sherman, P.A. 1977. "Why so Few Occupational Programs?" *Focus.*

Silk, L., and Vogel, D. 1976. *Ethics and Profit: The Crisis of Confidence in American Business*. New York: Simon and Shuster.

Simon, H.A. 1955. "Recent Advances in Organization Theory." In *Research Frontiers in Politics and Government: Brooking Lectures, 1955*, edited by S.K. Bailey et al. Washington, D.C.: Brookings Institute.

Simonds, R.H., and Shafai-Sahrai, Y. 1977. "Factors Apparently Affecting Injury Frequency in Eleven Matched Pairs of Companies." *Journal of Safety Research*, no. 3, 9:120-127.

Smart, R.G. 1974. "Employed Alcoholics Treated Voluntarily and under Constructive Coercion—A Followup Study." *Quarterly Journal of Studies on Alcohol* 35:196-209.

_____. 1975-1976. "Spontaneous Recovery in Alcoholics: A Review and Analysis of the Available Research." *Drug and Alcohol Dependency* 1:277-285.

Somers, G.G. 1978. "Alcohol and the Just Cause for Discharge." *Proceedings of the 28th Annual Meeting of the National Academy of Arbitrators*. Bureau of National Affairs, Washington, D.C.

Suurvali, H., and Shain, M. 1978. "The May Street Referral Trend Study." Employee-Assistance Programs Research Unit, Addiction Research Foundation, 33 Russell Street, Toronto. Mimeograph.

Swisher, J. 1977. Testimony to the U.S. Senate Committee on Labor and Public Welfare: Subcommittee on Alcoholism and Drug Abuse.

Task Force on Employee-Assistance Programs Report. 1978. Addiction Research Foundation, 33 Russell Street, Toronto, Ontario.

Task Force to the Secretary of Health, Education and Welfare. 1973. J. O'Toole, Chairman. *Work in America*. Cambridge, Mass.: MIT Press.

Taylor, F.W. 1911. *Principles of Scientific Management*. New York: Harper and Row.

Trice, H.M. 1962. "The Job Behavior of Problem Drinkers." In *Society, Culture and Drinking Patterns,* edited by D.J. Pittman and C.R. Snyder. New York: Wiley, pp. 493-510.

_____. 1978. "Testimony to the Task Force on Employee-Assistance Programs, February 1978." Addiction Research Foundation of Ontario Task Force Report.

Trice, H.M., and Belasco, J. 1966. *Emotional Health and Employer Responsibility*. Bulletin #57. New York State School of Industrial and Labor Relations.

Trice, H.M., and Beyer, J.M. 1977. "Differential Use of an Alcoholism Policy in Federal Organizations by Skill Level of Employees." In *Alcoholism and Its Treatment in Industry*, edited by C.J. Schramm. Baltimore: Johns Hopkins University Press.

Trice, H.M., and Roman, P.M. 1978. *Spirits and Demons at Work: Alcohol and Other Drugs on the Job*. Ithaca: Cornell University Press.

Trist, E.L., and Bamforth, K.W. 1951. "Some Social and Psychological Consequences of the Long-Wall Method of Coal-Getting." *Human Relations*, vol. 4.

Trist, E.L., and Murray, H. 1948. "Work Organization at the Coal Face: A Comparative Study of Mining Systems." Tavistock Institute of Human Relations Document #506.

Vicary, J.R. 1978. "Substance Abuse Programs in Business, Industry and Labor: Implications for Prevention." Addictions Prevention Laboratory, Division of Counseling and Educational Psychology, the Pennsylvania State University.

Von Bertalannfy, L. 1950. "The Theory of Open Systems in Physics and Biology." *Science* 111:23-29.

Von Wiegand, R. 1976. "A Loss Control Program for Alcoholism." In *Loss Control Management*, edited by F.E. Bird and R.G. Loftus. Loganville, Ga.: Institute Press.

Weber, M. 1946. "From Max Weber." In *Essays in Sociology*, edited by H.H. Gerth and C.W. Mills London: Oxford University Press.

Weiler, J.M. 1976."Non-culpable Cause for Discharge: A New Perspective." Paper presented at seminar on Current Issues in Grievance Arbitration, November 26 and 27.

Williams, R.L., and Tramontana, J. 1977. "The Evaluation of Occupational Alcoholism Programs." In *Alcoholism and Its Treatment in Industry*, edited by C.J. Schramm. Baltimore: Johns Hopkins University Press.

Winslow, W.W., Hayes, L., Prentice, L., Powles, W.E., Seeman, W., and Ross, W.D. 1966. "Some Economic Estimates of Job Disruption from an Industrial Mental Health Project." *Archives of Environmental Health* 13:213-219.

Wolkenberg, R.C., Gold, C., and Tichauer, E.R. 1975. "Delayed Effects of Acute Alcoholic Intoxication on Performance with Reference to Work Safety." *Journal of Safety Research*, no. 3, 7:104-118.

Woodruff, R.L. 1970. "Human Resources Accounting." *Canadian Chartered Accountant*.

Woodward, J., ed. 1965. *Industrial Organization: Theory and Practice*. New York: Oxford University Press.

———. 1970. *Industrial Organization: Behavior and Control*. New York: Oxford University Press.

Index

About the Authors

Martin Shain is head of the Employee-Assistance Program Research Unit at the Alcoholism and Drug Addiction Research Foundation of Ontario. His background includes a master's degree in jurisprudence from Oxford University, a diploma in criminology from Cambridge, and more than thirteen years of experience in the planning, development, and evaluation of services for such diverse groups as black gangs, young drug users, delinquents, alcoholics, schoolchildren, parents, native peoples, and others. He is coauthor of *Influence, Choice and Drugs* (Lexington Books, 1977), which explores the role of the family and the school in the genesis and prevention of drug use among schoolchildren, and he has written numerous articles in the field of addictions.

Judith Groeneveld received the B.A. in economics from Simon Fraser University in British Columbia in 1971. Since 1971 she has been with the Alcoholism and Drug Addiction Research Foundation of Ontario and is currently a senior staff member of the Employee-Assistance Program Research Unit.